Early Years Pioneers in Context

This accessible text provid... ...lished
the foundation for earl... ...r twentieth centuries. It places ... ...o help
the reader understand ho... ...e have
evolved over time.

Early Years Pioneers in C... ...orking
with parents, scaffolding ch... ...lect on
the differences and simila... ...o practice today. Pioneers covered ...

- Frederick Froebel;
- Elizabeth Peabody;
- Susan Blow;
- Rudolf Steiner;
- Margaret McMillan;
- Maria Montessori;
- Susan Isaacs;
- Loris Malaguzzi.

Featuring student integ... ...actice,
this will be essential reading ... ...degree
courses.

Pam Jarvis is a chartered ps... ...Trinity
University, and her key res... ...young
people and their families. She ... ...omen-
tal, social science and social policy modules ... ...pment pro... ...nes in
higher education.

Louise Swiniarski is a Professor Emerita in the School of Education at Salem State University, Massachusetts, USA, where she currently directs the Northeast Global Education Center to promote global literacy in Massachusetts' schools and educators' professional development programmes.

Wendy Holland is involved in the mentoring, training and assessing of early years teachers at Bradford College, UK. She is also currently working in the Teaching, Health and Care sector at Bradford College, developing and producing modules for the BA (Hons) in Early Years Studies.

Early Years Pioneers in Context

Their lives, lasting influence and impact on practice today

Pam Jarvis, Louise Swiniarski and Wendy Holland

Routledge
Taylor & Francis Group

LONDON AND NEW YORK

First published 2017

by Routledge
2 Park Square, Milton Park, Abingdon, Oxon OX14 4RN

and by Routledge
711 Third Avenue, New York, NY 10017

Routledge is an imprint of the Taylor & Francis Group, an informa business

British Library Cataloguing in Publication Data
A catalogue record for this book is available from the British Library

Library of Congress Cataloging in Publication Data
Names: Jarvis, Pam, author. | Swiniarski, Louise Boyle, author. | Holland, Wendy, author.
Title: Early years pioneers in context : their lives, lasting influence and impact on practice today / Pam Jarvis, Louise Swiniarski and Wendy Holland.
Description: New York, NY : Routledge, 2016. | Includes bibliographical references.
Identifiers: LCCN 2016011803| ISBN 9781138815049 (hardback) | ISBN 9781138815056 (pbk.) | ISBN 9781315747026 (ebook)
Subjects: LCSH: Early childhood educators—Biography. | Early childhood education—History--19th century. | Early childhood education—History—20th century.
Classification: LCC LB1139.23 .J369 2016 | DDC 372.21—dc23
LC record available at https://lccn.loc.gov/2016011803

ISBN: 978-1-138-81504-9 (hbk)
ISBN: 978-1-138-81505-6 (pbk)
ISBN: 978-1-315-74702-6 (ebk)

Typeset in Palatino
by Swales & Willis Ltd, Exeter, Devon, UK

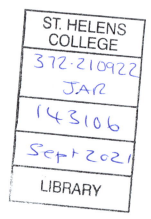

Dedication

Pam Jarvis:
For Chris, who was there at the beginning.

Louise Swiniarski:
For Joe, who encourages me to write and supports me through the process.

Wendy Holland:
This book is dedicated to all those young children it has been my delight to know and share in the 'awe and wonder' that is early childhood. During my time in early years education, the insight, honesty and imagination of young children have never ceased to amaze and encourage me. I would like to make this dedication especially to my grandchildren, Joseph, George and Alice, whose young lives continue to reinforce for me the richness in every child.

Contents

Acknowledgements   viii
About the authors and contributor   x
Foreword by Jonathan Doherty   xii

1. An introduction to early years pioneers in context   1
   PAM JARVIS, LOUISE SWINIARSKI AND WENDY HOLLAND

2. Early years pioneers: in the beginning   16
   PAM JARVIS

3. Frederick Froebel (1782–1852): the "garden of children"   31
   LOUISE SWINIARSKI

4. Elizabeth Peabody (1804–94): implementing Froebel's
   play-based learning   48
   LOUISE SWINIARSKI

5. Susan Blow (1843–1916): funding kindergartens and training
   professionals for American kindergartens in public education   65
   LOUISE SWINIARSKI

6. Rudolf Steiner (1861–1925): the anthroposophical approach   79
   WENDY HOLLAND

7. Margaret McMillan (1860–1931): the original 'liberatory pedagogue'   97
   PAM JARVIS AND BETTY LIEBOVICH

8. Maria Montessori (1870–1952): scientific pedagogy   120
   WENDY HOLLAND

9. Susan Isaacs (1885–1948): a message in a bottle   139
   PAM JARVIS

10. Loris Malaguzzi (1920–94): liberatory pedagogy for democracy   155
    WENDY HOLLAND

11. What now for the pioneers?   168
    PAM JARVIS, LOUISE SWINIARSKI AND WENDY HOLLAND

Index   178

Acknowledgements

Pam Jarvis:

My first acknowledgements are for the people who have hugely contributed to this book:

Betty Liebovich, EdD, my co-writer on Chapter 7 (Margaret McMillan). Betty is Lecturer in Early Years Education at Goldsmiths University, UK, an expert on the history of the open-air nursery, particularly the Rachel McMillan Nursery in South London, and a researcher of the history of early childhood teacher education in England and the USA. Thanks also to TACTYC (The Association for Professional Development in Early Years) at whose conference we met. With her ongoing professional connection to the Rachel McMillan Nursery, Betty transported me out of the library, and brought Margaret and Rachel McMillan to life for me, giving rise to a wonderful article and chapter, of which I hope they would both approve.

Jonathan Doherty, EdD, who is not only my colleague at Leeds Trinity University but also my academic 'brother', from our days of doctoral study under the inspirational guidance of Professor Kathy Hall at Leeds Metropolitan (now Beckett) University. Thank you so much for all your patient and helpful suggestions for this book, Jonathan, and for your Foreword that captures the spirit of the pioneers, and of the ethos we share.

Jane George, MEd, Head of Faculty for Social Care and Community Practice (Higher Education) at Bradford College, and in the words of Lucy Maud Montgomery, my 'kindred spirit' of the past twenty years; there is nothing that I have achieved professionally that has not been positively influenced by her unwavering support and friendship, including her meticulous proofreading of this book and always pertinent suggestions for improvements.

Many thanks to the New Lanark Trust, who so generously allowed us to use their beautiful pictures as illustrations in this book.

On a personal note, I should also like to thank my family who put up with me while I write and edit, especially my husband, to whom this book is dedicated. I have to offer huge thanks to my children Claire, Sian and Andrew whose development through play into the talented adults they have all become will always be my most enduring life-lesson. I should also thank my grandsons Lennon and Frankie, who have provided lessons in play in the twenty-first century; not least how to paint on an iPad! Thanks also go to their fathers, Chris and Adam, who have brought their own playfulness into the family, and Tammy who staunchly supports Andrew's ongoing play-in-work; after following Bruner's spiral curriculum of play-based learning from junk modelling and Lego, he has graduated to engineering cars which race in every hemisphere of the world.

Thanks also go to my colleagues at Leeds Trinity University, to Dr Sue Elmer who was always there to offer friendship and support when the climb to completing this book became steep, and to Dr Rosemary Mitchell who generously read early drafts of my writing about the McMillan sisters, and made very helpful comments.

Final thanks to my collaborators Dr Louise Swiniarski and Wendy Holland, whose hard work and scholarship made this book a reality.

Louise Swiniarski:

As the American author of this book, I would like to thank Dr Pam Jarvis for asking me to join with her and Wendy Holland in co-authoring this book. I also appreciate the guidance of Annamarie Kino and her staff at Routledge during the publication process of our book. Likewise, I wish to acknowledge Susan Edwards, Archivist of the Salem State University Archives and Special Collections, for her support in selecting appropriate early period photos of kindergarten children from the public Common School at Salem State Normal School.

Wendy Holland:

The very nature of early years practice is founded on good teamwork, and I would like to acknowledge all the help, support and inspiration I've received from the dedicated early years teams I have worked with both in mainstream and special school settings in Yorkshire and Lancashire. I would also like to acknowledge my current early years colleagues for their support and dedicated attitude to Quality First Practice, both in settings and with the students at Bradford University College, and Leeds Trinity University. Finally, my sincere thanks go to my collaborators in this venture, Dr Pam Jarvis, Dr Louise Swiniarski, Jane George and Dr Jonathan Doherty, for giving their time and sharing their knowledge and expertise to create something so uniquely knowledgeable and diverse for the early years 'pioneers' of the future.

About the authors and contributor

Dr Pam Jarvis is a Chartered Psychologist and Historian. Her key research focus is that of 'well-being' in education across all age ranges and academic levels. She has twenty years of experience of creating and teaching developmental, social science and social policy modules for Education/Child Development programmes in higher education. Pam currently leads the BA (Hons) in Child and Family Welfare at Leeds Trinity University, UK. She has Qualified Teacher Status, an MA in History and an MEd, and was awarded a PhD by Leeds Metropolitan University in 2005 for her thesis 'The Role of Rough and Tumble Play in Children's Social and Gender Role Development in The Early Years of Primary School'. Pam is a member of the academic advisory team for the National Save Childhood Movement and 'Too Much, Too Soon' campaign in the UK. Her recent publications include *The Complete Companion for Teaching and Leading Practice in the Early Years* (Routledge, 2016, with J. George, W. Holland and J. Doherty), 'British Nurseries, Head and Heart: McMillan, Owen and the Genesis of the Education/ Care Dichotomy' (*Women's History Review*, 2015, with B. Liebovich), 'On "Becoming Social": The Importance of Collaborative Free Play in Childhood' (*International Journal of Play*, 2014, with S. Newman and L. Swiniarski) and *Perspectives on Play: Learning for Life* (Routledge, 2014, with A. Brock and Y. Olusoga).

Louise Swiniarski is Professor Emerita at Salem State University, Massachusetts. As a Professor in its School of Education, Dr Swiniarski coordinated the Salem State Student Teaching Program in England, and the Early Childhood Education Undergraduate and Graduate Programs. She was named as a Visiting Professor at Leeds Beckett University in the UK and selected as a Visiting Practitioner at Harvard University's Graduate School of Education's Principal Center. Currently, she directs programmes for the Northeast Global Education Center at Salem State University. Her research interests include comparative early education programmes, the rights of the child, curriculum development and philosophical foundations. As an author and researcher, she presents her work at many international and national conferences and serves on the editorial board of the *Early Childhood Education Journal*. She has been a recipient of several awards for her research and teaching, including an International Research Scholarship from the Government of Finland for International Scholars and recognition awards for professional achievements from the Commonwealth of Massachusetts, the CAYL Service 2013 Fellowship Award and Salem State Alumni Awards. As a graduate from Boston College for her PhD in Philosophy of Education and a BS in Education, Dr Swiniarski was distinguished by being named as one of the *Fifty Faces of the Lynch School of Education.*

Wendy Holland, MA, has experience of teaching in mainstream nurseries, primary and special schools for over thirty years. From the 1970s onwards, her focus has been around inclusive provision and practice for children aged 0 to 8 years. Through the establishment of mother and toddler groups and playgroups for children with particular needs, and integrated mainstream provision for hearing and hearing-impaired nursery and primary-aged children, she has pursued her particular interests around the inclusion of parents/carers in the caring and educative process. The importance of the role of the reflective practitioner as an agent for change in early years practice is another of her interests. She is currently working in the Teaching, Health and Care sector at Bradford College in the UK, developing and producing modules for the BA (Hons) with Qualified Teacher Status degree and the BA (Hons) Educational Studies degree, alongside supporting students engaged in a range of undergraduate and master's-level programmes. Her recent publications include *The Complete Companion for Teaching and Leading Practice in the Early Years* (Routledge, 2016, with J. George, P. Jarvis and J. Doherty), 'The Patchwork Quilt' (in *A Story to Tell*, G. Murphy and M. Power, Trentham Books, 2009), 'The Early Years Professional and the Children's Centre: At the Hub of the "Big Society"?' (in *Making It Work for the Child*, A. Brock and C. Rankin, Continuum, 2011) and *Research in the Early Years Setting: A Step By Step Guide* (Harlow, 2012, with P. Jarvis, S. Newman and J. George).

Betty Liebovich, EdD, is Lecturer in Early Years Education at Goldsmiths University, UK, an expert on the history of the open-air nursery, particularly the Rachel McMillan Nursery in South London, and a researcher of the history of early childhood teacher education in England and the USA.

Foreword
Jonathan Doherty

It is a real pleasure for me to write the Foreword to this inspiring and exciting book. In the early years there continues to be a proliferation of new books aimed at a market of readers that embrace students, teachers, trainee teachers, practitioners, senior leaders and parents. The content of many of these books is often curriculum based, offering insights into play, child development, working with parents, multi-agency support, the learning environment and current educational policy. To readers they offer yet another piece of a jigsaw that somehow we have to fit together ourselves. This book is different as it essentially gives readers the first piece of the jigsaw, that of the early pioneers. Without a detailed investigation into the lives of the great leaders in early education of the past, their lives, their motivations and inspirations, we would not have the high-quality frameworks for early education we have in the UK and USA that we proudly possess today. It is no coincidence, therefore, that our current frameworks and the curricula for our youngest children are based upon sound foundations that have more than stood the test of time; they have evolved over time to create what we have in place today.

The word 'pioneers' in the title of the book implies individuals who are the 'movers and shakers' of their day. True leaders whose wisdom as well as their drive and outstanding resilience in the face of adversity inspire us through their charting of new territories and new ideas. It would be foolhardy to divorce the past from the present: where early years is today is our legacy of the past given to us by the likes of Montessori, Steiner, Isaacs and McMillan. It might also be tempting to look back at the past with a rose-tinted sense of nostalgia, whereas we should be thinking of how nostalgia enables us through reflection to critique the present and learn from it. The principles underpinning *quality* early education are its hallmarks, that of a relevant and appropriate curriculum and an enabling framework which is supported by knowledgeable adults in stimulating environments that offer warmth and security. Here, expectations for all learners are high but realistic, children are respected and given choice and are at the centre of learning, co-constructing it with adults who understand how children learn and develop and respond to their needs with pedagogies that are inclusive while offering challenge and promoting progression. Education for our children in primary and secondary schools is suffering the acute pressures of neoliberalism; that of accountability of its teachers, high-stakes testing, politicisation of teaching and a global drive for higher standards and measurable results in increasingly narrowed curricula. Social democracy, children's voices, a whole-child approach, understanding of developmental trajectories and meeting of individual needs seem sadly to be fading fast. For the principles that constitute quality learning, one has to turn to the early years and in doing so one is reminded of the teachings of the great pioneers that are described so eloquently by the authors of this book.

The authors skilfully take us on a journey and offer readers a piece of that jigsaw in every chapter. Froebel shows us the importance of learning through play and the fact that the needs of our younger children are different to older peers. Pestalozzi's ideas of an integrated curriculum emphasise the notion of the whole child we value so much today. This education places high value on the hand, the head and the heart of each child. Margaret McMillan's personal experiences and observations provide us with an enduring justification of the value of outdoor play. There are immediate parallels between the four principles of the early years foundation stage (EYFS) in England and Montessori's approach to education. Within each child lies hidden individual potential (Unique Child); parents as first educators and the value of partnership in learning (Positive Relationships); environments that support children's self-construction (Enabling Environments); and children as active learners who flourish when given opportunities to explore and experiment (Learning and Development). Similarly, Rudolf Steiner emphasises the need to understand child development with carefully planned learning, and describes how child-friendly environments supported and scaffolded by adults allow a child's natural capacities to unfold, which is at the very heart of child-centred education.

This book also prompts us to take a wider view of early education, contextualised by the authors in the UK and USA. Not only do the pioneers encourage us to look back; the book also encourages us to look broadly and become familiar with the experiences of other countries. There is a global flow of ideas in early childhood education and care (ECEC) which increases our knowledge base considerably, but it takes a discriminatory reader to ask *why* these ideas have developed, *why* they work, *why* they might not work if transported wholesale into a different context and *what* conditions are necessary to embed them successfully into a new context or culture.

The book is a scholarly and well-researched text and an excellent contribution to the field. Its narrative reads easily but at the same time its authority is evident. It communicates very clearly the uniqueness of each of the pioneers and their philosophies and teachings. It connects history with current policy and practice in early years. Its features almost demand readers to reflect on this connection and on their own practice. The legacy of these influential thinkers of the past provides us with a blueprint to take forward in the twenty-first century. By standing on the shoulders of such giants, the view of the future becomes much clearer.

Jonathan Doherty

An introduction to early years pioneers in context

Pam Jarvis, Louise Swiniarski and Wendy Holland

Introduction

Early Years Pioneers in Context is an international study of critical educational leaders who established the foundation for early childhood education across continents in the nineteenth and early twentieth centuries. The book's chapters are composed of biographies that introduce leading thinkers of the past whose theories still impact upon current educational policies and practices.

The book is written by academics/professionals committed to the field of early education in both the United Kingdom and the United States. To set a global tone, the chapters capture each author's voice by using their nation's version of English spelling and writing styles. The chapters cover an international scope of what "early years education and care" has consisted of in the United States and some areas of Europe, both in the past and present, in various settings for young children from birth to eight years old. American and British glossaries are provided to assist the reader in understanding the professional terminology used on both sides of the Atlantic, and the current differences in the structure of provision.

The need for such a book became evident and noted in situations whenever early educators from the United States and United Kingdom exchanged their concerns on the currently changing climate for teaching and caring for young children in both nations. One US kindergarten teacher recently remarked that she sensed her children are no longer as calm as students she taught in previous years because they seem constantly driven to complete a paper or task (Swiniarski 2016, unpublished interview). In the United Kingdom and in England in particular, concerns have been expressed about the heavy emphasis upon the development of academic skills at a very young age, giving rise to the "Too Much, Too Soon" campaign (see http://www.toomuchtoosoon.org/). The emphasis on preschool and kindergarten education is no longer centered on the child but focused on the content of very advanced academic curriculums. In professional conversations, early educators in both England and the US share the same worries that children's needs have been replaced by top-down mandates from governmental agencies (see Jarvis, Newman and Swiniarski 2014). In both nations, the current educational goals are not focused on the whole child. No longer is instruction designed to fit the child; rather, standards are now set that require the child to fit the instructions. As a result, engaged and spontaneous experiences for social and emotional development, creative thinking and artistic expression, once encouraged in a guided child-centered curriculum with opportunity for playful learning, have given way to directed teaching of subject matter authored by publishing houses and assessed by their tests. Professional development programs provided for teachers, administrators and higher education personnel aim at "Developing Strategic Pathways to College and Career Success at a Birth through Age Eight Policy Forum" (Massachusetts Department of Elementary and Secondary Education, May 16, 2014).

In England, young children are entered into a program of statutory assessments, principally focused on competence in literacy and numeracy. There is an overall assessment when they leave the statutory early years foundation stage (EYFS) (DFE 2014) aged five, alongside a "progress check" for overall development at the age of two. There is a test of phonics recognition during the school year in which the child turns six; while this is outside the EYFS and into the first year of the English National Curriculum, there is a deep impact upon practice in the EYFS in terms of settings' concern that children will be "ready" to perform to the "expected" level (which is set by the English Government Department for Education [DFE]). In England, children are admitted to reception at the start of the school year in which they turn five. The school year runs from September to August, so this means that some of each cohort, the "summer birthdays," will be only just four at the point of admission. None of the statutory assessments administered within schools are gradated for calendar age. The results of all these statutory assessments are notified to the DFE to be recorded against both the name of the individual child and the setting. The statistics generated from the results of cohorts of children from year to year play an increasingly important role in the statutory inspection of the setting. They also inevitably impact upon the progression of the individual child, in the ways in which they are subsequently constructed by teachers and head teachers, and grouped within the cohort. The assessment process in Wales is similar, while the policies of Scotland and Northern Ireland are currently evolving.

This book takes the reader back to the dawn of early years education, to consider early years pedagogical innovations developed by those who first conceived the provision of programs of education for children under eight. Each chapter tracks the ideas introduced by the relevant "pioneer" through to the present, considering how they have been developed for modern practice. Too frequently we are led to the conclusion that the current emphasis on transmission-based practice has removed much of the richness of holistic pedagogies that focus on the development of independent learning skills, rather than the transmission of disembedded knowledge and skills. This chapter will set the pioneers within their historical context, and provide underpinning knowledge of the relevant historical milieu to aid readers' understanding of the times and places in which the "pioneers" operated.

Historical notes

The United States of America is currently a huge nation composed of a federation of fifty states. However, the original thirteen "Crown Colonies" were created between the sixteenth and eighteenth century, principally by immigrants from Europe, with many from Great Britain (the historical name for the United Kingdom) and Ireland. They are located along the Eastern Atlantic seaboard of the nation and comprise Delaware, Pennsylvania, New Jersey, Connecticut, Massachusetts, Maryland, New Hampshire, Virginia, New York, Georgia, South Carolina, North Carolina and Rhode Island. These were originally ruled by Great Britain but following a successful collective declaration of independence from the British Crown, they became the first US states. Following the War of Independence between 1775 and 1783, the US became a new Federal Republic; a unitary nation composed of a number of states with some amount of freedom for self-determination under one unitary Constitution, which was ratified by all thirteen states in 1788. The United States of America was subsequently colonized by further immigrants, again principally from Europe over the period of the nineteenth and twentieth century, and further states were added as people moved out across the continent, to the borders of Canada in the North, Mexico in the South and to the Western Pacific seaboard. You will read in Chapter 2 of the sons of British "pioneer" Robert Owen, who became naturalized Americans, each playing a historically documented role in this process. The last two states were added to the union as recently as 1959; Hawaii and Alaska. Britain and America have continued to share close cultural ties, and of course a common language. Education is an area in which there have been many parallels, which continue to the present day.

Factors in wider society inevitably impact upon education. In the past, this importantly included religion, in both the US and Great Britain; specifically Christianity, which played a central part in the lives of the whole population of the US and Great Britain until the middle of the twentieth century. Christianity began in the Middle East approximately 2000 years ago, and we use a dating system that was set from a historical point that approximates the birth of Jesus, the founder of the religion. BCE means "before Christian Era" and CE means "Christian Era"; you will find these terms are used in Chapter 2. Over the period of its history, Christianity has experienced two major schisms: the split between Roman Catholic and Eastern Orthodox sects in the eleventh century and the split between Roman Catholicism and Protestantism in the sixteenth century. Many Protestant sects arose, and continue to debate various issues among themselves to the present day. One particular Protestant sect, the Puritans, initially located in Great Britain, had many differences to Church of England Protestants. This caused great difficulty for them as the Church of England was and still is the religion espoused by the state in the United Kingdom, headed by the reigning monarch (currently Queen Elizabeth II). Many Puritans consequently played a large part in founding the United States through emigration from Great Britain; this again illustrates the common history shared by the two nations.

Additionally, the US Episcopalian church has direct roots within the Church of England and is one of many broadly "Anglican" sects worldwide that sprung up from the basis of Church of England colonists who settled in many different nations. One of the "pioneers" in this book, **Susan Blow**, converted to Episcopalianism from Presbyterianism (another branch of Protestantism that originates in Scotland). **Elizabeth Peabody**, another of the "pioneers," embraced **Transcendentalism**, an American spiritual movement which rose from the Christian sect of **Unitarianism**, which has roots in Eastern Europe; however, its spread into the US came via an English Unitarian movement that began in London in the 1770s. British and American Transcendentalists agreed with the Unitarian view that God is one entity, and that Jesus was a human being rather than divine. However, they further added ideas from philosophy that celebrated human individuality and intense spiritual experience, viewing humankind as at one with nature. Froebel demonstrated similar leanings in his creation of the concept of **Gliedganzes**, which you will meet in Chapter 3. This was in turn based upon the concept of **Pantheism**, the belief that God is present in all living beings. Gliedganzes described how the divine human nature might be accessed by educational practices; an idea which **Rudolf Steiner** was later to extend, in the first instance through the use of **Theosophy** in his pedagogy. Theosophy views human intellectual functioning as the unification of body, mind and spirit. As such, Theosophists propose that by sufficiently developing spirituality alongside intellect, humankind would have the potential to gain access to other currently invisible "planes" that co-exist alongside the visible, physical world; Steiner used this idea in the development of his pedagogical framework. However, he later disagreed with some of the more extreme ideas that were being subsumed into Theosophy, in particular those that were derived from non-Christian religious thought. He therefore developed **Anthroposophy** as a breakaway sect, which maintained purely Christian beliefs at its core, but continued to advance the idea that the development of spirituality could bestow the ability to access elements of "hidden wisdom" that enhanced ethical and moral understanding. **Margaret McMillan** was very interested in Rudolf Steiner's linking of spirituality to education; however, she did not endorse his specific views.

Susan Isaacs was raised in a Methodist family, a Protestant sect with its roots in England, before declaring herself an atheist at the age of fourteen – someone with no belief in God at all. This was viewed as quite an extreme belief in the early twentieth century. In contrast, the **McMillan sisters**, who had roots within a Presbyterian Scottish family, became Christian Socialists in early adulthood. Christian Socialism was a blend of religion and socialist politics, very much rooted in the specific time and place of Victorian Britain. It focused on the immorality of the condition in which poor people lived in the industrial society that had emerged during the late eighteenth and early nineteenth century in Great Britain; this is further explored in Chapter 2.

While inequality has always been present in human societies, the conditions in which the poorest people lived and worked after the advent of industrialization eventually gave rise to alarm, in both Great Britain and the US. The cotton trade is a useful example of this situation due to the intimate links that sprang up between Britain and the US with respect to this initiative. Cotton was grown in the South-Eastern states of the US, and before the advent of sophisticated agricultural technology, the planting and harvesting of this crop was an unpleasant, labor-intensive task. A solution for meeting the demand for the substantial workforce required to farm cotton on an industrial scale developed between the two nations; that of using slaves imported from Africa. British ships sailed to Africa to buy slaves from tribal chiefs; they then transported the slaves to the US, who were purchased by the cotton plantation owners to work on their land. The empty British ships were then loaded with bales of raw cotton, which they transported back to Britain to be woven into cloth in mills staffed by very poor people, sometimes children, who were paid such low wages that malnutrition became endemic. The population of the US fought a Civil War between 1861 and 1865, Southern against Northern states, which brought an end to the use of slavery on the southern cotton plantations, while Britain passed a series of laws throughout the nineteenth century to curtail child labor and rationalize working hours for all. However, working conditions in British industry were still very harsh at the beginning of the twentieth century, and you will read in Chapter 7 of Margaret McMillan's enormous efforts during this era to improve the conditions in which working class families lived and worked. Indeed, D'Souza (1996, p. 89) proposes that "[US] slaves were, in material terms of diet, health and shelter, slightly better off than northern [English] industrial workers." This suggestion has been the source of much debate over many years; however, what is not in doubt is the huge amount of suffering experienced by ordinary people across the world in pursuit of profit through industrial production, and eventually, in early- to mid-twentieth-century Europe, from the industrialized warfare of World Wars I and II. This is further explored in this book in the chapters relating to Rudolf Steiner, Maria Montessori and Loris Malaguzzi.

You will find that the process of industrialization heavily impacted upon all of the "pioneers" in this book, albeit mediated by the time and place in which they lived and worked. They were also influenced by empirical studies and theories that emerged from the worlds of psychology and philosophy from the late seventeenth to the mid-twentieth century. As such, the section below briefly outlines some key concepts from these areas of research; those that had the greatest impact upon the pedagogies developed by the "pioneers."

Theorists who informed the policies and practice of the pioneers

The theories of some famous philosophers and psychologists are referred to in several chapters of this book. You will find a brief outline of the work of these people below:

John Locke (1632–1704): English philosopher Locke proposed that "No man's knowledge here can go beyond his experience" (Locke 1689). Where the biblical construction of the child that dominated Western Europe (and therefore European immigrants to the US) was as a being contaminated by "original sin," hence with an inherent tendency to revert to evil thoughts and behaviors, Locke rejected this idea. He proposed instead that each child was a neutral "blank slate" whose development would completely depend upon the input they received.

Jean-Jacques Rousseau (1712–78): French philosopher Rousseau was the first of his academic discipline to have a focused interest in early childhood. He, like Locke, proposed that the Christian perspective of the child was in error. However, unlike Locke, Rousseau proposed that human nature was instead inherently *good*, and could be nurtured within the child from this perspective.

John Dewey (1859–1952): American philosopher and psychologist Dewey proposed that education was not just the communication of ideas from a teacher to a pupil, but an interaction *between* them. He believed that pupils should be able to relate the information they were taught to previous experience, and make full sense of it in this respect. In this way, he believed that schools could be places in which independent thought and democratic understanding could be developed. He proposed that the learning process for human beings is inevitably one of "continuous construction" (Dewey 1902). This view was espoused in many different ways by all of the "pioneers" in this book.

Jean Piaget (1896–1980): Swiss psychologist Piaget was the first to develop a comprehensive stage theory of child development. His exhaustive program of empirical investigations indicated that children's thought was qualitatively different at different stages of development; this has been informative in the study of children's development of mathematical, technological and scientific understanding. His theory is called "constructivism" because, like Dewey's theory, it proposes that children have to construct their understanding of the world within their own thought processes throughout the period of development. Piaget was the first to develop a theory of *how* this might be accomplished. His stages of development are briefly as follows:

- *Sensori-motor stage* (birth to eighteen months) in which children develop an ability to physically coordinate their bodies and the information from their senses.
- *Pre-operational stage* (eighteen months to seven years) in which children develop an ability to conceive of the logical movements and state changes of objects beyond their own sensory experience, and to understand other people as beings with thoughts and intentions that are different from their own.

- *Concrete operational stage* (seven to twelve) in which children develop an ability to create logical predictions about the movement and state changes of objects, given the ability to manipulate them in a concrete (real-world) environment.

- *Formal operational stage* (twelve plus) marks the development of an adult ability to logically theorize the world of objects, which now has to be practiced by application to different examples.

Lev Vygotsky (1896–1934): Russian philosopher and psychologist Vygotsky was also a constructivist, proposing that children have to construct the world in which they live within their own thoughts to effectively operate within it. However, unlike Piaget, Vygotsky principally focused on the *social* world, proposing that the most important drivers of thought were rooted in interactions between the child and other people rather than their operations on non-animate objects. The most important Vygotskian concept for early years professionals is the "Zone of Proximal Development" which describes the area into which a child can progress when they are able to talk through a problem with other people. American psychologist **Jerome Bruner**, born in 1915 and 100 years old at the time of writing (early 2016), introduced Vygotsky's theories to the English-speaking nations during the 1970s, and went on to develop his own theories from this basis. These importantly include:

- *Scaffolding*: the carefully judged help a teacher or more able peer provides for a learner, so it remains within their zone of proximal development and thus enables them to progress.

- *The Spiral Curriculum*: where a learner visits a problem again and again in the process of learning, each time at a more advanced level. For example, a child who eventually becomes an accomplished architect will make constructions with junk materials and large construction bricks in early childhood, moving on to more advanced construction toys in later childhood, such as Lego, Meccano, etc. It is only by this gradual, repetitive experience which gradually increases in complexity (i.e. a *spiral* process) that they will eventually move on to full professional competence in building objects.

The following section will summarize the current situation in early years education and care in the US and UK; it is this perspective from which we currently look back at the "pioneers."

Contemporary early years education and care in the US and UK

Early years education and care in the US

The early years education and care situation in the United States is complicated. It is one of the largest nations in the world both in terms of population and land mass; a huge federation of states which are currently inhabited by approximately

320 million people. As such, the way that education is funded has created a national "patchwork quilt" of practices for the early years. The national government is known as the Federal Government, through which the US Department of Education mandates educational policies, practices and funding. Likewise, each of the fifty states has its own Department of Education and in each state, local governments have their own school district boards. Because the Federal Government administers only 8 percent of national spending on education, its mandates are tied to limited subsidies. The lower governmental bodies are responsible for raising the remaining 92 percent of the costs of education in their districts and states. Most states apply for federal assistance because otherwise they would lack sufficient funds to run their schools. In some cases, states have rejected national mandates and forfeited federal financial backing, which creates an unequal distribution of monies. Some states require that each local school system provide kindergartens; others do not. While most parents tend to send their children to kindergarten, they are not required to do so. Children enter kindergarten if they are age five before the September of the relevant school year. The authorized school entry age varies among the fifty states, but it is usually age six for entering Grade One.

A few states provide universal preschools for children age three or four. Fees can be charged to families in some communities for attendance in extended day kindergartens and preschool opportunities. Care for children under five across most of the US is principally funded by their families, although some projects are funded by charity and by grants from various sources that offer support in this respect. Some large companies also offer childcare facilities for their employees. Working parents may also get tax rebates set against the cost of childcare; this again varies considerably from state to state. There may be some changes in this situation in the relatively near future.

> The US government has recently shown a desire to move on in this respect in its passing of the Child Care and Development Block Grant Act in 2014. Ongoing information can be found on this topic on the US Office of Child Care website: http://www.acf.hhs.gov/programs/occ.
>
> (Jarvis 2016, p. 246)

Head Start (see http://www.acf.hhs.gov/programs/ohs) is a world-famous US project that focuses on care and education for young children living in conditions of socio-economic deprivation, which has been running nationally throughout the US since the 1960s. It is funded through federal grants and charitable donations. However, it is not a daycare provider as such; it offers holistic support to families, including adult education initiatives.

Early years education and care in the contemporary UK

The United Kingdom is currently a nation state of approximately 65 million people. It is composed of an ancient union of four nations under one monarch: England,

Scotland, Wales and Northern Ireland. This union was originally referred to as "Great Britain," a term that is still in use today, but it is now more commonly referred to as the "United Kingdom" (UK). Currently, 83.9 percent of the population of the UK is located in England, 8.4 percent in Scotland, 4.8 percent in Wales and 2.9 percent in Northern Ireland (Office for National Statistics 2014). The current monarch, Queen Elizabeth II, is the constitutional head of state of all four nations, and many key aspects of governance (for example, national taxation, which funds state education among many other things) are administered from Parliament in Westminster, London headed by the British Prime Minister and a "cabinet" of ministers. However, since the early 2000s, the nations of the UK have been undergoing a process of devolution, in which Wales, Scotland and Northern Ireland have been given greater independence of governance. This has impacted heavily upon the organization of education, which is one of the primary devolved powers.

The statutory early years foundation stage framework (DFE 2014), which is referred to several times in this book, is therefore applied to children between birth and five years *only in England*. Additionally, Ofsted (the Office for Standards in Education, Children's Services and Skills), which was set up to cover the whole of the UK in 1993, now only inspects schools and settings in England. The other UK nations have their own education inspectorates, for example Education Scotland, ESTYN (Her Majesty's Inspectorate for Education and Training in Wales) and ETI (The Education and Training Inspectorate) in Northern Ireland. In terms of frameworks and curriculums for children in the early years, Wales has the statutory early years foundation phase for three to seven-year-olds (http://gov.wales/docs/dcells/publications/141111-framework-for-childrens-learning-for-3-to-7-year-olds-en.pdf), with no formal framework for under threes. Scotland's Curriculum for Excellence covers provision for children aged three to eighteen years (http://www.educationscotland.gov.uk/learningandteaching/thecurriculum/whatis curriculumforexcellence/index.asp); again, there is no formal framework for under threes. Northern Ireland has non-statutory Curricular Guidance for Pre-school Education (http://ccea.org.uk/sites/default/files/docs/curriculum/pre_school/preschool_guidance.pdf). England is thus alone among the UK nations in providing a statutory framework from birth. The situation relating to early years frameworks/curriculums continues to unfold within the UK, and further discussion on this topic can be found in *The Complete Companion for Teaching and Leading Practice in the Early Years* by Pam Jarvis, Jane George, Wendy Holland and Jonathan Doherty (2016, Routledge).

Much of the policy for children, young people and families within the UK and for England in particular is in a constant state of flux, amidst not a little confusion. The creation and subsequent development/non-development of Children's Centres, and the ongoing debate about funding early years care and education, are useful illustrations of the current situation. Children's Centres were created throughout the UK via "Sure Start Local" projects under the direction of the New Labour Government 1997–2010; in the first instance, it was suggested that this process had been inspired by the US Head Start enrichment program. At that time, funding for Sure Start projects was largely provided by the government, with the proviso that they would become self-sustaining within a few years; but how this was to happen was never clearly specified, and became even less clear following the global economic recession that began in 2007.

The stated purpose for the Children's Centres was also somewhat problematic, in that the New Labour Government intended them to play a major role in the provision of universal daycare, but at the same time to additionally address socio-economic disadvantage; these two agendas quickly became confused. The Conservative-Liberal Coalition Government 2010–15 removed the agenda to provide universal daycare, but re-emphasized the mission to support children in families experiencing socio-economic disadvantage, a policy change which Prime Minister David Cameron stated was to take Sure Start "back to its original purpose" (Coalition Government 2010, p. 10). This led to the closure of many Children's Centres in areas that were not designated as "disadvantaged," and the selling off of their daycare provision to private providers. There are currently complaints of underfunding from those that remain.

In England, three and four-year-olds are entitled to fifteen hours of state-funded education and care for thirty-eight weeks of the year; in Wales they are entitled to ten hours a week; in Scotland the entitlement is 600 hours of free childcare a year, while in Northern Ireland it is 12.5 hours a week during school terms. In all UK countries, this care may be accessed from any registered setting, in various combinations. With respect only to England, the government has recently legislated to raise the hours of state-funded care to thirty hours a week for thirty-eight weeks of the year for three and four-year-olds. This is currently (early 2016) causing huge concern to privately run settings, as they propose that the fee per hour paid by the government is insufficient to cover their costs. When the statutory provision was fifteen state-funded hours, they were able to remain solvent by charging parents a higher fee for the extra hours that most needed to use; however, many families will not need to buy extra hours if the statutory provision is doubled, leaving settings with nowhere to recoup the shortfall (see http://www.daynurseries.co.uk/news/article.cfm/id/1573877/Most-nurseries-may-not-offer-30-hours-free-childcare).

Introducing the "pioneers"

The intent of this book's eleven chapters is to map pathways to equable systems for the provision of education and care for young children. The biography of each pioneer presents a legacy as a "look back to move forward" for the well-being of all young children, and the pedagogy espoused by each pioneer is subsequently viewed from a contemporary vantage point, considering what relevance it has for current early years knowledge and practice. The chapters are historically ordered, beginning in Chapter 2 with the advent of child-centered education in **Pestalozzi's** attempts to create a practical model of education that adhered to the philosophy of

Rousseau. Chapter 2 also briefly considers a key British pedagogical experiment headed by industrialist **Robert Owen**, in his attempt to provide an ethical holistic education in the factory school that he developed for children destined to become workers in his factory in New Lanark, Scotland.

Chapter 3 considers the original kindergarten developed in Germany by **Friedrich Froebel** and tracks the continuing international successes of Froebelian-inspired pedagogy to the present day. This is followed by two chapters, 4 and 5, detailing the work of two Froebel-influenced early years pioneers in the United States, **Elizabeth Peabody** and **Susan Blow**, following their substantial contributions to the creation of a cohesive vision for structured but flexible early years provision across their new and rapidly expanding nation. We then turn back to Europe in Chapter 6 to consider the spiritually focused pedagogy of **Rudolf Steiner**, developed in Germany between World Wars I and II. Chapter 7 considers the work of Steiner's British contemporary, **Margaret McMillan**, who, after a number of false starts, created a world-famous "open air" nursery, introducing the concept of "educare" to the world. McMillan's unique program, which combined attention to both physical health and social development, never became a pedagogy in its own right, but nevertheless blazed a trail for practitioners working with children from deprived socio-economic backgrounds, the echoes of which can still be discerned in enrichment programs such as Head Start in the US and Sure Start in the UK. Chapter 8 moves on to Southern Europe, to the comprehensive "scientific pedagogy" developed by **Maria Montessori**, starting in Italy in the early years of the twentieth century. The Montessori Method became a worldwide operation, promoted throughout the twentieth century first by Maria Montessori herself, and later by her son, Mario Montessori. The Montessori project continues in the twenty-first century with 20,000 Montessori schools worldwide.

Chapter 9 moves on to a very different "pioneer"; one who did not bequeath a particular pedagogical program to the world, but whose ability to create a practical pedagogy rooted in theoretical psychological concepts focused on children's emotional well-being underlines her unique contribution to our current body of early

FIGURE 1.1 The New Lanark School and Institute. © New Lanark Trust

years skills and knowledge. **Susan Isaacs** was both an early years teacher and a Freudian psychologist, who had an exceptional literary talent that enabled her to express complex psychological concepts in clear prose, both for professionals working with children and for parents and families. Her development of the practice of detailed, focused observation to inform professionals of the individual needs of children, both with respect to education and care, secured her place in our collection of "early years pioneers."

Chapter 10 details the holistic, flexible child-centered pedagogy of the most recent pioneer in our book, **Loris Malaguzzi**, and his associates on the **Reggio Emilia** project. Initiated in 1945 as a local anti-fascist venture, Reggio Emilia schools have gained worldwide fame and recognition for the excellence of their practice. The Reggio "method" can be seen as the culmination of many practices introduced by the earlier pioneers, and its innovative approach is still informing early years practice in many nations around the world. While its pedagogical philosophy is clearly not culturally compatible with the current neo-liberal agenda of the US and UK, its endlessly flexible approach, which is nevertheless coupled with a steady focus on education for democracy, can be viewed as a target for both nations to strive towards. In this way, we are hopeful that the early years pioneers will continue to lead us into the future.

Glossary of terms

America

Public schools are schools supported by tax revenues from the local authority, state and federal governments.

Private schools are independent schools funded by fees, usually paid by the parents of the children attending.

High schools are secondary schools for grades 9–12 (children age fourteen to eighteen years).

Preparatory schools are secondary schools that prepare students for higher education at the college and university levels.

Middle schools are for grades 6 to 8 (children age eleven to thirteen years).

Grammar schools are elementary schools that can range for grades kindergarten to 5 or 8 (children age five to eleven or five to thirteen).

Elementary schools can include primary education of young children from age five to eight or from kindergarten to age thirteen.

Kindergartens are for children age five and are equivalent to the last year of nursery/preschool in other nations.

Preschools are also known as **nursery schools** for children age two to four.

Universal preschools are open to all children age two to four funded by fees, usually paid by the parents of the children attending.

Free universal preschools provide education for children age three to four with public funding.

Child Care Centers are for children from birth to age eight.

Early childhood education is the umbrella term for programs for children from birth to eight and also known as **early education and care**.

England

Reception classes are the point of entry to schooling for English children, a year earlier than in the US. There is one admission point, in September, for children who will turn five between 1st September and 31st August during that school year. While reception is technically the last year of the early years foundation stage, the pedagogical regime largely focuses upon the transmission of literacy and numeracy skills, in preparation for the completion of the EYFS profile at the end and the phonics test during the following school year.

State schools are schools supported by tax revenues from the local authority and the state. Across the UK, the usual age divisions are nursery (three to rising five) primary (rising five to rising twelve) and secondary (rising twelve to eighteen). A few districts continue to work on a tripartite system; in this case children leaving primary school attend a middle school between the ages of rising twelve to rising fifteen.

Academies are a new type of state school, which draw their funding directly from the national government. They are structured on a business model, with boards of directors rather than a panel of governors. There are an increasing number of academy chains that run on the model of a business with multiple outlets (for example McDonalds or Starbucks).

Private schools are independent schools funded by fees paid by the children's parents; they may be primary or secondary schools. Many offer education for three to eighteen-year-olds, although they will be divided into nursery, primary and secondary departments which may be housed on different sites. Many offer scholarships (fee waivers) to children, usually higher achievers whose parents are not able to pay.

Public schools are so-called because in ancient times, they were the alternative choice to home-based education for the education of boys from wealthy families over the age of twelve. They continue to be the most expensive private secondary schools in the UK; however, most now offer scholarships to children from less wealthy families who fit particular criteria, usually related to academic achievement. An increasing number are now co-educational.

Preparatory or "prep" schools are private schools that educate children from the age of three to eleven who are destined for public schools.

Year groups are the British equivalent of grades, where children are allocated to a year group on the basis of where their birthday falls on an academic year between September and August. Children start in reception in the school year in which their fifth birthday falls, and finish in year 13 in the school year in which their eighteenth birthday falls.

Nurseries may be independent schools in their own right, but across the UK, they are more likely to be housed in a classroom within a primary school, under the same management as the mainstream year groups. They take in children from three to rising five, and daily sessions are typically one half-day. A typical nursery day would run two sessions from 9am to 12 noon and from 1pm to 4pm, Monday to Friday, with a different cohort of children attending the morning and afternoon sessions.

Daycare provision is privately run, but publicly inspected. Daycare centers choose their own opening hours; they are typically open from 7am to 7pm, with some now branching into later hours and/or overnight care. They cater for children from around six months of age to the age of five. In England, they are inspected by the same body as schools and nurseries (Ofsted) and expected to offer education alongside care. Registered settings may offer all or part of a child's statutory funded care and education.

Child minders provide home-based childcare for children, generally under age seven, although this may be flexible in terms of sibling groups. They too are publicly inspected by Ofsted in England and expected to offer education alongside care. In England, they are expected to deliver the EYFS to children of the relevant age, with similar standards applied to those applied to professional settings.

Playschool is a blanket term for professional provision for children that typically runs in a multi-purpose center (e.g., church hall or community center). Hours of care offered are various, and the funding basis for the group may be private or managed by a group of parents, or a church council, etc. These groups are also publicly inspected, and in England, inspected by Ofsted on the basis of their delivery of the EYFS in terms of both care and education.

Children's Centres were created throughout the UK by the New Labour Government of 1997–2010, although their numbers were cut back by the Coalition Government of 2010–15. The Conservative Government elected in 2015 has stated that their principal purpose is to work with families experiencing socio-economic disadvantage.

Maternity leave lasts for 52 weeks across the United Kingdom at a 90 percent wage for the first six weeks; thereafter £139.58 or a 90 percent wage if lower for the next thirty-three weeks. The last thirteen weeks are statutory but unpaid. From April 2015, parents have been able to share this leave between them after the first twelve weeks.

References

Coalition Government (2010) *The Coalition: Our Programme For Government.* London: The Cabinet Office.

Dewey, J. (1902) *The Child and the Curriculum.* Chicago: University of Chicago Press. Available at: http://www.gutenberg.org/files/29259/29259-h/29259-h.htm (Accessed March 1, 2016).

DfE (2014) *The Early Years Foundation Stage Statutory Framework*. London: DfE Publications. Available at: https://www.gov.uk/government/uploads/system/uploads/attachment_data/file/335504/EYFS_framework_from_1_September_2014__with_clarification_note.pdf (Accessed February 29, 2016).

D'Souza, D. (1996) *The End of Racism*. New York: Simon and Schuster.

Jarvis, P. (2016) The child, the family and the state: international perspectives. In P. Jarvis, J. George, W. Holland and J. Doherty, *The Complete Companion for Teaching and Leading Practice in the Early Years*. Abingdon: Routledge.

Jarvis, P., Newman, S. and Swiniarski, L. (2014) On 'becoming social': the importance of collaborative free play in childhood. *International Journal of Play* Vol. 3, No. 1, pp. 53–68. DOI:10.1080/21594937.2013.863440. Available at: http://www.tandfonline.com/doi/pdf/10.1080/21594937.2013.863440 (Accessed May 23, 2016)

Locke, J. (1689) *An Essay Concerning Human Understanding*. Available at: http://www.gutenberg.org/cache/epub/10615/pg10615-images.html (Accessed March 1, 2016).

Office for National Statistics (2014) Population estimates for UK, England and Wales, Scotland and Northern Ireland. Available at: http://webarchive.national archives.gov.uk/20160105160709/http://www.ons.gov.uk/ons/rel/pop-estimate/population-estimates-for-uk-england-and-wales-scotland-and-northern-ireland/index.html (Accessed February 29, 2016).

Swiniarski, L. (2016) Teacher interview on impact of curriculum changes in kindergarten instruction. Unpublished notes.

Early years pioneers
In the beginning
Pam Jarvis

This chapter will explore the beginnings of formal education in Western Europe, and consider the antecedents of the work of the pioneers whose lives and work are explored in the later chapters of this book. This means that not all of the content of this chapter will specifically consider early years education or early years educators, although all the people and concepts covered in this chapter have clear relevance for the innovations that were later introduced by those who pioneered early years education.

The chapter will begin with a short history of childhood in ancient and medieval European society, moving on to briefly consider the pedagogical philosophies of two eighteenth-century philosophers, Jean-Jacques Rousseau from France and John Locke from England. It will conclude by exploring the work of two educators who set up pioneering schools at the beginning of the nineteenth century: Johann Heinrich Pestalozzi from Switzerland and Robert Owen from Wales.

Childhoods in the distant past

Sterns (2011, p. 164) proposes that 'childhood . . . depends first and foremost on economic systems'. What he means by this is that the way a culture views its children and provides for them, including education and training, depends upon how it functions in terms of the ways in which wealth and property are divided, and how basic needs such as food and shelter are resourced. He comments that life in ancient hunter-gatherer societies was very different to that within the agricultural societies that grew up after 9000 BCE, for both children and adults. Ten thousand years ago, the Earth had recently emerged from an ice age that had lasted approximately 15,000 years. The human population at that time would have found the land increasingly fertile, and instead of living a nomadic existence hunting and foraging for food as they had done for many thousands of years, they began to settle down on the land to farm. The Genographic project (2016) refers to this huge cultural change as 'The Neolithic Revolution'.

Sterns (2011, p. 18) comments that the evidence suggests that prior to the development of agriculture, it was unusual to find a family with more than four children. In a hunter-gatherer situation people would not have had routine access to animal milk, therefore women would have been likely to lactate for much longer with each child. There may also have been some attempt to postpone reproduction due to the pressure a small child would put upon the resources of the family and community, in a culture that existed in a 'hand-to-mouth' situation. There would also have been high rates of infant mortality, caused by disease and when poor food supply decreased mothers' ability to produce sufficient milk to supply the child's needs.

However, Sterns proposes, it would have been likely that adults had more leisure time to spend with children than in the farming culture which followed, which required intense work on the land. From studies of rare contemporary hunter-gatherer societies, we can deduce that children were the responsibility of women until boys were old enough to be 'apprenticed' into the hunting group and girls deemed old enough to marry and have their own children; in both cases around fourteen years of age. While this sounds very young to modern people, it must be remembered that life-expectancy in hunter-gatherer societies was well below forty years of age, and there would have been very few people over sixty in the population.

In agricultural societies, the practice of children being cared for and educated solely within the family continued (Cunningham 2006). There was a dependent infancy until around the age of seven, at which time children were expected to have learned enough to be able to engage in simple chores around the house if they were girls, or apprenticed to begin learning about agriculture or a trade if they were boys. Orme (2001, p. 307) comments that by the medieval period, from the fifth to the fifteenth century CE, it was traditional for boys as young as seven to be employed to chase away birds from newly planted fields, or herd geese.

While children were seldom the focus of written records of this time, Cunningham cites an anonymous text from the fifteenth century CE that indicates adults clearly understood that between the ages of three and seven, children's learning was deeply rooted in make-believe:

> *To play with flowers, to build houses with sticks and branches, to make a white horse of a wand or a sailing ship from broken bread, a spear from a ragwort stalk or a sword from a rush, and to make a beautiful lady from a cloth and decorate it with blossoms and cherish it.*
>
> *(Cunningham 2006, p. 47)*

There was no system of formal education, however, and as such, parents were expected to be the principal teachers of their children. In the middle and upper classes, this would importantly include reading and usually writing. There was 'an ancient tradition of fathers instructing their sons, sometimes by writing texts for them to read' (Orme 2001, p. 243).

This is not to say that formal education was wholly unheard of in the early medieval period. Alfred the Great of England (849–99) expressed a wish for children of 'free men' to be formally taught to read English and for those boys with the aptitude to 'be brought to higher office' to learn Latin (Cunningham 2006, p. 51). Boys needed Latin, the official written language throughout Europe at that time for careers as churchmen, merchants and administrators (Orme 2001, p. 247). Very few girls learned to read Latin, and those who did tended to be highly privileged, taught by private tutors engaged principally to teach their brothers. Girls were certainly not permitted to attend school in this historical period. 'Highly educated women were the exception' (Cunningham 2006, p. 88). Cunningham additionally quotes an ancient English proverb: 'A mayde shuld be seen but not herd' (p. 47). Even boys would not be expected to attend school before the age of seven or eight, so early years education, such as it was, would have been principally within the home for all social classes (Orme 2001, p. 307).

In the final years of the medieval period, both Henry Vlll of England (1491–1547) and his Chancellor Sir Thomas More (1478–1535) encouraged their daughters to become highly accomplished scholars. Henry's daughter Elizabeth I (1533–1603) was fluent in French, Latin, Spanish, Italian and Greek, and there are reports of her speaking to visitors in Welsh and Cornish Gaelic. More argued in his famous book, *Utopia*, that there should be a national education system for both boys and girls (Cunningham 2006, p. 87). A century later, Czech philosopher John Amos Comenius (1592–1670) again argued the point for the education of women: 'they are also formed in the image of God and share in his grace . . . they are endowed with equal sharpness of mind and capacity for knowledge' (Cunningham 2006, pp. 89–90). For many centuries following, however well educated girls were, adult life brought gender-segregated roles for all but a few, with women's principal destiny focused upon the role of wife and mother.

Religion, predictably, was central to European formal education in the Middle Ages. Schools were most frequently located in or attached to churches and staffed by clergy. Teaching proceeded along the lines of instruct-recite, and boys who were inattentive or who struggled to learn as quickly as their teachers thought they should were frequently beaten (Cunningham 2006). Orme (2001, p. 157) quotes a rhyme scribbled in a medieval school book:

> *O noble teacher now we you pray*
> *That you will grant to give us leave to play.*

However, this may have been a vain hope. Medieval Christians believed that it was adults' most important duty to lead children away from childishness as quickly as possible, instilling dutifulness alongside spiritual and moral responsibility. The route to this, they believed, was by hard work and self-discipline (Orme 2001, p. 306). The biblical concept of original sin was strong within medieval societies in Western Europe; it was believed that children were born tainted in this way, and that adults' most important role was to teach them to control their sinful urges.

The beginnings of mass formal education

By the end of the seventeenth century, young children between three and eight from the middle classes were beginning to attend local 'Dame schools', so named because they were usually run by women, often in a room in their own house. Here children would learn the rudiments of reading, counting and possibly writing before being apprenticed (or in the case of girls, sent into domestic service) at seven or eight. Girls were also taught to knit and sew (Cunningham 2006, p. 78). Such a brief education adequately prepared children for working and middle-class adult life in the agriculture and trade economy. The Industrial Revolution, which began in England at the end of the eighteenth century, transformed working life, creating the requirement for the average adult to draw upon more complex skills and abilities.

Additionally, by the end of the seventeenth century, ways of thinking about childhood had already begun to change through what we now call the age of 'Enlightenment'. Scientists began to make important discoveries that challenged much traditional religious thought by demonstrating how many natural phenomena actually 'worked', and this in turn led to developments in sociological and political thought. This cultural development eventually impacted upon the European concept of childhood, which had previously been constructed as steeped in original sin. French philosopher Jean-Jacques Rousseau (1712–78) proposed in *Émile ou De l'éducation* (Émile, or on Education), 1762:

> *Love childhood, indulge its sports, its pleasures, its delightful instincts. Who has not sometimes regretted that age when laughter was ever on the lips, and when the heart was ever at peace? Why rob these innocents of the joys which pass so quickly, of that precious gift which they cannot abuse?*
>
> *Why fill with bitterness the fleeting days of early childhood, days which will no more return for them than for you? Fathers, can you tell when death will call your children to him? Do not lay up sorrow for yourselves by robbing them of the short span which nature has allotted to them. As soon as they are aware of the joy of life, let them rejoice in it, so that whenever God calls them they may not die without having tasted the joy of life.*
>
> *(Rousseau 1762)*

Rousseau stringently challenged English philosopher John Locke (1632–1704) who had taken up the baton for public education by focusing upon, in Rousseau's opinion, 'what a man ought to know without asking what a child is capable of learning . . . always looking for the man in the child without considering what he is before he becomes a man' (Cunningham 2006, p. 113).

This, then, is the beginning of a debate that is still present in the twenty-first century; that is, should childhood be cherished as a life stage in its own right, or should it be seen principally as a journey to adulthood in a particular culture and economy? John Locke had no doubts about his orientation, proposing that the children of the poor were 'usually maintained in idleness' (Cunningham 2006, p. 108) and therefore that 'working schools' should be established in each parish to ensure that such children 'from their infancy be inured to work, which is of no small consequence to making them sober and industrious all their lives after' (Cunningham 2006, p. 109). Locke did not, however, agree with the inherently religious 'sinful child' hypothesis; instead he 'argued that children were blank slates at birth, open to learning . . . unless corrupted by outside influence' (Sterns 2011, p. 76). Logically, from this point of view, influences encouraging children to develop a good work ethic and a sober approach to life should be exerted as soon as possible.

With the advent of industrial production at the end of the eighteenth century, the pressure for general schooling became more intense. Sterns (2011, p. 71) proposes that industrialisation changed three cultural 'fundamentals' relating to childhood:

- A conversion of childhood from work to schooling, which changed the concept of children from relatively quick economic assets, as they had been throughout the agricultural period, back to long-term economic liabilities as had been the case in the hunter-gatherer age, for completely different reasons;
- The need to limit family size due to the requirement to invest more resources in each child (which again repeats the hunter-gatherer imperative, but within a very different situation);
- Increased access to high-quality nutrition for all but the poorest in society, resulting in a significant drop in the infant mortality rate.

These 'fundamentals' – 'school, less death, fewer children in the overall population' – (Sterns 2011, p. 75) led on to further consequences:

- A growing interest from nation states in children and childhood, with a less numerous population of children constructed as national investments, leading to a growing involvement of the state in childhood and education;
- A subtle change in the construction of the genders, with girls' greater obedience and tolerance for 'sitting and learning' leading to a growing awareness that in a mass-schooled society, this 'might give girls an edge' (Sterns 2011, p. 75).

The issue of academically precocious girls was in general seen as a potential problem for society, and this orientation endured into the mid-twentieth century, for example in the 1950s English practice of creating a lower threshold for boys to pass the 11+ exam that admitted them to high-quality selective secondary education (Goldstein 1986). Several centuries before state education, Comenius had pre-empted this 'problem' and consequently proposed that education should be differently structured for boys and girls: 'we are not advising that women be educated in such a way that their tendency to curiosity shall be developed . . . [but] chiefly in those things that enable her . . . to promote the welfare of her husband and family' (Cunningham 2006, pp. 89–90). The first state educators had very similar ideas, and these were enforced until the Western civil rights advances of the mid-twentieth century resulted in more general equality for women.

The new construction of children as either inherently good (Rousseau) or as 'blank slates' (Locke) who could effectively be 'made good' fired the imagination of the generation of educators born into the middle of the eighteenth century. We will conclude this chapter by briefly focusing upon two of the most famous of these, Johann Heinrich Pestalozzi (1746–1827) in Switzerland and Robert Owen (1771–1858) in Great Britain.

Johann Heinrich Pestalozzi

Pestalozzi was born into a middle-class family during a turbulent time in the history of Switzerland, which was occupied by a variety of foreign armies throughout his lifetime. He was an avid student of Rousseau's philosophy of education, and formed a lifelong ambition to create a school that focused upon the practical implementation of a Rousseau-inspired pedagogy. His route to this was, however, quite indirect. He began by studying theology, following his family tradition, but abandoned this, taking up agriculture at the age of twenty-three in 1769. This business soon collapsed, and by 1774 he was taking poor children into his house near Zurich to help them become self-supporting by spinning and weaving. This enterprise also eventually collapsed, as the products the children made did not sell very well (Silber 2016). Pestalozzi turned to writing and eventually produced a novel, *Leonard and Gertrude* (1801). In this he described the setting up of his concept of an ideal village school by a fictional, highly accomplished mother. The story pitches his protagonist Gertrude against many odds, principally created by people championing the old-fashioned process of education – correcting the natures of naturally 'sinful' children. In the novel, one of his characters reflects:

> We can do very little with people unless the next generation is to have a very different training from that our schools furnish. The school really ought to stand in the closest connection with the life of the home, instead of, as now, in strong contradiction to it . . . a true school should develop to the fullest extent all the faculties of the child's nature.
>
> (Pestalozzi 1801)

Pestalozzi emphasises that all Gertrude teaches is 'intimately connected with the realities of life', which consequently the children come 'to know so thoroughly that they were able to teach it' (1801). The book sold well, bringing in some welcome funds for Pestalozzi to draw upon, and he began to consider how he might turn his ideas into reality. Bruhlmeier (2010, p. 6) explains how Pestalozzi believed that the psyche was divided into thought, feeling and action, which he referred to as 'head, heart and hand'. In this, he emphasised the intelligence, the morality and the practicality of the human being, emphasising that 'all should be developed to the full in harmony' through a pedagogy that worked with the child's nature rather than against it.

Switzerland was invaded by the French in 1798, which led to some amount of modernisation, particularly with respect to initiatives relating to class equality and consequent interest in the provision of education to such ends. Pestalozzi was asked to organise higher education in Switzerland but refused, asking instead to start at the beginning with children. From 1800–4 he established and led a school at Burgdorf, but in 1803, a change in the way Switzerland was administered meant that a different regional government was appointed, which did not agree with Pestalozzi's methods, and consequently gave notice to his school to close. Pestalozzi then moved to Yverdon and opened a boarding school for boys. This was principally for paying pupils, but every third child was from a poor family, and admitted free of charge (Silber 2016). This school and its practice-led pedagogy became famous, and was visited by other European education pioneers, including Froebel and Owen, who you will read about later in this chapter.

At the height of its success, Yverdon housed 150 boys between seven and fifteen. They learned from practical work, which teachers facilitated either via setting reading from which the children then elicited practical projects, or by facilitating field trips, for example to study nature; a practical application of Pestalozzi's 'head, heart and hand' philosophy, which pre-empted the similar Reggio Emilia system by nearly 150 years. You will read about Reggio Emilia in Chapter 10.

In 1813, following Napoleon's defeat at Waterloo, the French left Switzerland and it was subsequently occupied by the Russian, Prussian and Austrian armies. The Russian Czar, Alexander l, was very impressed by Pestalozzi's pedagogical methods and asked him to set up a public schools system in Russia. However, by this time, Pestalozzi was sixty-seven, and consequently declined such an extensive endeavour and relocation. Thereafter, under a somewhat unstable national government, the Yverdon school went into a slow decline. It finally closed in 1825 after many differences of opinion between Pestalozzi and his staff. By this time Pestalozzi was in his late seventies. He died two years later in 1827 aged seventy-nine (Silber 2016).

Pestalozzi thus introduced many aspects of pedagogy that are still in practice today; most importantly, the concept of children learning by doing things that they enjoyed, supported by friendly, facilitating adults rather than being 'talked at' by stern teachers who punished them severely if they could not mechanically repeat the relevant 'lesson'. Pestalozzi's pedagogical ideas sparked interest across many other European nations, and we will now focus on an educator who was heavily influenced by Pestalozzi, but whose underpinning philosophy was rather different: the British industrial educator, Robert Owen.

Robert Owen

Robert Owen was born in 1771 in Newtown, Wales, the youngest of seven children. His family was principally connected with farming, but had turned their hand to inn-keeping and saddle-making when times were hard. He was not,

FIGURE 2.1 Robert Owen. © New Lanark Trust

therefore, from the middle classes like Pestalozzi, but from a working-class back-ground. There was, however, enough money to send Owen to the local school until he was eight. His quick intelligence impressed the staff there and he was made an 'usher' or 'monitor' (a child teaching assistant) towards the end of his time at the school. At ten years of age, Owen was sent to live with one of his older brothers, who had obtained an apprenticeship for him in a London-based linen and wool drapers. Owen then undertook a succession of jobs in the textile industry, moving into successively senior roles, until at seventeen he became a wholesale buyer in a drapery in Manchester. At this time, Manchester was rapidly evolving into a large, busy, industrial city: 'the speed and volume of technological change . . . won the town the tile of "Cottonopolis" and its wealth and population grew with remarka-ble rapidity' (Davis and O'Hagan 2010, p. 19).

By 1792, at twenty-one, Owen was employed as the superintendent of a new modern cotton mill in Manchester. Always an avid reader, he was now newly middle class and able to join the Manchester Literary and Philosophical Society, in which members wrote and discussed papers on a variety of topics, many relating to reflections on the rapid changes in the society and economy they inhabited. Through these connections, Owen was invited to visit other textile businesses across the nation. In Glasgow he met Caroline Dale, who invited him to visit her father's cotton factory in nearby New Lanark, with which Owen was greatly impressed. Dale had not only set up a factory, but was attempting to create a model community with improved housing and amenities. Such amenities included a school for the children of his factory workers to ensure they had sufficient skills, including literacy and numeracy, to cope with the requirements of their own eventual employment within the factory: 'a commercial and social experiment' (Davis and O'Hagan 2010, p. 35).

Owen subsequently married Caroline Dale, becoming a partner in his father-in-law's business in 1800. He had a keen interest in the school in particular, and carried out careful research to discover the most progressive, current pedagogical ideas. This eventually involved a visit to Pestalozzi in 1818. The two men did not wholly see eye to eye. Owen was impressed with Pestalozzi's attention to children's well-being and their sense of civic responsibility, and was especially interested in Pestalozzi's practical pedagogy. However, he had little patience with Pestalozzi's highly developed spiritual and somewhat mystical principles, thinking them impractical and over-romanticised.

'Robert Owen was essentially a man of practical action rather than a systematic philosophical or social theorist' (Davis and O'Hagan 2010, pp. 37–8). As such, what he deeply desired was a way to educate children for *industry*. In 1810, Owen determined that the New Lanark school would pioneer a new way of educating children 'to form the new character of the rising population' (Davis and O'Hagan 2010, p. 38). In this we can see an echo of Locke's orientation to education, rather than the Rousseau philosophy that Pestalozzi brought to his practical pedagogy. It must be emphasised here that unlike Pestalozzi, Owen was not the originator of this initiative against considerable environmental opposition, but by contrast, built upon what his father-in-law had already begun, particularly with respect to craft training: 'the objective [Dale] averred in 1790 was to fashion young people equipped to serve in a highly competitive labour market' (Davis and O'Hagan 2010, p. 78). Whether children should be educated in a way that holistically develops their knowledge and skills, or whether they should be educated in a way that quite narrowly prepares them for roles within a particular economy, is an issue we still debate today. This in turn creates two dichotomous models of the child – either as 'human capital' for the relevant economic environment or as a holistic, organic human being within the world in general.

Owen had a unique 'cross-over' approach in this respect. While he made no secret of the fact that he was preparing the children to become workers in his factory, his fervent belief was that they would be better workers if they were holistically developed by their education: 'Opposition to [man's] natural feelings and to all his exertions to attain happiness bring forth in time an abundant harvest of discontent, dislike, displeasure, envy, hatred, revenge and all the evil passions' (Owen 1991, p. 163). Owen insisted that children needed not only to learn basic reading, writing, arithmetic and the skills to do the job in the industry to which they would be allocated, but also to be more generally educated in areas such as history, geography and gardening, to avoid becoming mentally 'cramped and paralysed' which would 'render their moral character depraved and dangerous' to the extent that they could 'never become really useful subjects of the state' (Owen 1991, p. 163). He created an analogy of the worker as a biological machine: 'since the general introduction of the inanimate mechanism into British manufactories man, with few exceptions, has been treated as a secondary and inferior machine . . . you will find that man . . . as an instrument for the creation of wealth may still be greatly improved' (Owen 1991, p. 6).

In this sense, Owen used a rather odd mixture of Rousseau and Locke's very different philosophies, which drew upon a very practical orientation that additionally encompassed an enlightened perspective upon what we would nowadays term 'developmentally appropriate practice': 'no child should be employed within doors in any manufacture until he is twelve years of age . . . judicious farmers will not prematurely put their beasts of burden to work' (Owen 1991, p. 234). Over the period of the mid-nineteenth century, successive British governments passed laws to curtail the practice of employing children in occupations that were grossly unsuited to their stage of maturity. Sterns (2011, p. 77) comments that the practice of putting small children to work in factories was a feature of the transition from agriculture to industry; it gradually became obvious that while small children could do simple jobs in natural open-air environments, they were not sufficiently mature to be able to cope with complex industrial machines, a point that Owen had immediately intuited. He also had sufficient understanding of human development to structure education differently for children under seven: 'younger children were encouraged to explore their environment in order to recognize its many information-rich sources of meaning, directly filtered to the human inclination to enquire and make sense of the new experience' (Davis and O'Hagan 2010, p. 94). In this, Owen pre-empted the schema theory of Piaget, and the Vygotskian 'Zone of Proximal Development' (Jarvis et al. 2016), and of course the staged approaches to learning developed by Montessori and Steiner that you will read about in later chapters of this book.

Owen named his New Lanark school 'The Institute for the Formation of Character'. It was formally inaugurated in 1816, in a two-storey, five-room house, which he proposed could provide education for 600 children. The main room downstairs was laid out as a formal classroom with long rows of desks, but the room upstairs, directly above, was furnished so it could be used flexibly, for example for public lectures or for music and dancing. The other rooms were structured for teachers to work with small groups of children, for example learning to read or learning about history, geography or nature. This was a highly innovative approach, very much inspired by Pestalozzi.

Owen was particularly opposed to mechanical, skills-based approaches to literacy instruction, 'to avoid literacy becoming an end in its own right, to ensure that the ability to decode and print text was wedded to the capacity to comprehend and derive satisfaction from the act of reading' (Davis and O'Hagan 2010,

FIGURE 2.2 The New Lanark site, 1818. © New Lanark Trust

FIGURE 2.3 The institute façade. © New Lanark Trust

p. 94). This is an argument in which we still engage today, for example in debates relating to the recent all-encompassing emphasis upon phonics as the mechanism through which to teach literacy, and the English government's recent imposition of national phonics tests to ensure that is the way in which children are taught (Jarvis et al. 2016).

Children under seven, as in the traditional Dame schools, were taught co-educationally at New Lanark, while boys and girls over seven were segregated, except for music and dancing. Other innovations included specialist peripatetic teachers for music, dancing and physical education, and the allocation of groups of children to specific class teachers. The school's records for 1816 indicate that it housed 444 children aged between three and ten years. 'In taking forward the strongly vocational bent of Dale's methods, with their emphasis on practical, experiential learning, Owen discovered his own semi-independent route to an enlightened theory of classroom pedagogy' (Davis and O'Hagan 2010, p. 87).

Owen asserted that he had achieved 'improvements of the living machinery . . . producing a return exceeding 50 per cent profits equal to the percent on the original capital expended on them' (Owen 1991, p. 5). He justified this as 'the difference of the results between a mechanism which is neat, clean and well arranged . . . and that which is allowed to be dirty, in disorder' (Owen 1991, p. 4). He went on to explain that he was educating his workers rather than leaving them ignorant, ensuring that they were trained by intelligent people rather than ignorant ones, and further protecting his investment by ensuring that his young staff were employed in roles that did not push them beyond their strength and developmentally determined competence (Owen 1991, p. 169). He was keen to emphasise that his teachers were expected to 'provide intellectually absorbing objects and resources as the stimulus for lessons' (Davis and O'Hagan 2010, p. 86). One set of such resources was a huge collection of maps, both of the contemporary and ancient world, which Owen believed would help the children to conceive of people and places beyond their immediate surroundings. There is evidence that this had a highly formative impact upon at least one of the New Lanark children: Robert Owen's son, David Dale Owen (1807–60), who later became the geologist who led the first geological surveys of Indiana, Kentucky and Arkansas in the rapidly expanding United States of America (Lewis and Snell 2009, p. 216).

UNESCO dedicated the New Lanark site as a World Heritage Centre in 2001 (Historic Scotland 2016). Owen moved on to similar industrial community development projects in the United States in the 1820s, severing his connections with the New Lanark community in 1825. Unfortunately all of his initiatives in the United States failed. Owen returned to Britain and later championed the development of the cooperative movement in England, which still exists today (*The Guardian* 2014). In old age he returned to his birth place, Newtown in Wales, and died there in 1858, aged eighty-seven. His sons remained in the United States. His youngest son, Richard Dale Owen (1810–90), became the first president of Purdue University (Purdue University 2014) while his oldest son, Robert Dale Owen (1801–77), was elected to Congress, where he drafted the bill for the founding of the Smithsonian Institution (Encyclopedia of World Biography 2016). The careers of all of his sons were clearly influenced by their father's passionate commitment to the principled development of pedagogy for the industrial age.

Conclusion

In conclusion, it is clear that both Pestalozzi and Owen passionately believed that children should be holistically educated, a thread that runs through the pedagogy of all the pioneers to whom you will be introduced in this book. The philosophy behind these convictions was, however, rather different, with Owen approaching his pedagogical innovations through the lens of developing workers for industry, and Pestalozzi through a determination to directly translate Rousseau's child-centred philosophy into a practical reality. The core impetus for Pestalozzi's work sprang directly from Rousseau's insistence that the human spirit was essentially noble and benevolent, rather than shameful and sinful, while Owen was more allied to Locke in this respect, with a model of the child if not as a completely blank slate, then as a 'new' or 'clean' person who could be developed in a way that would fit them to their adult role, albeit as a well-rounded and generally well-educated individual.

So does childhood – and childhood education – depend largely upon economic factors underlying the society into which the child is born, as Sterns proposed (2011, p. 164)? It is likely that Owen would say 'yes' to this question, while Pestalozzi would say 'no'. This is a useful question from which to begin your study of the subsequent chapters in this book. You will find it particularly relevant when you meet Rudolf Steiner and Loris Malaguzzi, both of whom forged their pedagogies in the chaos following pan-European war on an industrial scale, respectively in 1918 and 1945. Owen's 'pedagogy for industry' is also highly relevant to the work of Margaret McMillan, who attempted to nurture young children in the squalid inner cities to which industrialisation eventually gave rise. Holland and Jarvis comment:

> *For Owen and McMillan, the impetus [for their pedagogy] sprang from issues arising from industrialisation, in the pursuit of blunting its potential for crushing the human spirit. At the beginning of the process, Owen hoped that education would be the answer; that it would be able to humanise industrial communities. Nearly a century later, McMillan had no such illusions; her impetus was to nurture the bodies, minds and spirits of children at the earliest possible point in development, in an attempt to give them the resilience to cope with working class adult lives in such an industrial society.*
>
> *(Holland and Jarvis 2016, p. 21)*

The work of the pioneers cannot always be viewed in the light of such obvious direct historical progression. However, as you meet each subsequent pioneer in this book, it is a good idea to acquaint yourself with the culture and time period in which they operated, as this inevitably had a significant influence upon their life and work. There are also clear threads of practice development across time, an important example being increasingly developmentally informed child-centred pedagogy. You will be able to follow these through the chapters, and we will then explore such connecting threads in more detail in the final chapter.

Student integration tasks

- Consider the differences and similarities between Pestalozzi and Owen. How do you think time and location impacted upon these?

- What very different factors fed into the limitation of family size and the construction of children as economic liabilities in both hunter-gatherer and industrial societies?

- Why do you think boys and girls were treated so unequally throughout the whole of human history, until the mid-twentieth century? Do you think we have effectively dealt with this issue now?

- Why do you think we are still having some of the same debates about the dichotomous 'organic human being' and 'human capital' approaches to educating children? Do you think we will ever fully resolve these?

- This chapter indicates that throughout history there seems to be a fairly general understanding from quite ancient times that young children under seven learn rather differently to older children. Do you think that this is effectively recognised by early years education systems and frameworks today?

- As you move through the following chapters, consider the impact of Rousseau and Pestalozzi upon the later pioneers.

References

Bruhlmeier, A. (2010) *Head, Heart and Hand: Education in the Spirit of Pestalozzi.* Cambridge: Sophia.

Cunningham, H. (2006) *The Invention of Childhood.* London: BBC Books.

Davis, R. and O'Hagan, F. (2010) *Robert Owen.* London: Bloomsbury.

Encyclopedia of World Biography (2016) *Robert Dale Owen.* Available at: http://www.encyclopedia.com/topic/Robert_Dale_Owen.aspx (Accessed 5 February 2016).

The Genographic Project (2016) *The Development of Agriculture.* Available at: https://genographic.nationalgeographic.com/development-of-agriculture/ (Accessed 3 February 2016).

Goldstein, H. (1986) *Gender Bias and Test Norms in Educational Selection.* Available at: http://www.bristol.ac.uk/media-library/sites/cmm/migrated/documents/gender-bias-in-selection.pdf (Accessed 3 February 2016).

The Guardian (2014) The History of the British Co-operative Movement – A Timeline. Available at: http://www.theguardian.com/social-enterprise-network/gallery/2014/jan/29/the-history-of-the-british-co-operative-movement-timeline (Accessed 5 February 2016).

Heritage Scotland (2016) *New Lanark.* Available at: http://www.historic-scotland.gov.uk/index/heritage/worldheritage/world-heritage-sites-in-scotland/new-lanark.htm (Accessed 5 February 2016).

Jarvis, P., George, J., Holland, W. and Doherty, J. (2016) *The Complete Companion for Teaching and Leading Practice in the Early Years.* Abingdon: Routledge.

Lewis, C. and Snell, D. (2009) *The Making of the Geological Society of London.* No. 317. London: The Geological Society.

Orme, N. (2001) *Medieval Children.* New Haven: Yale Press.

Owen, R. (1991) *A New View of Society and Other Writings.* London: Penguin Classics.

Pestalozzi, J. (1801) *Leonard and Gertrude*. Available at: https://archive.org/stream/pestalozzisleona00pestuoft/pestalozzisleona00pestuoft_djvu.txt (Accessed 3 February 2016).

Purdue University (2014) *Did You Know: Purdue's First President*. Available at: http://www.purdue.edu/newsroom/purduetoday/didyouknow/2014/Q3/did-you-know-purdues-first-president.html (Accessed 5 February 2016).

Rousseau, J. (1762) *Èmile, or on Education*. Available at http://oll.libertyfund.org/titles/2256 (Accessed 31 January 2015).

Royal.Gov (2016) *Elizabeth I*. Available at: http://www.royal.gov.uk/historyofthemonarchy/kingsandqueensofengland/thetudors/elizabethi.aspx (Accessed 5 February 2016).

Silber, K. (2016) *Johann Heinrich Pestalozzi, Swiss Educator*. Available at http://www.britannica.com/biography/Johann-Heinrich-Pestalozzi (Accessed 20 January 2015).

Sterns, P. (2011) *Childhood in World History* (2nd edn). Abingdon: Routledge.

3

Frederick Froebel (1782–1852)

The "garden of children"
Louise Swiniarski

Introduction: life, work, and the times

Frederick Froebel (1782–1852), a philosopher of German Idealism, an activist for educational change, and the founder of the kindergarten movement, was born near the beautiful forests of Oberweissbach, Thuringia to a Prussian family. His father was a Lutheran Pastor and his mother died before Froebel was to reach his first birthday. Both his family and birth-place had a lasting impact on his life. His religious beliefs shaped his embrace of German Idealism in his concept of God. His appreciation of nature was enhanced by his boyhood apprenticeship as a forester. His respect for motherhood developed over the years in his yearning for his own mother, and her love and attention. Froebel had several influential careers, which included serving in the Prussian military and as a student of architecture, before finding what he saw as his mission as an educator who established a school for young children known as the kindergarten. Froebel's major work, *The Education of Man*, postulates his life as a manifesto of his metaphorical concept of communal living with like-minded citizens who support a kindergarten (a garden of children) as the community's educational core.

This chapter will examine the man and his contributions to early childhood education that continue to resonate in today's pedagogy for child-centered models of education. As a German Idealist, and a student of Johann Heinrich Pestalozzi, Froebel's notions revolutionized *play* as the key to learning for young children. But he went beyond the dictates of his mentor when he connected each teaching experience to an inner philosophical and spiritual meaning. The chapter will likewise introduce his methodology for using his designs of materials and activities he created (*Gifts and Occupations*) as his curriculum frameworks, his philosophy for educating professional teachers of young children, and expected outcomes for establishing the kindergarten in a communal setting.

Throughout the world, Froebel's legacy remains in evidence in many early childhood education models. Since Froebel's native Prussian government were politically unsympathetic to his commune and educational practices, it banned his schools and settlement. His disciples felt forced to immigrate to more welcoming countries in Europe and the frontiers of America, where they could promote and re-establish Froebel ideals. The movement harvested international German kindergarten enclaves that in many instances stood the tests of time. Today, kindergartens prevail in most countries around the world as the foundation for children's formal education. While his philosophy and methodology have faced challenges throughout the past and present centuries, his perceptions have been modified and replicated in contemporary early childhood educational policies and practices. The chapter will highlight the recognition he received for his achievements and the influences he ingrained in highly successful exemplars.

Ancient forebears and the romantic age of kindergarten education

The notion of the importance of educating children at an early age did not originate with Froebel. Theoretically, the idea of early childhood education is in evidence well before the nineteenth century. The Ancient Greek philosopher, Plato, in his *Book VII of The Laws* calls for a concerned society to minister to its young. Plato believed that care should begin with pre-natal care and follow through the stages from birth through childhood with parents and highly trained nurses jointly attending to the child's subsequent development.

In Plato's seventh book of *The Laws*, he pushed for universal education so that each community would provide a "sanctuary" for children starting at age three, the age at which children begin to interact more with each other around organized and supervised play to age six, when children began formal schooling (Plato, p. 176). Plato is credited for the saying "as the tree is bent so grows the tree." He also stated that "The perfection of children's bodies must grow straight from their earliest days" (Plato, p. 170). Subsequent followers reiterated his belief in providing early education. The Roman educator, Quintilian (AD 35–97), considered the early years of childhood as foundational to all learning when in his *Institutio Oratoria* he wrote:

> The time gained in childhood is clear profit to the period of youth. Let us not therefore waste the earliest years.
>
> (Quintilian translation, Butler 1963, p. 29)

Both Plato and Quintilian required highly qualified educators, *nurses*, as teachers and role models so that young children would avoid later needing to relearn previous instruction. He would argue that habilitation is more favorable than rehabilitation.

John Amos Comenius (1525–1670) is noted for his promotion of educating the young and supporting the mother as a child's first teacher. Historians credit him for acknowledging the importance of early education. His mandates for education were written in his seminal work, *The Great Didactic*, first in Czech (1632) and printed in Latin (1841), then translated into English (1896). Comenius believed that the betterment of "mankind" would come only through a universal, but not identical, education, which must start at the early ages (Power 1970).

> *[Comenius] refers to the adage "As the twig is bent the tree is inclined," in stressing the necessity for education from the children's most infant years.*
>
> *(Power 1970, p. 428)*

Comenius divided his curriculum into four stages beginning with the Mother School for children from birth to six. He therefore believed that the mother needed an education as well to carry through her tasks. Comenius wrote *The School of Infancy*, a guide intended for parents that was predicated on a sound pedagogy centered around play experiences to be carried out at home rather than in a formal school setting. He departed from Plato and Quintilian when they required trained professional nurses as early childhood educators. For Comenius' model, mothers needed to have the sufficient literacy skills for teaching their children during the School of Infancy period, which would hopefully be gained during the Vernacular School, opened to girls and boys until entrance into the Latin School, which was intended only for selected teenage boys who would need to prepare for the final level, the University. Comenius' trust in motherhood is a theme that Froebel adapted into his practice for training women and mothers as kindergarten teachers. Froebel also embraced the notions of play that Comenius prescribes for the Mother School.

Froebel's philosophy: idealism defines the goodness within children and his theory of education

Introduction: the romantic age

The innovators who established the notions for starting early in education prompted the framework for the nineteenth century's romantic age in early education and care of children. Reacting to the negative seventeenth- and eighteenth-century religious beliefs about childhood, nineteenth-century philosophers viewed children as naturally good but in need of guidance to fulfill their potential.

History places Froebel as one of the voices of the romantic age for his Idealism and commitment to allowing children's self-activities as modes for learning in his kindergarten (Power 1969). He and like-minded colleagues sustained the romantic age, which spread beyond school rooms to influences from the music of nineteenth-century composers, the art of painters like the Impressionists, and authors and illustrators like Kate Douglas Wiggin and Kate Greenaway, who were among the first to design children's clothes to give freer movements while at play. All these endeavors were formed by the philosophies of the era and their optimistic views of childhood.

Idealism

Froebel built his kindergarten around his notions of Idealism, which held that children are born with innate ideas and a natural goodness to be cultivated at an early age to avoid any negations. The kindergarten experience began the process for children at the age of three.

Froebel's methodology was predicated on this philosophy. His teaching practices were structured around its assumptions. The techniques he used were centered on prescribed play activities, music, poetry, and nature studies. All learning experiences had a spiritual meaning as well as educational implications.

His pedagogy, *Gifts and Occupations*, was the framework for his curriculum and activities that guided the instruction of young children. The philosophy was the cornerstone for every detail including the layout of the classroom and the atmosphere in which learning takes place. Coached by extensive instructions, teachers learned how to organize effective teaching sessions that led to cognitive development and understanding of spiritual tendencies. For example, the children sat in circles for their instruction to learn not only the tasks of the day but also to realize when in a circle, the child experiences the wholeness of being complete within oneself, while being a part of a greater whole. The children then learned the meaning of being *the one and the many* at the same time. Mothers were also instructed in the methodology to guide the child's pre-kindergarten years of development at home.

Froebel borrowed the dialectical view of reality from the German philosopher Hegel, and "the relationships between human beings and the external world" from the German philosopher Schelling (Lilley 1967, p. 9). In his metaphysics, Froebel sees the learner as "the active agent in the process of acquiring knowledge and truth" (Swiniarski 1976, p. 11). In his epistemology, he ascertains that "the learner grows and learns through self-activity" (Swiniarski 1976, p. 11).

Pantheism's influence on Froebel's philosophy of education

"Pantheism holds to the belief that God, the author of all being, exists in all creation, including humans. So, each one of us is divine as an extension of God's spirit" (Breitborde and Swiniarski 2006, p. 85). Froebel shaped Pantheism into his doctrine known as *Gliedganzes*, which deemed that ideas cultivate spiritual meaning and connections to educational practices. He followed many thinkers of his time; Pantheism was well imbedded among several religions and philosophies of the early nineteenth century.

Froebel lived in a period that spanned the heyday of speculative philosophy and was impressed with the Idealists' attempts to express a unified concept of reality as they sought to avoid duality in their interpretation of life through a systematic approach to philosophical inquiry. In Absolute Idealism the dilemma of duality was resolved by defining reality as a product of thought which could be explained by rational principles and synthesized in a total system.

(Swiniarski 1976, p. 9)

Froebel's kindergarten: a garden of children at play

Introduction

Prior to Froebel, theorists had speculated about the importance of play. Theorists valued play as an incentive or reward for learning. Froebel's unique treatment of play was his understanding of its value beyond an intrinsic mechanism. . . . Through play children learn about their world, themselves and others. Play allows them to solve problems, explore ideas, socialize and communicate.

(Breitborde and Swiniarski 2006, p. 85)

Play in the garden of children

Froebel established his school in 1840 to provide the proper environment that would guide the direction of a child's development in accordance with his philosophy and epistemology. He named his school the kindergarten – a metaphor for a garden of children cultivated in harmony with nature and God (Lilley 1967, p. 117). As plant life has its laws governing growth, so do children. The school's environment was based on nature and respectful of its laws. Likewise, the kindergarten was designed to be sensitive to the child's needs from age three to six and not a preparatory stage for later educational years. The kindergarten was intended as the first stage in promoting the child's development in a comprehensive educational program. Since it was the first school experience for the child, it was of foundational importance to all subsequent learning.

The purpose of this earliest stage of schooling was to develop awareness of the dwelling divine in each child through self-activity. Metaphorically, Froebel's school was a garden and its teachers and children were the gardeners. Children were free to explore self-activity in play. The garden was the setting. Play was the core for the child's development. But play was to be guided by the *gifts and occupations* designed by Froebel. Play was not a reward or a mere recreational experience. It was the medium through which children learn and develop cognitively. While the child was free to engage in self-activity, care was given to provide play activities and explorations for appropriate learning experiences.

Each activity had specific objectives and various levels of knowledge. Teachers needed to incorporate and order the levels for the selection of play experiences while trying not to deviate from Froebel's curriculum. Teachers established actual gardens for children as a part of their curriculum. In Froebel's communes for community living, the children grew their own vegetables as part of the kindergarten's curriculum that included mathematics, environmental studies, and promotion of healthy eating habits (Froebelweb 2016a).

Symbolic play: the spiritual side of teaching and learning

Symbolism is inherent in all Froebel's play activities to enhance the spiritual side of knowledge. Froebel believed higher degrees of knowledge were attained through the understanding of symbols. Each movement, linguistic pattern, or geometric object symbolized the principles of truth. The ball, for example, symbolizes unity and by playing with it, the child gains this insight. While American promoters of Froebel like Susan Blow highlighted the importance of symbolic education in their creed, later educators would question the earlier practitioners' positions on Froebel's insistence on using symbolic play. In universities such as Columbia University's Teachers College, these criticisms caused a later rift in the kindergarten movement.

To ensure optimum growth in each child, the teacher's task was to insure that each playful learning experience corresponded to the child's momentary period of unfoldment. Froebel believed play must be carefully fashioned and designed for specific objectives which he called gifts and occupations. Taken together, his gifts and occupations symbolically represent the principles of unity, connectedness, contrast, and development.

Gifts and occupations

Froebel's teaching materials and activities were published in his work, *The Education of Man*, as a guide for teachers. The materials and activities were his *Gifts and Occupations*.

> *The ten gifts included uses of colored worsted balls, natural wood blocks shaped as cylinders, cubes, rectangular, square and triangular wood blocks of various sizes. The occupations involved four areas of studies,* Solids, Surfaces, Lines and Points, *which children investigated with various materials such as clay, paper, cardboard, wood, and natural items of peas, beans, sticks, straw, and pebbles in carefully allocated activities including weaving, drawing, folding, paper cutting, wood work, stringing of beads, and performing.*
>
> *(Weber 1969, p. 12)*

The replication of Froebel's gifts and occupations was kept alive by his followers when they implemented his methodology and philosophy of Idealism in their schools' instructions. The gifts and occupations were adapted in the United States by Elizabeth Peabody, Kate Douglas Wiggin, and Nora Archibald Smith to be used in the home as well as at school. Wiggin and Smith made more distinctions in the specific meanings of what were to considered gifts when compared to the occupations. Froebel was not so detailed and sometimes blended gifts and occupations as one activity, which caused confusion to some of his disciples.

Critical perspectives: father of the kindergarten movement

Introduction

Internationally Froebel is affectionately named the Father of the Kindergarten as founder and philosopher of the kindergarten movement. Most followers were in agreement with his principles and tried to replicate his precise directions. While his followers were very dogmatic in their attempts to keep his premises pure in their practices, they could not avoid the adaptations that emerged from the cultures and needs of their diverse students.

When his disciples moved beyond the kindergarten established in Froebel's Prussian commune, several interpretations took place. Multiple languages required translations of his book, *The Education of Man*. The translators tried to stay faithful to Froebel's intents but culture and geography shaped contextual meanings and the physical formation of learning environments. However, according to one educational historian, Froebel's unique contribution of social education has had a lasting impact:

FIGURE 3.1 An American kindergarten class picture. Courtesy of Salem State University Archives and Special Collections.

> *Froebel made two outstanding contributions to modern education. One was the kin-*
> *dergarten: the other was social education. . . . No educator before Froebel . . . per-*
> *ceived more clearly than he the importance of human relations and the role schools*
> *could play in advancing them.*

> *(Power 1970, p. 515)*

Froebel's kindergarten: an international model

Froebel established his initial school, *Anstalt fur Kleinkinderpflege*, in 1837, but later changed its name in 1840 to the *Kindergarten*. However, in the 1840s, the Prussian government closed many of their liberal schools, including Froebel's kindergarten, and forced his followers to immigrate across Europe, beyond to Great Britain and eventually to America and Asia to establish kindergartens in more conducive and welcoming settlements (University of Roehampton 2016).

The opening of available land in America made this destination a favorable country to settle for the German followers. Froebel was hopeful for success in the new country. The earliest American kindergartens were primarily for children living in German-speaking communities. In 1856, Margarethe Schurz was credited with being the first in the United States to launch her kindergarten primarily for her own child, Agatha, and local neighborhood children. Her school grew as it opened to more families, who enrolled their children to benefit from the advantages of Froebel's educational program. Later, prominent early childhood education pioneers such as Elizabeth Peabody and Susan Blow adapted and adopted English-speaking public kindergartens for all young American children, both native-born and immigrants.

On the European continent, the Baroness von Marenholtz-Buelow founded her school and training program for its teachers in 1871 in Florence, Italy, while Henriette Schrader-Breymann managed to institute the Pestalozzi-Froebel Haus to educate teachers in Berlin for the remaining German kindergartens in 1873. Other countries that followed suit in setting up kindergartens included Austria, Russia and Japan. The 1870s also ushered in the Froebel Society, which was first established in both Manchester and London, England. Today, the Froebel Society offers grants to scholars for research into Froebel's issues to continue Froebel's goals and holds biennial conferences to outreach to committed educators globally. The most recent conference is scheduled for Kassel, Germany in June 2016. Conferences have been held in Dublin, Ireland and at Wheelock College in Boston, the United States (see http://www.froebelweb.org//linepost.html).

Theoretical and critical perspectives

There are still many loyal international followers of Froebel's philosophy, but with diversity also comes discourse. The twentieth century marked a shift in early education needs and practices. Innovations of the child study movement and the changing impact of the industrial age on twentieth-century childhood brought new challenges. Early childhood educators of the twentieth century questioned the notions of nineteenth-century romanticism in the arts, literature, and educational endeavors. Emerging sciences and academic studies such as psychology and sociology brought new horizons to educational methodology, policies, and practices that replaced many of Froebel's mandates for early education programs. As Froebel's kindergarten spread globally, his critics' voices were also heard and adapted in early childhood education, even though later history points out:

> *[Froebel's] attention to steps of development in the learning process made Froebel a forerunner in psychology and in some ways an anticipator of the progressive movement in education.*
>
> *(Power 1970, p. 514)*

Great Britain

In Great Britain, one formidable critic of Froebel's theory of education was Margaret McMillan (see Chapter 7), who in 1923 was the first president of the newly established Nursery School Association. Margaret and her sister, Rachel McMillan, led the nursery school movement in Great Britain to combat the high rates of infant mortality and promote educational opportunities for poor urban children. Despite the sisters' lack of professional training as early educators, their work in cities such as London in the south of England and Bradford in Yorkshire was very successful. Their infants and young children survived with proper care and educational opportunities to grow physically, cognitively, and socially. Margaret McMillan debated with professional early childhood educators that her approaches were more successful than those found in Froebel's models. The McMillans' mission was a response against the use of child labor in the coal mines and factories of the Industrial Revolution throughout Great Britain. As social activists and members of Britain's Labour Party, the sisters disregarded Froebel's symbolic meanings and his philosophy of Idealism.

United States of America

In the United States, the campaign to protect and promote Froebel practices was carried on by Kate Douglas Wiggin (1856–1923), a protégée of Elizabeth Peabody and her teacher, Emma Marwedel, who brought Froebel's kindergarten movement to Los Angeles, California. Kate Douglas Wiggin became the "creative interpreter of Froebel when she wrote and published four professional books on Froebel with a convincing style and skills" (Snyder, p. 115). With the kindergarten established from coast to coast by the twentieth century, Wiggin's work was a major national booster of Froebel's ideas.

Kate Douglas Wiggin was and still is a highly regarded author, known for her children's books that are now classics in American literary circles. She wrote and sold one of her most popular books, *The Birds' Christmas Carol*, to raise monies to keep the kindergarten viable in California (Wiggin 2001).

Despite Wiggin's valiant efforts, the tide moved against her. Beginning with John Dewey and his followers Alice Temple (1871–1946) in Chicago and Patty Smith Hill (1868–1946) at Columbia University in New York, new early childhood education practices began to grow in other universities such as Stanford University in California on the west coast and across America to the east coast at prestigious women's colleges such as Wheaton College, Smith College, and Wellesley College, all in Massachusetts. In these scholarly environments, early education's pedagogical theories became based on scientific research and the child studies movement, a field of psychology with new theories of child developmental stages.

Italy

In the early twentieth century Froebel's kindergarten also encountered an emerging competitive early education methodology developing under the skillful direction of a female Italian medical doctor, Maria Montessori (1870–1952, see Chapter 8). Although the Montessori method has in-depth coverage in a subsequent chapter in this book, it is prudent to note here the challenges Maria Montessori placed on earlier established efforts to spread Froebel's message throughout the then recently unified country of Italy.

Maria Montessori was concerned with similar issues in educating children in poverty the McMillan sisters held. Dr. Montessori worked with children confronted by disabilities in sight and hearing before she turned to assist the poor Italian children of the industrial age, who at the time were diagnosed as being cognitively impaired. At her *Casa die Bambini*, Dr. Montessori observed her urban children and concluded that they were lacking in proper care, not intellectual capacities. Montessori came to realize that these children needed a new approach to teaching and learning.

Dr. Montessori placed scientific findings at the core of her methodology to address children's educational issues. One of her biographers claims that "Dr. Montessori described herself as an empiricist" (Lillard 2005, p. IX). Montessori likewise considered her *Casa dei Bambini* as "not simply a place where children are kept, but a true school for their education" (Martin 1992, p. 12). She wanted her school to be a *home* where children felt safe to learn and a place where she could further study how children learned.

Her curriculum was centered on self-teaching materials that she created based on sensorial experiences and designated as *didactic materials*. She devised for her staff an instructional guide to accompany her methodology that became the *Montessori Method*. Maria called her teachers *directresses*, because they would direct the children on how to use their facility and its materials. Among educators today, Montessori training programs for professionals are highly regarded. She highlighted the importance of the directress roles in achieving success.

It is true that the child develops in his environment through activity itself, but he needs material means, guidance and an indispensable understanding. It is the adult who provides these necessities crucial to his development. The adult must give and do what is necessary for the child to act for himself.

(Montessori 1970, p. 154)

While Montessori agreed with Froebel that children should be active and autonomous in their learning experiences, she questioned Froebel's philosophy of Idealism, especially his symbolism in play activities. It is interesting to note that "play" was not a word Montessori ever used in her methodology. Indeed, she was very doctrinaire about the use of her didactic materials and scripted her guidelines. Children were not allowed to experiment with the materials in fantasy play or creative uses.

The Montessori method moved forward internationally into the twenty-first century, holding on to its interpretation of its twentieth-century scientific protocol. It remains a popular choice in Italy and in countries around the world as an alternative approach to kindergarten education.

FIGURE 3.2 Child playing at home with Montessori sound cylinders. © Louise Swiniarski

Relevance to contemporary practices: Froebel's legacy

Introduction

It is difficult to think about Frederick Froebel without remembering the many ideas he brought to education with his kindergarten. The kindergarten is now regarded as the foundation year in many school systems worldwide. Even though some of Froebel's ideas have been replaced by new technologies and methodologies, there are still institutions that follow or adapt his pedagogy.

Froebel's practices for today's child

Froebel's healthy respect for play and his sense that children should be actively engaged in their learning experiences are endorsed in many kindergarten and pre-school programs today. An American program that respects his ideas on play and "teaching to the needs of young children" is the national Head Start Program. Since the 1960s, during President Johnson's administration, the growing number of Head Start programs have adapted some of Froebel's mandates into their practices. A most notable practice is the outreach to and involvement of families in Head Start centers.

Froebel's influence is found in some private schools across America that continue to value play. Such private schools hold to the tradition of teaching around the developmental stages of children. They follow the mandates of the National Association for the Education of Young Children (NAEYC) that identify national standards and requirements to be an accredited preschool and/or kindergarten. This organization sets the benchmarks for quality education of children from three to six years of age. NAEYC provides teaching and curriculum standards for appropriate practices that echo the voice of Froebel on self-activity, social experiences, and guidelines for play activities that promote a sense of well-being in young children. Recommended "best practices" include the use of blocks and building materials, construction, art experiences with clay, and circle time (Swiniarski 2006).

There are international movements that resist the overemphasis on the current trend of academic-only studies in preschools and kindergartens. The Save Childhood Movement is such an organization in the United Kingdom (see http://www.savechildhood.net/). Its members are concerned by the diminished opportunities for today's child to play in or outside of school. The movement has revived the concept of National Children's Day (see http://www.educationscotland.gov.uk/resources/i/internationalchildrensday.asp), sponsoring activities to celebrate childhood across the nation on the relevant weekend and collating a list of recent readings, principally available online, supporting the need for play in childhood (see http://www.nationalchildrensdayuk.com/).

Parents and teachers also voice concerns about the inflated importance of academics in kindergartens. They call for more creative play when they point to Finland, which has received international applause for their national early education and care policies from organizations like the Organization of Economic Co-operation and Development (OECD). During visits to Finnish child care centers, one notices that some of Froebel's ideas have been consistently practiced throughout the twentieth and twenty-first centuries. Froebel's fine motor development exercises are still emphasized in the curriculum. Young children do weaving activities, stitchery, and craft work. Likewise, cognitive concepts and language development continue to be taught through the visual and performing arts such as painting, music, dance, drama, and puppetry (Swiniarski 1984, 2006, 2013, unpublished interviews in Finland).

> *Finland has maintained a long tradition of equity in access to early education and care, where play, language, and the arts are the basis of the early curriculum and balanced by goals of social and cognitive development.*
>
> *(Swiniarski 2014, p. 10)*

Internationally, professional psychologists, guidance counselors, and tutors agree with Froebel's emphasis on the significance of play in the well-being of children. They use play therapy with children in their counseling and tutoring sessions. Likewise, both at school and at home with family members, tutors have adapted contemporary versions of gifts and occupations models in block play. Tutors find the materials helpful in the study of math concepts and the application of creative thinking in tasks for problem solving.

As a former forest ranger, Froebel was aware of the importance of nature and being connected to one's physical environment. He recognized the need for children to work in a garden, whether it was a small city plot setting or a country allotment. He understood that lessons from nature are boundless and such interactions promote the well-being of children. There are still schools that plant gardens with their children, regardless of any restrictions a location might present.

As a student taught by German architects, Froebel knew of the importance of how to design, build, and arrange an open environment. He created spaces that filled a place for children to reflect alone and/or to share with others. His kindergarten included the indoors and outdoors as welcoming sites to explore and learn. His work influenced future architects including America's famous architect, Frank Lloyd Wright, who as a child used the gifts and occupations model under the guidance of his mother (Froebelweb 2016).

Teacher education for the early years

Froebel's name lives on primarily for his establishment of the kindergarten and its timeless practices, some of which find a home not only in today's primary schools but also in teacher education institutions of higher education. Froebel recognized the importance of teacher education programs for the professional development of his staff. Like Plato and Quintilian of Ancient Greece and Rome, Froebel wanted the "best and brightest" teachers for his kindergarten. Today, there is a growing global trend to establish professional degrees in early childhood education at leading universities and colleges. At Helsinki University in Finland, early childhood education majors are required to earn a bachelor's degree to teach in a Finnish preschool or child care program. Admission to the university's early education and care program is very competitive and only the most successful candidates are accepted.

In the United States, efforts are being made to increase the number of doctoral degrees in early childhood education for professional leadership roles and faculty positions in institutions of higher education. Although there are many prestigious MEd programs in early education in American universities, only a few graduate school programs grant a PhD in early childhood education. There is a PhD program at East Tennessee State University in Johnson City, Tennessee that serves as a recently approved exemplar.

In the United Kingdom, Froebel's specific pedagogy continues to be revered and offered at the University of Roehampton in London, England. Choices at the University of Roehampton allow students to pursue an academic liberal arts and science major at the university combined with their professional study at Froebel College through its Departments of Dance and Education (see http://www. roehampton.ac.uk/Colleges/Froebel/Froebel-History).

Legacy of gifts and occupations

Other documentaries of Froebel's lasting impressions on early education include his impact on the development of educational teaching materials and toys for young children. In the nineteenth century, Elizabeth Palmer Peabody's kindergarten used Froebel's materials for teaching his gifts and occupations in her Boston kindergartens. She persuaded the toy manufacturer, Milton Bradley of Springfield, Massachusetts, to produce the materials that Froebel designed. Currently, other manufacturers continue to market their versions of Froebel's materials for today's classroom and at home.

Conclusion: Froebel's memorials

Frederick Froebel died June 21, 1852 and was buried in Germany. The design for his memorial was based on his *Second Gift: The Sphere, Cylinder and Cube* which for Froebel represented "Knowledge, Beauty and Life" (see http://www.froebelweb. org/images/stein.html). This tribute honored his skill as an architect, educator, and protector of childhood. Other memorials include a stamp printed in December 1949 by the *Deutsche Post* (The German Mail) to respect his contributions to childhood (see http://www.froebelweb.org/images/stamp.html).

In conclusion, Froebel's living memorials are the kindergartens housed in schools around the globe and in his native country of Germany. The Prussian government eventually allowed the Keilhau Froebel School to continue as a living tribute to his accomplishments (see http://www.friedrichfroebel.com/keilhau/moore.html).

Student integration tasks

- For a complete view of Frederick Froebel's *Gifts and Occupations* as they are presented in current classrooms and homes, search for Froebel Gifts on Google Images.

- Another resource for finding information on gift materials is through the company Uncle Goose Toys of Grand Rapids, Michigan-49504. Identify any materials that are familiar to you. List where you have seen them, for example in a classroom, home, or at a store. List ways in which the materials were used by children, parents, and teachers. How would you use these materials with young children? Do you think Froebel would agree with their uses today?

- To learn more about what current educators are doing with Froebel's legacy, research the International Froebel Society's website, *Promoting Child-Centered Kindergarten & Early Education Worldwide*: http://www.ifsfroebel.com/?page.

- To learn more about Kate Douglas Wiggin and her books for young children, search online for new or used editions of her books, or visit your local book store, library, or school library to see what editions they have available for teachers and children. How might you implement them in your teaching?

- The following are primary sources of books written by or about Frederick Froebel to broaden your understanding of child-centered teaching and learning:

  Education of Man, English translation by Josephine Jarvis with an introduction by Elizabeth Peabody, is still available in paperback.

  Paradise of Childhood, first published in the United States by Milton Bradley.

  The Republic of Childhood-Froebel's Gifts by K. Wiggin and N. Archibald Smith.

- The Froebel Trust offers grants for research on Froebel. To learn about applying, see: http://www.froebel.org.uk/grants.

References

Breitborde, M. and Swiniarski, L. (2006). *Teaching on principle and promise: The foundations of education*. Boston: Houghton Mifflin Company.

Comenius, J.A. (1956). *The school of infancy*. Edited by E.M. Eller. Chapel Hill, NC: University of North Carolina Press.

Froebel, F. (1892). *The education of man*. Translated by W.N. Herbert. New York: Appleton-Century-Crofts, Inc.

Froebelweb (2016a). Friedrich Froebel created kindergarten. Available at: http://www.froebelweb.org. Retrieved May 25, 2014.

Froebelweb (2016b). Frank Lloyd Wright. Available at: http://www.froebelweb.org/web2000.html. Retrieved February 25, 2016.

Greenaway, K. (1886). *A for apple pie: Reproduction of original*. New York: Merrimack Publishing Corporation.

Lillard, A. (2005). *Montessori: The science behind the genius.* Cambridge: Cambridge University Press.

Lilley, I. (1967). *Frederick Froebel: A selection from his writings.* Cambridge: Cambridge University Press.

Martin, J. (1992). *The school home: Rethinking schools for changing families.* Cambridge, MA: Harvard University Press.

Montessori, M. (1970). *The child in the family.* Translated by N.R. Cirillo. New York: Avon Books.

Plato. (1960). *The laws.* Translated by A.H. Taylor. New York: J.M. Dent and Sons.

Power, E. (1969). *Evolution of educational doctrine: Major educational theorists of the western world.* New York: Appleton-Century-Crofts.

Power, E. (1970). *Main currents in the history of education.* New York: McGraw-Hill.

Quintilian. (1963). *Institutio Oratoria, Vol. 1.* Translated by H.E. Butler. Cambridge, MA: Harvard University Press.

Snyder, A. (1972). *Dauntless women in childhood education: 1856–1931.* Washington, DC: Association for Early Childhood Education International.

Swiniarski, L. (1976). *A comparative study of Elizabeth Peabody and Susan Blow by examination of their work and writing.* An unpublished PhD dissertation. The Graduate School of Boston College, Chestnut Hill, MA.

Swiniarski, L. (January/February 1984). Daycare in Finland: A national commitment. *Childhood Education: Journal of the Association for Childhood Education International,* 60, 3, 185–188.

Swiniarski, L. (2006). *Breaking news: Preschool is happening in your school.* An unpublished presentation to the Schott Foundation Principals' Institute in Early Care and Education, Milton, MA.

Swiniarski, L. (2006–13). Unpublished interviews in Finland.

Swiniarski, L. (2014). (Ed.). *The evolution of universal preschool in a global age.* World Class Initiatives and Practices in Early Education: Dordrecht, The Netherlands: Springer.

University of Roehampton. (2016). Friedrich Froebel. Available at: http://www.roehampton.ac.uk/Colleges/Froebel/Froebel-History. Retrieved February 25, 2016.

Weber, E. (1969). *The kindergarten: Its encounter with educational thought in America.* New York: Alfred A. Knopf.

Wiggin, D. (2001). *The birds' Christmas carol.* New York: Welcome Books.

Websites

http://www.froebelweb.org. Retrieved May 25, 2014.

http://www.roehampton.ac.uk/Colleges/Froebel/Froebel/History. Retrieved October 25, 2015.

http://www.froebelweb.org/onlinepost.html. Retrieved October 25, 2015.

http://www.leedstrinity.ac.uk/news_events_blogs/pages/%27saving-children%27 27. Retrieved September 13, 2014.

http://www.froebelweb.org/images/stein.html. Retrieved January 5, 2016.

http://www.froebelweb.org/web2008.html. Retrieved January 5, 2016.

http://www.froebel.org.uk/grants. Retrieved October 20, 2015.

http://www.communityplaythings.co.uk/learning-library/articles/freidrich-froebel. Retrieved May 25, 2014.

https://www.google.com/search?q=froebel+gifts&biw+1024&bih+isch&tbo=u&. Retrieved January 5, 2016.

http://www.froebelweb.org/images/stamp.html. Retrieved January 5, 2016.

http://www.ifsfroebel.com/?page. Retrieved October 25, 2015.

https://www.google.co.uk/search?q=froebel+gifts&sa=X&biw=1600&bih=740&site=imghp&tbm=isch&tbo=u&source=univ&ved=0ahUKEwilx9zE7pLLAhXBPg8KHc2aCqUQsAQILg. Retrieved February 25, 2016.

Elizabeth Peabody (1804–94)

Implementing Froebel's play-based learning

Louise Swiniarski

A historical, philosophical, cultural, and socio-political context: nineteenth-century America and the framework of Elizabeth Peabody's world

Elizabeth Peabody's lifespan of ninety years (1804–94) extended throughout most of the nineteenth century – a century that was charged:

- politically, with the development of a new Republic of the United States of America;
- economically, in a global period of industrial revolutions and technological changes;
- culturally, with a growing national population of new immigrants and cultures across the ever-expanding national boundaries;
- socially, with a divided citizenry on civil rights and governance;
- philosophically, with a romantic age in its literature, the arts, religions and educational theory.

These factors, which contributed to the making of a new nation, the United States of America, defined the many roles of Elizabeth Peabody and why she came to be a teacher, philosopher, linguist, writer, publisher, book-seller, and social activist.

Life and work: ancestry and antecedent influences

Elizabeth Palmer Peabody was born in May 1804 into two prominent American families: her maternal Palmer family and her paternal Peabody relations. She was the first child of Elizabeth Palmer Peabody and Nathanial Peabody. Her maternal great-grandfather was a Revolutionary War-time hero and Boston Tea Party member, who lost his fortune after the colonies' independence was granted (Marshall 2005). His son and Elizabeth's grandfather, Joseph Palmer, tried his hand at business, farming, and the tradition of teaching for a livelihood. Although Joseph had only meager success as an educator, he provided a foundation to establish schools as financial support for future generations.

Elizabeth's grandfather on her father's side of the family was a New Hampshire farmer of little financial means with limited educational opportunities, but a member of the highly regarded Peabody family, whose influence continues into contemporary times (Marshall 2005, Hoyt 1968). In turn, his son, Nathaniel, a Dartmouth College graduate, was a Latin teacher at the prestigious Andover Academy, when he met his future wife, a "preceptress" at North Andover Academy for Girls (Wineapple 2003). Later he continued his education to include medicine and dentistry at the bidding of his wife to support their growing family of additional children, Mary, Sophia, Nathaniel, George, and Wellington.

The early years of the American republic were challenging times economically and politically. Salem, Massachusetts, the on and off again perennial "home town" of Elizabeth's branch of the Peabody family, was economically diminished as a major sea-port by President Thomas Jefferson's *Embargo Act of 1807* which closed Salem's trade with England, France, the Caribbean, and Asia. Then the city was hit by President James Madison's War of 1812 with England, the former Mother Country. Salem, the once vibrant North Atlantic hub of wealthy sea captains and merchants, lost its primary sources of income.

During this period, the Peabody family lived in the Salem neighborhood bordering the once busy wharfs, so in turn their family finances were adversely affected. Yet they survived the economic upheaval since both parents had the skills and professional background to home school their daughters to be sufficient scholars for entrance into intellectually elite circles as young adults, and their sons gained admission into Salem Latin School and Harvard College (Swiniarski 1976). Contrary to family expectations, the three Peabody sisters sustained the family's lifestyle, while their brothers struggled throughout their adult lives to support themselves. The family ties to Salem and Boston communities also helped to make appropriate social contacts for all members of the family.

Mrs. Peabody set up her schools in her home wherever they lived to teach local children as well as her own children (Swiniarski 1976). While living in Salem, Mrs. Peabody enrolled many neighbors, including the sister of Nathaniel Hawthorne. The young school friends made livelong relationships. Mrs. Peabody's schools served as models for her own daughters, when at eighteen, Elizabeth and Mary both followed their mother's profession into establishing schools to enhance the family income.

The sisters, Elizabeth and Mary, moved to settle their schools in the Boston area, where they met and made close personal connections with leading thinkers in the Boston-Cambridge-Concord enclaves. As a young man, Ralph Waldo Emerson was Elizabeth's Greek and Latin tutor, foreshadowing her interest in languages to study French, German, and the then lesser-known Spanish and Basque languages (Swiniarski 1987). Likewise, her mentor, the Unitarian Rev. William Ellery Channing, had a lasting influence on her religious and philosophical dispositions that led her to Transcendentalism, which in turn paved her way to embrace Froebelian thought.

> In her last years of the 1820s Elizabeth Peabody was groping toward her own distinctive intellectual position. . . . From her Unitarian family and culture she drew a sense of orderliness of the cosmos and a belief in universal truth . . . William Ellery Channing expanded Peabody's intellectual range . . . showing her how emotions can have a place in liberal religion.
>
> (Ronda 1999, pp. 74–5)

Another Boston force in Elizabeth Peabody's life was her long-term relationships with the Bronson Alcott family, made globally famous by their daughter, Louisa May Alcott and her book, *Little Women*. By the mid-1830s Elizabeth Peabody had joined Bronson Alcott in the establishment of his controversial Temple School, the subject of her first major publication, *Record of a School*. While the two educators disagreed on several issues and split their relationship over arguments on the practices at the Temple School, Elizabeth was intertwined with the Alcotts throughout her life. On occasion she lived with them, argued with them, and ultimately during the later years of her life, she joined Bronson in his last endeavor, the Concord School of Philosophy.

In her early twenties, as an experienced teacher, Elizabeth expanded her horizons by living as a governess with wealthy families in Maine, where she drew upon their extensive libraries to enhance her own academic background. Upon her return to the Boston area in 1825 she began her international correspondence with William Wordsworth, later known as Britain's Poet Laureate. Not confident that she would receive a response to her first letter, she waited two years before mailing it. Wordsworth did reply and their correspondence continued for the next twenty years.

Since Wordsworth received lots of "fan mail" that he typically did not recognize, the question has been asked: Why did he elect to answer Elizabeth Peabody, a twenty-one-year-old unknown from Boston? His biographer, Stephen Gill (1989), suggests that both Elizabeth and Wordsworth shared a reverence for spirituality in nature and childhood. Wordsworth saved eight of her letters over the two decades of correspondence, beginning with the first, which was "particularly pleasing as it revealed an ardent spirit in sympathy with what he believed to be the essence of his poetry" (Gill 1989, p. 348). The common bond Elizabeth shared with Wordsworth impacted her beliefs not only as an educator but also as a writer and philosopher. These exchanges shaped her thoughts about childhood and her disposition toward creative ways of teaching.

Both Elizabeth and Mary met the recent widower and the first appointed Secretary of Massachusetts State Board of Education, Horace Mann, as fellow residents at the Clarkes' boarding home at 3 Somerset Court in Boston. The sisters rented two rooms. They used one as a schoolroom, where they shared their interests and expertise in education with Horace Mann, who was then in the process of restructuring schools and teacher training programs throughout the Commonwealth of Massachusetts.

It has been said that both sisters were infatuated with Mann. But Mary married Mann several years after the other Peabody sister, Sophia, married Nathaniel Hawthorne, incidentally another close male friend of Elizabeth. Much speculation has been made of Elizabeth's love life and love triangles within the family over the two men. However, it appears that in the end, Elizabeth opted out of any male relations. She seemed to have preferred the freedom that allowed a single nineteenth-century woman to pursue her numerous interests as a social advocate, educator, philosopher, writer, publisher, and highly regarded book-seller.

Elizabeth led fellow Transcendentalists by promoting their philosophy, which she found consistent with German Idealism, and would later recognize Transcendentalism as compatible with the philosophy of Frederick Froebel. She is credited with giving Transcendentalism its name (Marshall 2006) and endorsing its teachings as a publisher and book-seller.

In 1840, Elizabeth left teaching to open a book store on West Street in Boston, which also served as a publishing house. The combination of these two businesses was common practice in the nineteenth century. In her book store, she published and sold the Transcendentalists' quarterly the *Dial*, to which she contributed several essays. She also published Henry David Thoreau's *On the Duty of Civil Disobedience*, the book that a century later influenced Dr. Martin Luther King as he led his Civil Rights movement and Mahatma Gandhi in his struggles to liberate India from the British Empire. Additionally, Elizabeth was a voice for the Abolitionists' movement against American slavery, when she published the pamphlet, *Emancipation*.

Her book store became a meeting place for prominent women from Boston to voice their ideas. At her book store, she hosted a lecture series for women intellectuals in partnership with her colleague, the *New York Tribune* literary editor and columnist, Margaret Fuller (Marshall 2013). This endeavor helped Elizabeth develop the organizational skills she needed for her leadership role in founding the first English-speaking kindergarten in America.

Life and work: the kindergarten movement

Prototypes

After the closing of her book store (1840–52), Elizabeth became disillusioned with her former schools and business ventures and disheartened by America's state of the union. The country was in turmoil amidst the rumbles of an impending civil war. Slavery, state rights, and Federal governmental jurisdictions were in question. Furthermore, there was disagreement among the Peabody family members on moral and political issues. While most Peabody family members were against slavery, Sophia and her husband, Nathaniel Hawthorne, believed time would eventually solve the problem, when they argued with family members that a civil war was to be avoided at all costs. In addition, Elizabeth felt her influence on her students had been negligible in moral issues and doubted the effectiveness of her past teaching endeavors. She searched for an educational framework that would resolve compelling problems facing the next generation in America's new democracy.

In 1859, Elizabeth met the German educator, Margarethe Schurz, and her young daughter Agatha at a Boston lecture in which Mrs. Schurz introduced the community to Frederick Froebel's kindergarten (Snyder 1972). The talk inspired Elizabeth to learn as much as possible about Froebel by reading his major thesis, *The Education of Man*. An experienced advocate for social reform and fund raising, Elizabeth then solicited financial support from her friends and colleagues to open the first adapted American-based kindergarten. Most kindergartens in the USA at that time were established by German immigrants, who came to America with the ideals of Froebel to teach their own children in their native language.

One person alone cannot effect change. Elizabeth's experimental kindergarten received backing from many walks of life, including influential governmental leaders (Snyder 1972). Before the meeting at the Schurz lecture, Dr. Henry Barnard, the United States Commissioner of Education, was praising the kindergarten experiences he observed during visits to centers in Europe (Weber 1969). Fondly known as the Father of the American Kindergarten, he wrote about his observations of Froebel's kindergartens and later encouraged Elizabeth to carry on her endorsements for American kindergartens.

Elizabeth's sister, Mary Mann, now the widow of Horace Mann, joined her to open their English-speaking kindergarten at 15 Pinckney Street in Boston, Massachusetts in 1860 (Swiniarski 1987). The sisters also co-authored circulars, books, and professional journal articles. In 1862, the *Atlantic Monthly Journal* published Elizabeth's article, *Kindergarten: What Is It?* Two years later, Mary and Elizabeth together finished their first edition of their *Moral Culture in Infancy and Kindergarten Guide*. These publications caught the attention of other educators such as Edward A. Sheldon at the Oswego Normal School in New York, who invited Elizabeth to speak about her school to his constituents (Swiniarski 1987).

The kindergarten curriculum: what is it and what is it not?

The German model for the education of young children, from three to seven years of age, was predicated on a philosophy kindred to Elizabeth Peabody's Transcendentalism in its belief of innate ideas and a universal goodness in all humans. Elizabeth intended to replicate Froebel's approaches and philosophy and blend his ideas with her goals. Her school was to distinguish itself from the existing primary public school, which relied on rote learning and feedback responses (Swiniarski 1987). Rather, her kindergarten, like the German kindergarten model, was to have three major components in its curriculum, namely: a play-based approach, language instruction central to all learning, and Froebel's *Gifts and Occupation*. Added to this core were subject areas such as gymnastic instruction, nature study, art, French, and songs and poems published in Froebel's book, *Mother Play*. All of these components were integrated into a holistic teaching approach (Swiniarski 1987).

Despite her adherence to Froebel's pedagogy, Elizabeth remained dissatisfied with the results of her new endeavor. She held a firm belief that a proper educational system enhanced society; yet she could find no evidence of improvement in her kindergarten or her students' attitudes. So she took herself to Germany to learn first-hand from the experts, who would guide her in the reconstruction of the next stage for her kindergarten. Mary remained at home to carry on and initiate the new members of staff Elizabeth recruited from abroad.

Elizabeth's fifteen-month search in Europe for the true kindergarten took her beyond Germany into Italy and England, where she met key educators in the movement, some of whom she convinced to join Mary in their Boston venture. Eventually, Elizabeth returned home with new directions, insights, and an abundance of confidence.

Reforms: teacher training

Key to Elizabeth Peabody's reform efforts was teacher training. The German staff, who Elizabeth introduced to her new school, assisted in modeling an authentic teacher education program that offered a balance between theory and practice. The new faculty renewed the training and formation of kindergarten teachers, known as *kindergarteners*. These German instructors based their pedagogy on Froebel's belief that women had the best dispositions for teaching young children and agreed with him that mothers were natural teachers. To be effective *kindergarteners*, teachers needed to intrinsically believe and be thoroughly imbued in Froebel's methodology, philosophy, and mandatory practices.

Elizabeth drew on other resources along with her capable German staff. Having worked with her brother-in-law, Horace Mann, Elizabeth was very familiar with the Normal School movement and its practices, but was careful to adapt only the appropriate methods for her early childhood clientele. Likewise, she borrowed ideas from Pestalozzi, Comenius, and the ancient educators, such as Plato and Quintilian, who required their teachers of young children to be the "best and brightest" candidates. Elizabeth felt the teaching of young children was intellectually more demanding than of that of older children (Swiniarski 1987). She held high standards for admission into her training programs, which she fashioned on "the first English training school for kindergarteners located in Manchester, England" (Swiniarski 1987, p. 224). Her challenging schedule included:

> *Monday – Drawing, Theory and Application of the Kindergarten System; Tuesday – Singing, Science of Education; Thursday – Theory and Application of the Kindergarten Systems; Friday – Physiology and Science, Health, Natural History.*
> *(Swiniarski 1987, p. 224)*

Added to this study program were subject areas such as history of education, the classics, games, storytelling, philosophy, theology, and all of the Arts.

Elizabeth sought the rigor and prestige that medicine and law held in educating their trainees. Her education of a *kindergartener* was a life-long learning process that needed continuous professional development.

> *Teachers, like lawyers, theologians and medical men, must study for their profession as long as they live.*
>
> (*Peabody*, Salem Gazette, *February 21, 1882*)

Reading and language

The teaching of reading was paramount in the educational process. Elizabeth was a writer of children's books as well as philosophical and professional publications. Hence as a writer, she considered language as central to the stages of intellectual growth and key to cognitive development. She maintained that formal instruction of reading should not begin before the age of seven. Much like today's programs in Nordic nations such as Finland, Sweden, Denmark, and Norway, her kindergarten deferred directed formal reading instruction until the age of seven. Rather, she blended literacy in all teachable moments through play activities and when using Froebel's prescribed instructional materials.

Reading was embedded throughout the curriculum in the tone and climate of her kindergarten's settings. Listening to, telling, and interpreting stories were building blocks to reading and language development. Additionally, she required the teaching of French and Latin under the directions of teachers who were specialists in their languages. She realized the importance of thinking and structuring thought in more than one language to conceptualize multiple points of view and acquire various modes of expression of one's ideas.

Symbolic teaching and learning

Most of the kindergarten's routines and activities held symbolic meanings. Some were religious and others, philosophical. Even today, kindergarten children typically sit in a circle for morning meetings, story time, or show and tell. The reasons for doing so are many. For example, a circle formation is a good strategy for maintaining attention through eye contact and easy access to one another. However, in Froebel's kindergartens, this arrangement had additional philosophical undertones. Namely, each child learned that by sitting in a circle you are a whole person, while at the same time, you are also part of a bigger whole (see Chapter 3). This notion of "being the one and many simultaneously" is a basic tenet of German Idealism and an abstract symbol physically represented by the circle. Such abstract concepts were taught through concrete experiences each day. All trainees were well versed in Froebel's philosophy and the symbolic nature of his pedagogy. Teachers and children were expected to learn the subtle philosophical undertones of each activity and instructional exercise.

Kindergartener alumni

Elizabeth's training program was successful. She recruited a talented group of trainees. While Louisa May Alcott declined the invitation, well-known pioneers in American education accepted, namely Lucy Wheelock, the founder of Wheelock College, still a teaching institution for early years educators in Boston, and Mary Garland, who broadened higher education opportunities for women through her Garland Junior College.

Reforms: outreach for equal professional status of kindergarten educators

Once Froebel's newly configured reforms were instituted with Elizabeth's and Mary's directives, the renewed kindergarten training program was under the administration of the mother and daughter team from Germany, Matilde and Alma Kriege. The Krieges in turn hired Mary Garland, Elizabeth's former student, as a member of their staff. Eventually, Mary moved the Krieges' training school into Garland Junior College (Swiniarski 1976).

Elizabeth left the role of teacher to work on projects that promoted her re-constructed kindergarten mode and to concentrate more on her writing. Along with Mary she updated a second edition of the *Moral Culture in Infancy and Kindergarten Guide.* Elizabeth then initiated a monthly journal, *The Kindergarten Messenger*, to inform readers of the continuous new reforms and happenings in the profession (Swiniarski 1987). The intent of these publications was to inform and reach out to families and professionals as members in kindergarten organizations.

Impressed with the original Froebel Union and the English Kindergarten Union Elizabeth visited during her trips to Europe, she campaigned for an American Froebel Union which was a model for the formation of the International Kindergarten Union (IKU). Today, the IKU is known as the Association for Childhood Education International and still operates in the United States from its headquarters in Washington, DC. The adapted name of the organization speaks to its current broader audience of professionals and educators which now stretches from the early to middle years of childhood rather than the traditional kindergarten ages of three to seven.

The goals of the professional organizations were to improve professional status through continued scholarship in the field and fund and sustain the ongoing training and improved payment of teachers. To insure the equity and equality for all teachers and students, Elizabeth demanded adequate salaries to attract talented women of modest financial means rather than be dependent upon only wealthy women who could afford to freely volunteer their services. Teachers from all levels of society were fairly compensated to work together. Otherwise, she "feared that an elite group would dominate the mass" (Swiniarski 1987, p. 227).

The quality of our education should rise, or at least not sink below that of the nations that have educated the few to dominate over the many.

(Peabody, Kindergarten Culture, *pp. 1–2)*

This message is as timely now as when it was published in the reprinted *Annual Report of the National Commission of Education* of 1870.

The picture below illustrates a Common School kindergarten child busy painting the Three Bears, a story still enjoyed by children today.

To further ensure equality and equity, Elizabeth built on the strength of Horace Mann's successful Common School mandates when she argued for the kindergarten to be the entry into primary education, placed under the jurisdiction of public education, and maintained through tax revenues. To accomplish these aims, she joined forces with a longtime friend, William T. Harris, Superintendent of Schools in St. Louis, Missouri, and a leading young kindergarten advocate from St. Louis, Susan Blow. She invited Harris and Blow as Missouri's representatives to the executive committee of the American Froebel Union. The three of them were to become major campaigners for tax-supported kindergartens and teacher education programs. (For further information see Chapter 5.)

Critical perspectives

Elizabeth Peabody is credited by historians with dedicating herself to a lifetime of humanitarian endeavors. She was always ready to right a wrong, support the

FIGURE 4.1 Child painting three bears. Courtesy of Salem State University Archives and Special Collections.

disenfranchised or lobby for a cause. When President Abraham Lincoln suffered from the reproach of New England constituents for his Union Army's early losses in the American Civil War, Elizabeth gave him the benefit of the doubt. Dismayed by the depth of the criticism, Elizabeth went to Washington, DC to advise the President on how to explain and defend his convictions and goals. Lincoln was actually grateful for her support and heeded her wise counsel (Snyder 1972).

It was during this visit to the nation's capital that Elizabeth witnessed the appalling conditions of the Civil War and was horrified by the treatment of abandoned slave children. With her usual determination, she immediately set about trying to improve their circumstances. Through her contacts with members in Congress, the generosity of her wealthy influential friends, and her own fund-raising efforts, she managed to raise sufficient revenue to secure a safe home for the children and remedy the ills of their former lifestyles (Snyder 1972). Elizabeth later continued her support of improving the children's education by defending and assisting Myrtilla Miner's struggles to maintain the first normal school in Washington, DC for black women in a letter to Emily Howland on March 9th (Peabody 1865).

Elizabeth Peabody also worked to promote Native American causes when she attended to the plight of the Piute people. Ageing did not impede Elizabeth's missions. Well beyond her eightieth birthday, she still labored on to assert her influence and campaign for the less fortunate native peoples. She managed to raise funds for the Piute Princess Winnemucca's innovative school that questioned the ongoing practices of the established Native American boarding schools, the focus on vocational education, and the disregard for the natives' first languages, customs, and cultural legacies.

In 1886, Elizabeth initiated a meeting with President Grover Cleveland to discuss the "maladministration of the Indian office" (Ronda 1999, p. 332). During her conference with President Cleveland, she requested he provide land and appropriate educational opportunities for "her friends," the Piute nation of Nevada (Baylor 1968). While Elizabeth was encouraged when President Cleveland agreed, she did not attain her goals. Unfortunately, even with a Presidential endorsement, the venture did not materialize. According to Peabody's biographer, Bruce Ronda (1999, p. 333), "the school was on shaky grounds [and] . . . no governmental agency recognized its existence."

Historians have questioned the integrity of Princess Winnemucca when she could not account for the many donations given for the management of the school. Rumors spread that her husband had gambled away some of the monies. "Yet, the embarrassment of the affair did not hinder Elizabeth from her persistent pleas to improve the lives for the Piute" (Swiniarski 1976, p. 71).

Elizabeth, however, was not equally sympathetic to all causes. She turned a blind eye to the nineteenth-century immigrants from Ireland who lived in her own community and worked in the New England households, caring for children and families' needs. Regardless of her reputation as a very assertive and aggressive champion of social justice, Elizabeth appeared not to be sympathetic to Irish causes. In her assessment of childcare nurses, particularly those employed in her prominent friends' homes to care for their young children, Elizabeth singled out the Irish as being inappropriate for the positions. In her published *Lecture, 61*, she stated:

> *It is but justice to the latter (uncultured servant maids) to say that there are occa-sionally found among the Irish nurses those who could teach many mothers. The Irish nature is not altogether bad material for the production of good motherly nurse, but it must not be left wild.*

(*Swiniarski 1987, p. 224*)

Peabody's perceptions of the Irish are compatible with those of her peers. Her bias is reflective of the prevailing nineteenth-century anti-Irish sentiments held by elite members of American social and political circles. The negative attitudes were particularly strong in places like Boston, New York, and Salem. Historical documents show that the Irish were chastised for their religious commitment to Catholicism and their social status in coming from the lower classes of a British colonial country.

Some Americans insist that the prejudice against the Irish prevailed until the 1960s, when President John F. Kennedy was elected as the first Catholic Irish-American President. At the same time, an ever-increasing number of Irish Catholics gained status in the mainstream American middle and highly educated classes. Ironically, many of these successful Irish immigrants began their early education in the very public school kindergartens Elizabeth established and in the programs founded in the settlement house named in her honor. One might speculate that these early years experiences propelled many Irish children to continue their edu-cation and eventually number among the future generations in professional ranks of civic leaders, successful entrepreneurs, scholars, educators, writers, artists, and performers.

Elizabeth was a complex woman of her times. In some regards, she was a vision-ary, but she was also influenced by others. She lived in an age when American courts had to demand that textbooks with derogatory references to the Irish be expunged by public school districts like New York City and when the Catholic Ursuline Convent in Somerville, Massachusetts was torched by an unruly crowd.

Theoretical and practice legacy

A personal legacy of many dimensions

Elizabeth Peabody's legacy impacts multiple spheres of influence. Scholarly publi-cations extoll her contributions to Transcendentalism. She numbered as one of the few women admitted to the Concord School of Philosophy. Her twenty years of correspondence with the British Poet Laureate William Wordsworth underscored her international status as a noted writer and educator. Her scholarly publications on philosophy and her insightful pedagogy for early childhood education were received with high regard on both sides of the Atlantic, when she made ocean crossings to promote other authors such as Nathaniel Hawthorne and Ralph Waldo Emerson to a British audience and to create permanent links with British literary publishers and respected writers.

Locally, a memorial for her advocacy of Boston families' and children's well-being was initiated with the naming of the Elizabeth Peabody Settlement House, established in Boston and later moved to Somerville, Massachusetts where it is still in operation. When she died, the city of Boston bestowed upon her the title of "the Grandmother of Boston" to commemorate her numerous contributions to the city's children.

The kindergarten legacy

Unquestionably, Elizabeth Peabody's defining accomplishment is the establishment of the kindergarten as the basis for early education in American schools. She brought to the kindergarten all the talents and resources she had acquired throughout her life. The kindergarten movement needed a leader of her status with multiple abilities.

Elizabeth Peabody's kindergartens became beacons of light throughout the United States as models for future early education practices. Her kindergarten was an extended-day, multi-age setting for young children from three to seven. Since Elizabeth believed that early education began at home, she included parental involvement in her daily kindergarten practices.

Peabody's kindergartens prefigured today's Full Service Schools. She charted the path to help needy families and children with services provided beyond the walls of the schools and the hours in classrooms. She gave parents and families a network and a collective voice in her Parent Unions, fashioned after the American Froebel Union for teachers.

In keeping with Froebel's optimistic view of childhood, Elizabeth promulgated a child-centered approach to teaching a comprehensive curriculum built on play experiences rather than a dogmatic curriculum focused on drill and memorization. Her standards were defined and fashioned by the needs of the learner. She understood that learning takes place when instruction is designed to fit the child. Elizabeth adapted the American kindergarten to link "the individualism of the American spirit" to the belief "that all children can learn through a personalized program of instruction" (Swiniarski 2005, pp. 219–20).

Elizabeth was dauntless when she sought to secure mandatory kindergartens to be provided equally in all states throughout America. Unfortunately, statistics show her goal is not yet met, but her plea is still honored.

> *Six states don't require schools to provide kindergarten. . . . Alaska, Idaho, Michigan, New Jersey, New York and Pennsylvania [while] 11 states and Washington, D.C. require public schools to provide free, full day kindergarten by law.*
>
> *(Covert, February 26th, 2014, pp. 1–2)*

An advocate for justice and equity throughout her life, Elizabeth died in 1894. She was buried in Sleepy Hollow Cemetery in Concord, Massachusetts, where on her grave is an apt inscription:

> *Every human cause had her sympathy*
> *And many her active aid.*

Relevance to contemporary practice

Is Elizabeth Peabody a leadership model for today's educators?

Nineteenth-century America was a culturally constricted country in many regards. Elizabeth Peabody found herself bound by the nineteenth century's manners and mores, rules of etiquette, and lifetime expectations. For example, her position as a feminist is debated. In the kindergarten movement, Elizabeth modeled an international leadership role for women. She offered women everywhere a new opportunity to pursue higher education as a *kindergartener* with a professional salary. She valued the role of motherhood and the continuous education of mothers.

In her personal life, Elizabeth removed barriers to enter into male sanctuaries. She was accepted as a spokeswoman for the Transcendentalists. She crossed the threshold to be the first woman publisher in Massachusetts. The owner of a bookshop for ten years, she and Margaret Fuller held "conversations" for other women seeking a place to share their ideas. Yet some biographers feel that Peabody was not a feminist as she held some beliefs that differed from feminism:

> *A feminist, Peabody was definitely not one, [she] saw the picture very differently [than her feminist friends] over a broad range of issues – education, vocation, activism in reform, religion, property rights, suffrage.*
>
> *(Ronda 1990, p. 259)*

Researchers of her publications and personal letters find her to be equal among her male peers in formal discourse; yet in personal correspondences, she can be deferential to men (Neussendorfer 1984, Swiniarski 2011, Davies et al. 2012). Like many of her contemporary Victorian women associates, Elizabeth approached William Wordsworth's correspondence with an acquiescent tone. It took nearly twenty years of friendship for Elizabeth to find a confident voice in her letters (Swiniarski 2012).

Elizabeth Peabody's kindergarten vs. kindergartens in today's USA

Elizabeth Peabody's wanted to insure the kindergarten's position in America's public schools, and build upon the ideal of Horace Mann with the Common School as the melting pot of a common culture for all children. Just as Mann provided a uniform school, Elizabeth based her kindergarten on the sole philosophical framework of Froebel's Idealism to form her cornerstone. A comparative study of today's American kindergartens' policies documents the differences.

Today in the United States, there exists a patchwork quilt approach to the kindergarten. The support of public education is primarily paid by a combination of local, state and federal government revenues. The federal government under the US Department of Education contributes approximately 8 percent of the funding for educational programs. Local education authorities and states pay the remaining 92 percent. Some communities have full-school-day kindergarten programs; others provide a half day. Parents are charged fees for the extended-day program in one town, while in neighboring communities full-day kindergartens are free. The local policies are based upon available monetary support from the state's funding and local municipal budgets. While there are national curriculum standards from preschool to grade 12, now known as the Common Core, each state is required to compete for the additional funding from the federal government's program, Race to the Top, to contribute to the costs of mandates.

Other patches in the quilt involve how the curriculum is implemented and how achievement is assessed. Like Elizabeth Peabody did in the past, some public and private kindergarten programs still maintain a child-centered philosophy with an emphasis on individualized instruction in the context of play opportunities. Conversely, more of today's kindergartens are building their curriculum around class presentations of academic skills and scripted instruction. There is movement to assess kindergarten children on standardized tests much like those designed for older children in elementary grades. These tests measure primarily academic knowledge. Test preparation becomes drill sessions that take most of the instructional time in a school day.

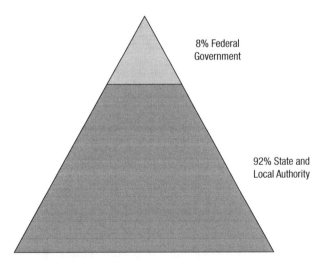

8% Federal Government

92% State and Local Authority

FIGURE 4.2 The current federal funding for the education system in the USA. Courtesy of Michael Swiniarski.

A current controversial assessment package is the Partnership for Assessment of Readiness for College and Careers (PARCC) published by Pearson and used with the federal government's standards known as the Common Core. The PARCC tests are given annually in grades 3 to 8 for mathematics and reading skills developed by the Common Core standard curriculum. Plans are in place to begin the PARCC assessments of achievements in kindergarten. Teachers and parents have questioned the reliability of these assessments as they mourn the loss of local control over curriculum content. Some states have withdrawn from or not accepted Common Core money from the US Department of Education. The current governor of Massachusetts (Charlie Baker, elected January 8th, 2015) is now reviewing the Common Core and PARCC for the commonwealth's public schools. There are daily newspaper articles about parents and educators who are lobbying for changes in the testing criteria. Meanwhile, young children are being trained to excel as test takers.

The National Governors Association Center for Best Practices has been working on a national policy to improve early education through grade 3. Massachusetts was selected as one of the six states to join in the mission. The Massachusetts Department of Early Education and Care drafted at a forum the following competencies for:

> *Cognitive Development and General Knowledge*
> *Social and Emotional Development*
> *Language and Communication*
> *Play and Learning*
> *Physical Development and Well-Being.*
>
> (*Department of Early Education and Care Draft,*
> *Commonwealth of Massachusetts, May 5th, 2014, p. 2*)

The competencies are viewed as generic and in keeping with traditional early education thought and practice. However, developing goals for early education as stepping stones "to college and career" is not seen as compatible with Elizabeth Peabody's intentions for her kindergarten.

The notion of linking early education and care instruction to pathways for career and college goals is a recent policy influenced by the US Department of Education. Successful international competition with other nations for producing future competent workers in a global economy is the ultimate target. Such values were not apparent in the foundation of the kindergarten movement or expressed in the work and writing of Elizabeth Peabody.

The technology of today has also changed preschool and kindergarten programs. Today's children can be seen working with tablets as well as electronic books, and the ubiquitous worksheets that would not be available in Elizabeth Peabody's programs. However, Elizabeth was a pathfinder in promoting the manufacturing of educational materials. She convinced Milton Bradley, a USA toy company, to procure the rights to produce Froebel's *Gifts and Occupations*, materials, and activities. Interestingly, these instructional materials became classical equipment for the kindergarten that are still found in early educational settings around the globe.

Closing thoughts

When left to their own devices, children choose to play. They explore undefined territories and freely test their limits in their own imaginary activities. Recognition of the value of play as the medium through which children learn and develop is still important. Research substantiates that the loss of free and open play in childhood has adversely affected the social development of today's children (Jarvis, Newman and Swiniarski 2014). Elizabeth Peabody realized the significance of play in childhood by observing her students growing throughout the multiple-age groupings she offered in her kindergarten. Her insights are still in print and available. Contemporary practitioners can learn from her time-tested ways of teaching and measuring success. Perhaps it is time to revisit the past to inform the best practices for the future.

Student integration tasks

- List your favorite play experiences and their worth in your development as an adult and a professional.

- Visit different early education centers that still replicate some of Elizabeth Peabody's schools' practices such as multi-age groupings or contextual play-based approaches to the curriculum. List how such centers differ in their teaching and learning from mainstream contemporary practices.

- Read for review one of Elizabeth Peabody's works mentioned in the chapter. Compare her thoughts with your ideas of an ideal kindergarten experience.

References

Baylor, R. (1965). *Elizabeth Palmer Peabody: Kindergarten Pioneer*. Philadelphia: University of Pennsylvania Press.

Covert, B. (February 26, 2014). *Six States Don't Require Schools to Provide Kindergarten*. Available at: http://thinkprogress.org/education/2014/02/26/3331631/day-. Retrieved February 8, 2015.

Davies, J., Edwards, J., Cowton, J., Connolly, J., Sinclair, H. and Black, E. (2012). *Beyond Words: Understanding and Sharing the Meanings of Manuscripts*. Grasmere: The Wordsworth Trust.

Gill, S. (2001). *William Wordsworth: A Life*. Oxford: Oxford University Press.

Hoyt, E. (1968). *The Peabody Influence*. New York: Dodd, Mead & Co.

Jarvis, P. Newman, S. and Swiniarski, L. (2014). On becoming social: The importance of collaborative free play in childhood. *International Journal of Play*, 3, 1, 53–68.

Marshall, M. (2005). *The Peabody Sisters: Three Women Who Ignited American Romanticism*. Boston: Houghton Mifflin Company.

Marshall, M. (2006). Elizabeth Palmer Peabody: The first Transcendentalist? *The Massachusetts Historical Review*, 8, 1–15.

Marshall, M. (2013). *Margaret Fuller: A New American Life*. Boston: Houghton Mifflin Company.

Massachusetts Department of Early Education and Care (May 2014). *Draft: Building the Foundation for College and Career Success for Children from Birth through Grade 3*. Boston: MDEEC.

Neussendorfer, M. (1984). Elizabeth Palmer Peabody to William Wordsworth: Eight letters, 1825–1845. In Myerson, J. (Ed.) *Studies in the American Renaissance* (pp. 181–211). Charlottesville: University of Virginia Press.

Peabody, E. (1865). *Letter to Emily Howland*, March 9. Available at: https://mail.salemstate.edu/owa/?ae=Item*t=IPM.NOTE&id=RgAAAADmZVzSZie0SZIP. Retrieved June 12, 2014.

Peabody, E. (1870). *Kindergarten Culture*. Reprinted from the Annual Report for 1870 of the National Commissioner of Education. Washington, DC: The National Series of Educational Tracts.

Peabody, E. (February 21, 1882). Miss Peabody on pedagogic reform: An index to Dr. Henry Barnard's journal. Salem, MA. *Salem Gazette* (np).

Ronda, B. (1999). *Elizabeth Palmer Peabody: A Reformer in Her Own Terms*. Cambridge, MA: Harvard University Press.

Snyder, A. (1972). *Dauntless Women in Childhood Education: 1856– 1931*. Washington, DC: Association for Childhood Education International.

Swiniarski, L. (1976). *A Comparative Study of Elizabeth Peabody and Susan Blow by Examination of Their Work and Writing*. An unpublished PhD dissertation. The Graduate School of Boston College, Chestnut Hill, MA.

Swiniarski, L. (April 1987). A pioneer in the kindergarten movement in America. *Instructive and Amusing: Essays on Toys, Games, and Education in New England: Essex Institute Historical Collections*, 123, 2, 206–229.

Swiniarski, L. (February 2005). On behalf of children: Elizabeth P. Peabody's bicentennial birthday: A celebration of a past legacy and a future vision for kindergarten. *Early Childhood Educational Journal*, 32, 4, 219–220.

Swiniarski, L. (March 2011). *Letters to a Poet Laureate, Elizabeth Peabody to William Wordsworth, 1825–1845*. An unpublished presentation at the Innovative Interpretation of Manuscripts Conference, Wordsworth Trust, UK.

Swiniarski, L. (April 2012). *"Mr. Wordsworth, Dear Sir": An Analysis and Interpretation of the Physicality of Elizabeth Peabody's Letters to William Wordsworth for Meanings Beyond*, An unpublished presentation at the Conference on Words and on the Page and Meanings Beyond, Wordsworth Trust, UK.

Thoreau, H. (1960 Ed.). *On the Duty of Civil Disobedience*. New York: Signet.

Weber, E. (1969). *The Kindergarten: Its Encounter with Education Thought in America*. New York: Teachers College Press.

Wineapple, B. (2003). *Hawthorne: A Life*. New York: Alfred A. Knopf.

Susan Blow (1843–1916)

Funding kindergartens and training professionals for American kindergartens in public education

Louise Swiniarski

A historical, philosophical, cultural, and socio-political context: Susan Blow's world bridges the nineteenth and twentieth centuries

Susan Blow was born a mid-westerner in St. Louis, Missouri, a critical state in determining preliminary conditions leading to the outbreak of America's Civil War in 1861. Her family became immersed in the legal outcomes of the 1820 *Missouri Compromise* controversial decisions, which identified Missouri as a slave-owning state to balance the acknowledgment of Maine as a free state.

The Blow family had migrated to Missouri from the states of Virginia and Alabama with their slave, Dred Scott, who was sold rather than freed as presumably intended by his owner, Peter Blow (Maltz 2007). Scott later moved to the free state of Indiana where he was free, but regrettably returned to St. Louis to pursue his assumed right of freedom in the courts' system. He ultimately lost his case and appeals when the US Supreme Court decided against him. His situation then became a cause for the northern states, the Abolitionist movement, and the Blow family. In 1857, Taylor Blow, Susan's uncle, righted the wrong, when he took on Dred Scott's case and finally freed him from the bonds of slavery (Maltz 2007). These social and philosophical dynamics shaped the young Susan Blow's sense of civic responsibility for her lifelong endeavors to bring social justice and equity to all.

Life and work: the kindergarten movement

Although Susan Blow's family was highly regarded and considered quite wealthy in St. Louis, Susan was educated briefly in private schools. She was primarily taught by family members, governesses, and tutors at home. While her father studied at

St. Louis University as a lawyer and successful businessman, he did not deem it necessary for his daughters to pursue higher educational studies. Nevertheless, Susan's life experiences seem to have filled that gap.

Her father was an appointed diplomat by President Lincoln during and after the Civil War in 1861 as the American representative for Venezuela and by President Grant as the US Minister for Brazil in 1869. He was also elected to the US Congress in Washington, DC as the representative from his Congressional District. Fortunately, the family accompanied him on his global travels or struck out on their own. His gifted daughter, Susan, became a linguist and student of multiple languages. It was during a family visit to Europe that Susan became acquainted with Frederick Froebel's followers and the German kindergarten movement, which inspired her lifelong mission to properly educate the young child. During time in France, she began her professional training in Froebel's practices. The frequent international experiences broadened her perspective of the world and transformed her into being a globally literate educator.

Upon her return to St. Louis, she was determined to move kindergarten education and training of kindergarten teachers (called kindergarteners) into the public school domain. To do so, she continued her study of Froebel's pedagogy and philosophy with Maria Kraus-Boelte in the New York Institute for Kindergartens and joined the kindergarten cause with Elizabeth Peabody. Working together as partners, she and Elizabeth Peabody persuaded their mutual friend and St. Louis Superintendent of Schools, William Torrey Harris, to support their idea of using public funds from tax revenues to support St. Louis kindergartens and educate their teachers in Froebel's methodology.

Elizabeth Peabody's kindergartens in the Boston public school system were patterned on the goals of the Common School, established by her brother-in-law, Horace Mann, to be free and open to all children. Ideally, Elizabeth had her kindergarten children, age three to seven, begin their schooling with a staff of Froebelian trained teachers before their entrance into the Common School. However, Elizabeth's early kindergarten endeavors in Boston were either private schools, maintained by tuitions, or public kindergartens, financially backed by philanthropic donations, not sustained through revenues from taxation. So when Susan Blow's father offered to finance the St. Louis project, Susan declined his help. Both she and Elizabeth Peabody recognized the value of having the kindergarten be a publicly supported venture. Despite limited available municipal funding, both women worked together to convince St. Louis city officials and their mutual friend, Superintendent William Torrey Harris, that kindergartens were for the national good as well as the city's welfare. They further argued that tax revenue support had far-reaching consequences in securing a democracy throughout America. Citizens as tax-payers needed to be vested in the kindergartens as they were for the common schools (Swiniarski 1976). All peoples had to be stakeholders if the kindergarten movement was to provide more opportunities to educate women, improve family conditions, and ameliorate the social and moral values of young children at an early age when their natural innocence was just beginning to develop. The goal of public kindergartens was to insure equal opportunity for all, whereas private and charity kindergartens generally served only limited or selected populations.

While the training for teachers in kindergartens was to fall under the mantle of public education, Susan and Elizabeth recognized that teacher education for the kindergarten could also be enhanced by the normal schools, women's academies, and seminaries. However, in such settings, the kindergartners' training in philosophy and practice was to remain distinct from the traditional elementary teacher education programs and based only on Froebel's methods. Otherwise, Blow and Peabody both feared kindergartens would become a mere preparation for the higher primary and elementary grades.

Their insightful concerns became realities in future school practices and policies. When the kindergartens and training programs were no longer under their direct jurisdiction, many kindergartens did become and remain preparatory experiences for subsequent higher levels of schooling. Furthermore, in many public programs today, there is no longer the intent of basing kindergarten instruction on the stages of development realized through *unfolding*.

Life and work: the 1873 public kindergarten

The year 1873 found America in the throes of an economic panic, yet the citizenry was determined to forge ahead in its struggle for national unity and survival. The

FIGURE 5.1 A public common school's kindergarten orchestra conducted by a girl to prefigure women's leadership role into the new century. Courtesy of Salem State University Archives and Special Collections.

country was still recovering from the shock of its Civil War, the assassination of one president and the impeachment of another. The agonies of the reconstruction of southern life after losing to the northern states in the Civil War of 1861–5, the impact of burgeoning populations of newly arrived immigrants in northern cities and the formidable obstacles of western expansion were but some of the problems that beset the country. The optimistic American looked to humanitarian reforms and education as the country's hope for a brighter future. Susan Blow was such an American (Swiniarski 1976).

In 1873, the public kindergartens Susan Blow established in St. Louis were the first in the nation to be funded by local taxation and to fiscally support the training of kindergarten teachers in the city's public schools. Making kindergarten the entrance level to public education in St. Louis was a monumental achievement. It set the benchmark for the state of Missouri and other communities throughout the nation. By 1904, Susan Blow cited in her publication, *Kindergarten Education*, the following cities as offering "the most fully developed systems of public kindergartens":

> *Boston, Chicago, St. Louis, Philadelphia, New York, Brooklyn, Milwaukee, Indianapolis, Rochester, Des Moines, Grand Rapids, Brookline, Newark, Jamestown, Los Angeles.*
> *(Blow 1904, p. 42)*

The future goal for the national movement was to have each state mandate kindergartens for all American children.

Curriculum development and teacher training programs

Ms. Blow's training classes were free and opened initially as part of the kindergarten experience in St. Louis at the Des Peres School in Carondelet. Her student teachers came for a general education as well as professional training. Blow upheld the tradition of a combined rigorous curriculum with a hands-on practical experience. The course of study used Froebel's *Mother Play and Nursery Songs* as a reference for the play-centered curriculum, which was based on the implementation of Froebel's *Gifts and Occupations*, his songs and games as carefully prescribed teaching strategies. Classical literature was also fundamental in the training programs and practicum. Susan borrowed from the humanities to use literature as the core of her student's liberal arts education. The liberal arts studies included:

> *Greek tragedies: the Iliad, the Odyssey, Herodotus, Shakespeare's dramas, Dante, Faust, the philosophy of history and psychology.*
> *(Blow, letter to Harris, August 29th, 1891)*

In addition, mathematics, biology, art, grammar, logic, and history completed the list of core studies. The goal of Blow's liberal arts curriculum was to develop "habits of the mind" rather than a disconnected acquisition of isolated facts and chunks of knowledge (Swiniarski 1976).

The teacher training programs advanced to a second graduate course level in classes assisted by Mrs. Clara Benson Hubbard, who served as the director of the kindergarten for Saturday morning training sessions held at the Eads Kindergarten (Fisher 1924). The study of world languages was then included. The advanced graduate students' language proficiencies were sufficient enough for them to work on amending the German to English translations of Froebel's *Mother's Play*. The goal of translation assignments was to have students gain insights into the symbolic meanings of each play activity. The students' editions were used in instructional sessions until Josephine Jarvis and Susan expanded their translations of 1896. Jarvis' and Blow's renewed editions presented "American translations [of] poems, games, and songs that [Blow] felt exemplified the spirit of Froebel and at the same time reflected the personality of the American child" (Swiniarski 1976, p. 137).

Outreach to community in family policies and practices

Susan taught in the St. Louis kindergartens without pay for eleven years. During this time, she paved the way for establishing her schools and training programs with enough confident students who assumed roles as instructors. Her student practitioners included mothers with no professional aspirations, who worked as aides with professional trainees. Both groups read her publications and attended her nationwide lecture series, especially those given in Chicago.

Susan Blow's most famous lectures were delivered in Chicago where a program to educate women for motherhood was successfully established. Blow concurred with Elizabeth Peabody to follow Froebel's call to all women as teachers of young children. Additionally, she and Elizabeth promoted Froebel's concern for defining, developing, and teaching the arts of motherhood. Although one might think that their adulations of motherhood were romantic and sentimental, their ambitions for parent programs were practical and realistic. Along with many of her followers, Susan believed motherhood studies had a legitimate place in teacher education. Elizabeth agreed.

Both Elizabeth and Susan were encouraged by their program graduates who competently staffed the growing number of kindergartens, published professional books and articles on the movement, and consequently directed their own teacher training programs. Likewise, Susan and Elizabeth were equally pleased that study classes and training programs attracted women without professional ambitions, but who wanted the benefits of an education. The kindergarten movement was not only for children. It was also a social cause committed to the rights of women as well as young children. Educational opportunities were limited for nineteenth-century women. Elizabeth and Susan remedied the situation by moving multiple early childhood education opportunities beyond the classroom to home visits (Swiniarski 1976).

Some contemporaries complained that Susan's notions of classes for mothers were too ambitiously conceived (Swiniarski 1976). Blow advocated to establish a department for mothers in institutions of higher education. Although her plan to have motherhood courses in higher education was a logical consequence, her adversaries compiled statistics and studies to discredit her endeavor. Susan Blow's aspirations prevailed. Designated departments for motherhood came into existence in higher education (Swiniarski 1976).

Susan and other sympathetic thinkers campaigned to promote Chicago Kindergarten College's unique program for mothers. Her numerous publications helped the cause. For example, her book, *Kindergarten Education*, extolled the school's effort to transform "a girls' college into a school for motherhood" (Blow 1904, p. 43). The data issued in *Kindergarten Education* clearly illustrated the Chicago Kindergarten College's program's impressive success, when it reported that "during the year, 1891–92, the department enrolled 725 mothers and during an eight-year period the college boasted of reaching almost 5,000 mothers participating in whole or partial courses" (Blow 1904, p. 43).

The college also hosted a yearly convocation for the discussion of child-nurture. This annual gathering was similar to conferences for professionals interested in child welfare projects. Susan Blow addressed these groups to educate parents in the culture of childhood and to advise families on available support services. "She believed that society's hope for betterment rested upon the success of the family, since in the last analysis, a society would be judged by its care of its young" (Swiniarski 1976, p. 146).

Susan Blow was a social advocate and reformer. She pushed the kindergarten cause beyond the school. Many of her ideas mirror today's missions of settlement houses founded in the late nineteenth and early twentieth centuries. She engaged all constituents with particular interests in the child's early years of education.

Susan Blow's teaching did not end with her St. Louis programs. She was invited to bring her message to Columbia Teachers College as a lecturer, despite her own limited formal education and lack of college degrees. There, she continued the promotion of Froebel's work in this institution's highly regarded halls of learning.

Critical perspectives: physical factors, religious assumptions, and philosophical discourse

Physical factors

After Susan Blow stepped down from teaching in her beloved kindergartens, she was suffering from an unknown condition that brought on a serious case of fatigue. Her illness became her major obstacle to continue her work in all aspects of the movement.

She suffered from Graves' disease, named by the Irish physician, Robert James Graves, for an exophthalmic goiter causing a malfunctioning thyroid (Swiniarski 1976). Laura Fisher, her former student, friend and biographer, convinced Susan to be evaluated at Massachusetts General Hospital in Boston. The hospital's Harvard University Medical School's affiliated doctors were able to correct her condition with their diagnosis and able surgical skills. Once Susan's health was restored and her energy was regained, she channeled all of her strengths into her lecture series, her teaching at Columbia University, and her scholarly leadership in the International Kindergarten Union.

Religious assumptions and conflicts

Susan grew up in a devotedly religious household where family beliefs held "a strict accordance with the dogmas and practice of 19th century Presbyterianism" (Fisher 1924, p. 186). Throughout her adult life as a disciple of Frederick Froebel, Susan struggled to reconcile her early years' religious training on the notion of "evil" with Froebel's philosophical Idealism and his fundamental commitment to developing the innate goodness of every child. Susan Blow outwardly endorsed the philosophy of Idealism as the mainstay of the kindergarten movement but she was always doubtful and questioned Froebel's pantheism and its notion of reality. Froebel believed that reality is an extension of the notion of God that dwelt in all creation. Thus, each child needed to be nurtured early in life to unfold the divine nature within everyone before distractions from the outside world took place (see Chapter 3).

Since Froebel's theories were in accord with those of Transcendentalism, Elizabeth Peabody could easily embrace his hypothesis. Susan questioned his assumptions and looked to Dante, Goethe, and Hegel's dialectical philosophy to interpret and blend her adaptations into Froebel's conceptions. Even though Presbyterian theology evolved in a range of different religious interpretations of conservative Christian positions to liberal points of view, Laura Fisher (1924, p. 187) maintained that Susan's later conversion to the Episcopal Church rendered "greater hope and peace in her final acceptance of Froebel."

Susan and Elizabeth both upheld the belief that the kindergarten had a religious base established by Froebel as its prophet when they spread his message together and "heaped public praise upon each other" (Swiniarski 1976, p. 189). But in private letters to William T. Harris, both women revealed the inner reservations they shared about each other. Elizabeth rejected Susan Blow's outlook on Froebel's theories and contended "it blurred the benevolence of Froebel's religion" (Baylor 1968, p. 106). Meanwhile, Susan, who could embrace some aspects of Transcendentalism, sensed the Transcendentalists, themselves, "had their heads in cloudland" (Swiniarski 1976, p. 189). Evelyn Weber, a noted early childhood education historian and author, speculated that neither Harris nor Blow assumed Elizabeth Peabody's "romantic reverence for childhood" (Weber 1969, p. 28). All of these subtle disparities foreshadowed the struggles ahead for Susan Blow in her campaign to preserve the dogma and true spirit of Froebel in the kindergarten movement.

Philosophical discourse

By the end of the nineteenth century, Froebel's practices were challenged by newer theories. John Dewey, who laid the ground work for the progressive movement in education, had an interest in early childhood education, but found Froebel's philosophy to be incompatible with his pragmatism and his scientific view of teaching practices (Dworkin 1959). In his 1916 publication, *Democracy of Education*, Dewey (1966, p. 58) praised Froebel for his "recognition of the native capacities of children" but felt he erred "when he conceived development to be the unfolding of a ready-made latent principle [and] failed to see growing is growth, [and] developing is development." Dewey was at Teachers College, Columbia, and familiar with Blow's disposition on Froebel, when he wrote this book in 1915. His critique was a significant defeat of Froebel's influence in early education programs and Blow's faithful following of Froebel in the emerging twentieth century.

Changes in child study programs happened in several prominent women's colleges such as Wheaton College, Wellesley College, and Smith College. Their child study programs focused on the scientific findings in child development based in part on Dewey's progressive philosophy. By the 1920s the rising influence of psychology also spawned adaptations of British nursery schools in America such as Abigail Eliot's Ruggles Street Nursery School in Boston, later housed at Tuft University in Medford, Massachusetts. Susan Blow, however, carried on with Froebel's ideas and supported his kindergarten model until her death in 1916.

As a member of the International Kindergarten Union's Advisory Board from 1895–1916, Susan Blow maintained the conservative view of Froebel against the emerging child study movement. She brought her position to Teachers College Columbia University, where Dean James Earl Russell, anxious to have both schools of thought presented, invited Patty Smith Hill, an outspoken liberal, to meet Susan Blow in a debate-lecture series at the university (Swiniarski 1976). Critics concede that Patty Smith Hill won the debate. Time and circumstance were on Smith Hill's side as a new faculty face at Teachers College Columbia. However, the two women respected each other and continued to teach as partners under the direction of Dean Russell, who wanted representation of divergent views at the university.

Theoretical and practice legacy

Susan Blow steered the kindergarten movement into the twentieth century. At times, it was a lonely pathway, especially when William Torrey Harris departed from St. Louis to become the US Commissioner of Education in Washington, DC. While Harris continued to support Susan in his new more powerful position, his daily available mentoring was sorely missed.

As Susan Blow approached the twentieth century, her validation of Froebel's legacy was spoken in a lonely voice without the echo of Elizabeth Peabody. Despite their differences, both women always upheld Froebel's pedagogy because they were equally convinced that the key to the betterment of humankind lay in Froebel's practices. His philosophy was embedded in their epistemology and social values. However, as Elizabeth grew older to face her death in 1894 at ninety years old, Susan carried the cause forward into the twentieth century. She accepted the challenge with dignity and passed on her own impressive legacy.

Susan Blow's legacy and recognition for her achievements

In her mission for equity in American education, Susan Blow secured early entrance into the public school system for all young children to be educated in kindergarten classrooms. In her teaching, she welcomed and placed all children as equals at the center of her instruction. Her legacy lives on into the twenty-first century with the following achievements.

Susan Blow adapted Froebel's child-center kindergarten in theory and practice to be based upon a guided play curriculum for American children and:

- captured the spirit of American childhood in her pedagogy;
- designed her kindergarten class' physical interiors with colorful decoration, comfortable furnishing, and plentiful room for youngsters to freely move about and experience learning;
- modeled a professional commitment of community engagement;
- heightened respect for the roles of motherhood and the parenting of children to a professional level;
- shared her scholarship for future generations through her prolific publications of books, journal articles, manuscript translations, and lectures;
- demonstrated a global perspective in her leadership role in the International Kindergarten Union;
- acknowledged teaching in kindergartens as a profession with special training and education at college and university levels.

For all of these reasons and more, Susan Blow was often recognized with awards and memorials for her reputation as a scholar, her skills as an educator, and her achievements as a social advocate. She tended to decline any public recognition as she considered her work a civic responsibility. She felt obliged as a citizen to contribute to her community and country. Nevertheless, the state of Missouri recognized her good deeds with a mural entitled *Let Us Live for the Children*, on display in its State Capitol to commemorate her accomplishments in the education of young children. The city of St. Louis cited her publicly when it built its St. Louis Walk of Fame to acknowledge her attainment of public funding for both their kindergartens and the specialized training of their teachers.

In 1879, Susan was accepted into the Concord School of Philosophy as one of the few women admitted to engage in scholarly discourse with a selected erudite gathering of American philosophers. At its opening event, she joined her close colleagues, William Torrey Harris, Elizabeth Palmer Peabody and a fellow St. Louis Hegelian Society philosopher, Denton Jacques Snider, along with the distinguished roster of Concord's leading Transcendentalists.

Critical for the development of Susan Blow's legacy were the efforts of her followers who spread her message nationally. After Harris went to Washington, DC, Susan Blow lost some of her local influence in the schools. She too left St. Louis to move east primarily for health reasons, but also in disagreement with the Board of Education's changes for more formal instruction, made by its newly appointed supervisor, Mary C. Cullough. Likewise dismayed by the focus on an academic-based curriculum, many of Susan's protégées moved on to new positions as well (Snyder 1972).

Laura Fisher, Blow's former student and later biographer, was named as the Director of Boston Public School Kindergarten. Cynthia Dozier, one of Blow's first kindergarteners in training, was the Supervisor of the New York Kindergarten Association. Mary Runyad was given the position of Head of the Kindergarten Department in Teachers College Columbia University. Caroline Hart Head went to the Training School of the Kindergarten Association of Baltimore along with Harriet Head who took a post in the Training School Kindergarten of Washington DC. Agnes Snyder contends in her book, *Dauntless Women in Childhood Education, 1857–1931*, that these young apostles of Susan Blow, who left St. Louis in protest, were highly regarded. Their departure was a loss for St. Louis. To the nation, however, they cultivated Susan Blow's theories on kindergarten education in prominent key positions throughout the USA (Snyder 1972, p. 66).

Today, Susan Blow's legacy continues to live online in the *My Hero Project* for her effective teaching of eleven years in the kindergarten and training programs of St. Louis that she designed and established in its public school system as a national model (see http://myhero.com/hero.asp?hero=S_Blow_moran_ms_2008).

As a prolific writer and committed scholar, Susan was a role model for her student teachers, families, reformers, and advocates. Her publications exemplify the demands she required of herself. Her published works still prove to be motivating for contemporary readers who seek a better world for all children.

Relevance to contemporary practice

Susan Blow's insistence on moving the kindergarten into the public school system with tax revenue support is as timely today as when she proposed it. While many states in the US mandate that communities provide public kindergartens, to date not all states have complied (see Chapter 4). Blow's campaign for consistent national tax support is still carried on by early educators and families. Parental and professional voices in today's daily news media call for petitions that support equal education opportunities for all young children. Families are also dismayed that time-honored successful child-centered practices have been replaced by academic models in time schedules that offer a shorter day with fewer play opportunities. Families are equally concerned about the increased number of standardized testing proposals. The current call for the Common Core curriculum and national testing of kindergarten children is as controversial as the St. Louis Board of Education's shift in curriculum design that prompted Susan Blow and her followers to leave the city in 1885.

Influences on Settlement House

In tandem with Elizabeth Peabody, Susan Blow's influences spread to the Settlement House movement. In 1889, Jane Addams and Elizabeth Gates Starr established the first Settlement House, Hull-House Settlement House, in Chicago as a worldwide model for social reform. Like the Peabody Settlement House in Boston and later in Somerville, Massachusetts, Addams and Starr were influenced by the kindergarten pioneers' innovations for working with families and young children in educational programs through social services. The Settlement House goals included providing support programs for immigrant families to transition into American society. They offered English language lessons to English language learners, and extended parenting education and early childhood education programs to families in need. These social activists turned to the work of Blow and others in the kindergarten movement as resources for guidelines and successful exemplars. Today, community social centers still work with newly arrived immigrants, help families in need, and provide early education and care of children.

Antecedent of Full Service Schools

Full Service Schools, also known as Community Schools, see their mission as extending beyond the walls of the school and its academic goals. Such schools are concerned with the development of the whole child and understand the importance of family and home in the education of youth. Their endeavor is to promote a multi-service approach that embraces the whole child and their family. Full Service Schools, much like Susan Blow's kindergartens, provide parent education. Likewise, Full Service Schools have adopted the motto that "parents are the child's first teachers" (Breitborde and Swiniarski 2006, p. 465).

> *Historically the kindergarten programs established in settlement houses and public schools during the nineteenth century were the precursors of the Full Service School. These twentieth-century early education efforts pioneered parental involvement, inclusion of social services in schools and the notion of educating the whole child. [Full Service Schools] seek to improve education by empowering families. Typically, Full Service Schools provide after-school programs, medical services, social services, parenting courses and counseling. Their mission is to meet the needs of their constituents . . . beyond the purview of the traditional schools.*
>
> *(Breitbode and Swiniarski 2006, pp. 465–6)*

In the United States, much of the groundwork for the Full Service movement was set by kindergarten pioneers such as Susan Blow. Her influence was felt into the twenty-first century through the leadership of people like Joy Dryfoos who "believes education does not happen in a vacuum" (Breitborde and Swiniarski 2006, p. 466). Dryfoos is especially concerned about improving education for at-risk students by collaborating with multiple services in the community. Today there are several models of partnerships between the school and community agencies in public and private sectors. Some Full Service Schools partner with medical agencies, institutions of higher education, and communities' social services. Their instructional projects can take place in the community in facilities beyond the school grounds.

Other Full Service Schools might take on the challenge of being established as a Charter School. Charter Schools are public schools because they are supported by public funds but are independent options within a school district, which offers families a selection of schools for their children. In some cases, Charter Schools have petitioned their states for charters that outline goals and plans with a Full Service climate. All Full Service Schools can extend from early childhood education years through to the final four years of high school.

Closing thoughts

Susan Blow's legacy lives on today. She provided the foundation for the public kindergarten throughout America. Her work resonates with educators and parents who still believe early education should center on the young child, in an environment conducive to their needs, under the guidance of highly educated teachers in schools, equally available for all families through public funding support.

In the United States the notion of public support for early childhood education programs is partially in place. Today, children can start their public schooling in kindergarten at age five, if kindergarten is offered in their state or community. To complement the early childhood education years, the new goal is to make universal preschool education available to all American children starting at age three. Susan Blow's kindergartens began with children age three in a full-day program. Her children had the advantage of staying in a multi-aged kindergarten until they moved on to elementary school at age seven.

American families find few public early childhood education funded programs available in the United States for children at the ages of three or four. Annually, politicians seeking local and national offices make promises to establish free universal preschool education funded by tax revenues as endorsed in 1996 by the international Organisation for Economic Co-operation and Development (OECD 1996). To date, however, in the USA only a few states deliver such a promise because there is no national mandate (Swiniarski 2014). Susan Blow's message – that everyone needs to be a stakeholder in funding the education of children by age three – is still as relevant today as it was in 1873.

Good ideas seep up. Susan Blow's outreach to family practices have been adapted into the upper levels of elementary school, middle school and high school education in many community education programs. In this regard, her mission as a social reformer surpassed her own expectations.

Susan Blow's scope was global. A fluent linguist in several languages, she appreciated the values of being multi-lingual, able to connect with others and communicate across boundaries. Her moral sense of citizenship and responsibilities to one's own country as well as to people worldwide defines her as a globally literate educator and an exemplary world citizen.

Student integration tasks

- For further information about Susan Blow and her effects on public kindergartens in St. Louis, visit the State Historical Society of Missouri's website for online photos and documentations: http://shs.umsystem.edu/historicmissourians/name/b/blow.

- To learn more about Full Service Schools, see Dryfoos, J. (1998). *Full service schools*. San Francisco: Jossey Publications.

- To see a Settlement House movement in action, you can view the DVD titled *An Experiment in Democracy*, published by Jane Addams Hull-House Museum in Chicago, Illinois. Information on the Hull-House Museum's listings can be found on its website. It includes the DVD along with numerous books written by Jane Addams. Jane Addams was not only one of the founders of Hull-House but also a path finder recognized worldwide as a promoter of many international causes. She was awarded the Nobel Peace Prize in 1931 for her work in the Peace Movement for women and children during the aftermath of World War One (Addams 2002). Like Susan Blow, Jane Addams was a complex woman who saw her mission as a global educator as well as an American social reformer: www.hullhousemuseum.org.

- Charter Schools are public school options for families. In the UK they have been called "Opting out Schools" or "Free Academies." Sweden has public-supported parent-run schools. Go online to find if there are such schools in your school districts that offer similar family services, parent education, and involvement in the education of their children. Visit the schools and volunteer to launch school and family partnerships where needed.

- John Dewey was a critical player who challenged Susan Blow's efforts in her final years' efforts to maintain the influence of Froebel's theories in American kindergartens. For further research on John Dewey's impact and his publications that shaped future kindergartens and twentieth-century educational practices in America, there is a collection of his works available for study at Southern Illinois University in Carbondale, Illinois: http://www.siu.edu/-deweycrt.

References

Addams, J. (2002). *Peace and bread in time of war*. Urbana and Chicago: University of Illinois Press.

Baylor, R. (1965). *Elizabeth Palmer Peabody: kindergarten pioneer*. Philadelphia: University of Pennsylvania Press.

Blow, S. (August 29, 1891). *Letter to William Torrey Harris.* St. Louis, MO: Missouri Historical Society, Harris Collection.

Blow, S. (1904). *Kindergarten education.* New York: Lyons.

Breitborde, M. and Swiniarski, L. (2006). *Teaching on principle and promise: The foundations of education.* Boston: Houghton Mifflin Company.

Dewey, J. (1944). *Democracy and education.* New York: The Free Press.

Dryfoos, J. (1968). *Full service schools:* San Francisco: Jossey Publications.

Dworkin, M. (1959). *Dewey on education selections.* New York: Teachers College Press.

Fisher, L. (1924). *Susan Elizabeth Blow: pioneers of the kindergarten in America.* New York: Century, pp. 184–203.

Maltz, E. (2007). *Dred Scott and the politics of slavery.* Lawrence, KS: University Press of Kansas.

Organisation for Economic Co-operation and Development. (1997). *Lifelong learning for all.* Paris, France: Organisation for Economic Co-operation and Development.

Schultz, R., Portincaso, D. and Strobel, M. (n.d.). *An experiment in democracy.* Chicago: Jane Addams Hull-House Museum.

Snyder, A. (1972). *Dauntless women in childhood education: 1856–1931.* Washington, DC: Association for Childhood Education International.

Swiniarski, L. (1976). *A comparative study of Elizabeth Peabody and Susan Blow by examination of their work and writing.* An unpublished PhD dissertation. The Graduate School of Boston College, Chestnut Hill, MA.

Swiniarski, L. (Ed). (2014). *World class initiatives and practices in early education: moving forward in a global age.* Dordrecht: Springer.

Swiniarski, L. (April 23, 2015). *Unintended consequences: gender, purpose and politics on the movement for professional education. Part 2: Founders of American kindergartens and training of kindergarteners.* Unpublished presentation at the International Society for Educational Biography 32nd Annual Conference, St. Louis, MO.

Swiniarski, L. (March 11, 2016). *Elizabeth Peabody and Susan Blow: 19th century educators and promoters for equal public support of the American kindergarten.* Accepted presentation for the University of Southern Mississippi, Long Beach, MS.

Weber, E. (1969). *The kindergarten: its encounter with education thought in America.* New York: Teachers College Press.

Websites

www.hullhousemuseum.org.

http://myhearo.com/go/hero.asp?hero=S Blow moran ms 2008.

http://shs.umsystem.edu/historicamissiourians/namr.b blow.

http://www.siu.edu/-deweycrt.

http://myhero.com/hero.asp?hero=S_Blow_moran_ms_2008.

6

Rudolf Steiner (1861–1925)
The anthroposophical approach
Wendy Holland

Introduction

Various pioneers of education have raised the idea that a child's education should be a holistic experience, and not simply an enactment of the reductivist view of the young child as human capital; however, such ideas are still generally considered to be 'alternative' in the contemporary United Kingdom. Some compromise attempts have been made over the century and a half since public education began in the UK to 'co-opt' certain elements of such holistic 'alternative' approaches into the mainstream. The English early years foundation stage (EYFS) in its original inception (2007), for example, mentions the need for a 'holistic' approach for children from birth to five years, but this is a poor match with the requirement to monitor children's 'outcomes' within a carefully structured framework of assessment. The impetus to grade, label, target, test and be accountable for children's 'outcomes' can be seen even more clearly in the revised EYFS (2012/14). Such 'weighing and measuring' of the individual would have been anathema to all the pioneers, who operated along a common theme that constructed childhood as a time in which the young child could naturally unfold, demonstrating the richness of human potential to those who were prepared to take the time to observe and listen.

Such a perspective was particularly the case for Rudolph Steiner (1861–1925) and this chapter will discuss his unique approach to human development, embedded within a specific spiritual view of humanity's place within the world, which led him to a concentrated focus on holistic development during the period of childhood. It will use the term 'Steiner schools' to refer to schools using the Steiner framework, both in the past and present, which is the British custom. American readers are advised that in the US, such schools are generally referred to as Waldorf Steiner schools or Waldorf Schools.

Rudolf Steiner: life and work

To understand the impact of Rudolf Steiner as a pioneer of alternative education, we need to look at the man holistically, seeing the influences that helped shape his ideas through his own childhood and adolescence, to the complex adult he later became. His lifespan, encompassing the latter half of the nineteenth century and the first quarter of the twentieth century, placed him to experience the end of one epoch and the beginning of another, and we now recognise that these times were turbulent, creative and at the same time destructive. The legacy of Rousseau's Romanticism (see Chapter 1) was still being felt in the late 1890s and this sat uneasily with the more scientific, mechanical philosophy of the 1900s.

Thanks to the ideas of Nietzsche, Darwin and the rise of the 'scientific method', there was a cultural movement towards the concept that God was 'dead' and there seemed no place for the spiritual, or acknowledgement of the human 'soul' (Steiner 1996). From quite early in his life, Rudolf Steiner set himself the quest of trying to unite these opposing philosophies. Having experienced what he described as moments of clairvoyance, which, he proposed, enabled him to see into the spirit world, Steiner thought the only means of salvation for the world crisis and the related spiritual and material misery of his times would be the 'spiritualisation' of natural science. Through deep self-reflection, he believed that human beings would rediscover a lost ability to bridge the material world and the spiritual. This approach has and continues to receive much criticism, but regardless of his contemporaries' ridicule, it became Steiner's life's work, as he tells us in his autobiography, *The Course of My Life* (1928), published posthumously by his second wife, Maria von Sivers (Steiner 1928).

This quest led him to study the ideas of such philosophers as Kant on idealism, Goethe on natural science, light and colour and Darwin, whose concept of evolution he rejected. The nearest to his ideas of 'spiritual science' he found in the theosophy movement, with its exploration of the spirit world, a belief in reincarnation and karma and expectations of the 'second coming' of a Messiah (Lachman 2012, also see Chapter 3). With customary zeal Steiner soon became one of theosophy's leading exponents in Germany, but later, after some vigorous disagreement with Annie Besant, the movement's vice-president, he split from the Theosophical Society and formed his own philosophical belief system. This he named Anthroposophy, which for Steiner meant an extended form of scientific cognition that connects man with the spiritual world (Ulrich 1994).

In trying to give credence to the life of the spirit, as well as scientific thought, he created an alternative approach to education that has not only survived his death, but grown as the numbers of Steiner schools are today increasing on a global scale. Contemporary statistics show 1,200 Steiner schools worldwide, with 2,000 early years settings in 60 countries, 35 of which are in the UK and Ireland (see http://www.steinerwaldorf.org). This growth has occurred in spite of real controversy around Steiner himself, according to the sources accessed. Some believe him to be a 'dilettante philosopher' whose theories on science, particularly physics, were dismissed as nonsensical, with Max von Laue (Nobel Prize winner for physics in 1914) mounting a scathing critique in 1922 of Steiner's ideas (Restivo 1985). Others have alternatively proclaimed him a true polymath, literary scholar, philosopher, social reformer, architect, playwright, lecturer, founder of the spiritual science movement of anthroposophy and inspirational founder of the educational movement of Waldorf/Steiner Schools (Lindenberg 2012).

Some of the seeds of Steiner's development of his unique alternative view of education can be traced back to his own account of his life.

As a young boy, according to his autobiography (1928), Steiner felt a real affinity to the natural beauty of the countryside around the village in which he was born, but even at this point his 'fascination with all things of a mechanical character overshadowed my childish soul' (Steiner 1928, p. 3). Here Steiner is referring to the railway his father worked for as a station master, which transected the rural landscape, the trains simultaneously disturbing and attracting Steiner with their noise and smoke 'that must always disappear into the far distance' (Steiner 1928, p. 3). This conflict between nature and the mechanical products of science and engineering and later technology can be seen reflected in his emergent ideas on education that were later to reject early exposure to technology in favour of the study of nature.

Steiner's own early education was far from conventional, partly due to his somewhat frail constitution. He was the child his parents considered 'precious' and was quite carefully protected by them during his formative years. After being abruptly removed from the village school he attended (as a result of being wrongly accused of dishonesty), his father attempted to home school him, with less than perfect results. Steiner realised from this early age that he would struggle to engage with 'what had to come to me by way of direct instruction' (Steiner 1928, p. 6). Again here we see how these early experiences begin to help form his later ideas around education, particularly the negative effect of 'transmission' teaching. He was interested in how things worked, visiting a local mill to watch the miller at work and trying to gain access to a local yarn factory, curious about how cloth was made; unfortunately, the owner was less accommodating. This curiosity and need to be actively involved in observing and learning is again seen embedded in his ideas on education.

His autobiography makes numerous references to influential adults who peopled his childhood, from the miller to the village priest and local doctor. The school teacher of another village school he later attended made a great impression on the young Steiner, teaching him a love of music and the mysteries of geometry that continued to engage his thoughts. This teacher also introduced him to 'form' in art by encouraging Steiner to copy images from an original drawing. Again this focus on and fascination with geometric patterns is an aspect of the curriculum that has been incorporated into the daily practices that Steiner later created for the Waldorf/Steiner schools.

These people he calls 'notables' often gathered at his home to discuss politics, philosophy, art and religion with his father, who was regarded as a 'free thinker', while Steiner's younger brother and sister (of whom he says very little) played and his mother 'knitted or crocheted' (Steiner 1928, p. 16). The young Steiner would listen to conversations and sometimes heated discussions about the works of Lessing, Goethe and Schiller, about concepts of beauty and ugliness. He describes, too, the impact on his emergent spiritual sensibilities when serving as an altar boy; the feelings and thoughts aroused during these activities began to form emergent ideas about the existence of a spiritual dimension which he could 'visit'. He later claimed this period marked the beginning of his clairvoyance. By the time he was ten years old he realised that he had some difficulties in the 'material' world, particularly with developing skills in reading and writing:

> *My relationship to reading and writing were entirely different . . . I passed rapidly over the words in reading; my mind went immediately to the concepts, the ideas, so that I got no feeling from reading for spelling or writing grammatically . . . in writing I had a tendency to fix the word forms in my mind by their sounds as I generally heard them spoken in the dialect.*
>
> (Steiner 1928, p. 18)

Again, if we look at the present-day approach to reading and writing in Steiner schools, there is a deliberate attempt made to delay the development of these literacy skills until a child transitions to 'Class 1' at the age of seven years.

Steiner's family were not wealthy, but his father was aware of his son's potential from the early days of childhood and had hopes of him becoming a railway engineer. When it came to deciding on Steiner's secondary education, his father sent him to the Realschule where science and modern languages were the focus, rather than the Gymnasium (the European equivalent of a grammar school at that time), which put an emphasis on the classics.

The autobiography builds a picture of a child both lonely in his need for a kindred 'spiritual' friend and involved in the practical activities of life:

> *Throughout all this I was not drawn away from whatever pertains to the actual doing of practical things and the development of human skills . . . gathering cherries, taking care of the orchard, preparing the potatoes for planting, cultivating the soil.*
>
> (Steiner 1928, p. 26)

Steiner learned book binding and stenography from one of his father's employees and worked with his brother and sister doing the necessary chores for the family's subsistence. Again, this is reflected in the rhythms of the seasons that are celebrated in the Steiner school curriculum, as well as the attention given to the development of physical skills such as knitting, bread making, gardening and growing produce.

But Steiner was also a boy who craved the company of adults with interesting ideas and conversation about art, music and mathematics, adults whom the young Steiner could 'model' himself upon (Steiner 1928, p. 21). This need to be with inspirational adults, coupled with the love of nature, the work and rhythms of agricultural life, concepts of beauty, musical forms, the power of art and geometry are all echoed in the structure of the Steiner schools, where nursery children aged between three and seven years rely upon, listen to and imitate the actions of one trusted adult through the routines of their day and children from seven to fourteen years stay with the same 'inspiring' adult through their primary and 'middle school' years.

As he approached transition to the Realschule, Steiner experienced a deepening spiritual belief which he describes thus: 'The reality of the spiritual world was as certain to me as that of the physical. I felt a need, however, for a sort of justification for this assumption' (Steiner 1928, p. 23).

Indeed, as mentioned earlier, in later life he would go on to form his own branch of theosophy known as anthroposophy (see http://www.anthroposophy. org.uk/). There are many references to the spirit world throughout Steiner's secondary education where he sought to understand the 'form' in nature as spiritual, even the study of mathematics and geometry, which, according to Steiner, were linked to the unseen spirit world, accessible to only a few. Another important influence at this time was his introduction to Kant and his *Critique of Pure Reason*, an author whose work he would return to later. Steiner's autobiography at this point reads like the journey of the adolescent boy that he once was, who seemingly gained little from the actual content of his school lessons and much more from the adults who introduced him to important thinkers of philosophy, literature and religion. Much of his spare time was spent in trying to absorb and understand the complex ideas they presented. He was also introspective and continued to struggle to define the mystical elements he believed co-existed with physical reality, as a result of his episodes of clairvoyance: 'to what extent is it possible to prove that in human thinking real spirit is the agent? . . . That the ego, which is itself spirit, lives in a world of spirits was for me a matter of direct perception' (Steiner 1928, p. 34).

By the age of fifteen, despite the ever-present struggle with his inner spiritual consciousness which often distracted him from his studies, he was considered to be a 'good scholar', having mastered his school subjects sufficiently to become a pupil teacher. Steiner describes the effect of teaching:

> In having to give to others in turn the matter which I had been taught, I myself became, as it were, awake to this . . . on the other hand this experience compelled me at an early age to concern myself with all things practical. I learnt the difficulties of the development of human minds through my pupils.
>
> (Steiner 1928, p. 36)

From these early experiences of teaching, we begin to see the model of a reflective teacher concerned with human development, two basic and important tenets that would later inform Steiner's programme for teacher training. Steiner's father, ever accommodating to his son's needs, asked to be moved to a small station near Vienna so Steiner could begin his university education at the Technical University there, while still benefitting from the daily support of his family.

At university Steiner chose to study mathematics, natural history and chemistry. Here, he fell under the influence of Karl Schroer, a professor of German literature.

It is through the presentations that Schroer demanded his students give that Steiner gained confidence in public speaking, something he would develop to what we would nowadays term a 'motivational' level in the lectures he later gave in many nations throughout the world. At university he was again seduced from his elective subjects to attend lectures on ethics by Robert Zimmerman, who he saw as another role model. Steiner reported that he also felt that his clairvoyance was growing in power at this time. After the death of a school friend, Steiner describes that he, too, 'followed . . . in the spiritual world' (Steiner 1928, p. 39). When he wrote to a former tutor, describing this experience in his letter, the tutor wrote back without acknowledging any such disclosure and Steiner began to realise this would be the normal reaction of others. They would happily discuss his ideas on Goethe and his views of colour, Kant's materialistic philosophy and the issues with Social Darwinism, but any talk of the spiritual world Steiner felt he inhabited would be met with silence.

Clearly in need of a kindred spirit, Steiner tells us at the age of twenty-one how he encountered a 'mystic' on his train journeys to and from university, who was versed in 'the spirituality of nature'. Through their regular discussions Steiner began to develop ideas around reincarnation. The mystic introduced him to another fellow traveller, who Steiner simply called the 'master', who introduced him to the work of the philosopher Johann Fichte. Again, contemporary critics of Steiner's educational approach raise issues about such ideas filtering into the 'hidden curriculum' that is used, but not mentioned, in contemporary Waldorf/Steiner schools.

From 1884 to 1890 Steiner supported himself through private tutoring; in particular he was employed by a prosperous Jewish family with four sons. He quickly discovered that one of the children was

> considered so subnormal in his physical and mental development that the family had doubts to his capacity for being educated . . . I was soon able to bring the child into a loving dependence upon me. This caused the mere intercourse between us to awaken his sleeping faculties of soul.
>
> *(Steiner 1928, p. 71)*

Steiner describes how through short bursts of instruction the boy began to respond to his teaching. This strengthened his belief in the 'association between the spiritual-mental and the bodily man'. However, he added that preparation for such an onerous task frequently took him a very long time, two hours for half an hour of instruction, reflecting that this impressed on him the idea that 'teaching and instruction must become an art in the genuine understanding of man' (Steiner 1928, p. 72).

This led Steiner on to create a schedule in which the days had to be 'properly' structured, with set times for instruction, so that the child's 'spirit' was not damaged. To avoid such 'spiritual damage' Steiner reported that he provided relief from the cognitive domain through short sessions of movement. He finally informs the reader that the child had a hydrocephalic condition, but in spite of this managed, through Steiner's careful teaching, to enter the school system, eventually gaining a place at the Gymnasium. What this particular passage shows is that some of Steiner's personal experiences of tutoring were again used in the foundation of the form, content and approach to teaching that is today embedded in Steiner schools worldwide. We see here the avoidance of too much pressure solely on the child's cognitive domain and also the curative use of sessions of movement, something he would later develop into eurhythmy (Lachman 2012).

It also suggests a spiritual and philosophical underpinning based on what Steiner termed a genuine understanding of the holistic human being; this he later explains in more detail in the ideas of his philosophical movement of anthroposophy. There is continued argument and contemporary debate as to what extent present-day Steiner schools embrace the teachings of anthroposophy. Some critics suggest it is so thoroughly embedded as to make a Steiner education a 'religious' one, with the resulting opposition to any government funding for Steiner schools (Dugan and Daar 1994).

It was while tutoring the children of the Jewish family that Steiner talks about experiencing the pleasure of play for the first time, at twenty-three years of age. He commented that throughout his life before this point, there had been little time and opportunity for play. But by engaging in a playtime which he had to order and organise for the children, he began to understand what play was and the potential impact upon the human being. He reflected that he had come very late to this understanding and that it was likely that most men would understand how play 'worked' 'before the 10th year' (Steiner 1928, p. 74). Again, his personal experience can be seen to impact upon his later professional practice; this time in extended periods of daily free play in the Steiner school.

In terms of Steiner's own education, his intention had been to complete his degree and to find work as a grammar-school teacher. However, some sources suggest he did not complete his studies, partly due to his preference for literature and philosophy. Other sources claim he graduated in 1883 (Ulrich 1994). It is, however, certain that around 1881 Joseph Kurschner, a friend of Steiner's long-time friend and mentor, Schroer, gave Steiner the prestigious task of editing Goethe's scientific writings. This resulted in a number of publications by Steiner, and one entitled 'Truth and Science' gained him a PhD in philosophy from the University of Rostock in 1891. From this point onwards he seems to have made a living from writing, teaching and delivering lectures. He also became involved with the Theosophical Society, whose spokesperson was Annie Besant, feeling that this group's acknowledgement of 'hidden wisdom or knowledge that offers the individual enlightenment and salvation' (Lindenberg 2012) fitted with his own ideas of spiritually free human beings.

An aspect of Steiner's life that is hardly mentioned in his autobiography or other biographies about Steiner is his first marriage in 1899 to a widow named Anna Eunike, whom he had lodged with while working in Weima. This episode in Steiner's life provides some critical insight into his persona. Critics called it a marriage of convenience, where he was given bed and board and nurtured by this woman, several years his senior, while he concentrated upon his writings. In 1902, he was elected general secretary of the German section of the Theosophical Society, which included undertaking many lecture tours across Europe. During this period he met the woman who was to become his second wife, Marie von Sivers, an ardent theosophist herself, who later helped him further develop his ideas on curative euthymic movement. Steiner's first wife Anna died in 1911 and he married Marie von Sivers in 1914. Like many other German-speaking theosophists, Marie broke with the Theosophical Society in 1913 and joined Steiner in his newly founded Anthroposophical Society.

In 1919 Steiner demonstrated his considerable architectural skills, and using the skills of local craftsmen, he organised the construction of a wooden building which he named the 'Goetheanum', which was to be used as a school of spiritual science in Dornach, Switzerland. It was an amazing building even by today's standards, and reflects Steiner's belief in the importance of the physical as well as the spiritual ambience of a learning environment, a belief that would later be reflected in the building of Steiner schools around the world.

Steiner's reasons for breaking away from Annie Besant and the theosophists concerned a point of dogma regarding the interpretation of the life of Jesus Christ. Steiner's view of Jesus not as the son of God, but as a 'sun god', in a pantheon of gods, would create problems for parents wanting to send their child to a supposedly non-denominational school. This too is a contemporary debate to which Steiner's critics keep returning.

The many lectures Steiner delivered internationally led to him being accused of becoming a 'charismatic leader of a new philosophical community . . . focused on his own personality' (Ullrich 1994). Steiner attempted to lay before his audience a programme for spiritual reform of life in its many aspects; art, education, economics, medicine, agriculture, the Christian religion and politics. There were, and remain today, issues around some of his ideas at this time, particularly on the subject of 'lightness' and 'darkness'. His philosophy envisaged two gods who embodied these contrasts. This was also linked to Steiner's ideas of a racial 'roots' theory, which implied that dark-skinned 'races' were at a lower level of spiritual evolution, and that the light-skinned Aryan races were examples of a higher spiritual evolution, capable of 'seeing' the spirit world that Steiner claimed to have witnessed. This has led over time to accusations of racial intolerance, something contemporary followers of anthroposophy attempt to ameliorate with references to the 'zeitgeist' or prevailing ideas held during the period in which Steiner first introduced his views. However, contemporary critics maintain that there is a definite preference of light colours over dark in Steiner schools, even down to the elimination of dark-coloured crayons and paints in nursery children's art work, the 'wet' painting techniques that produce an evanescence, and the preponderance of light colours in Steiner schools' architecture, with their pastel walls and woodwork. Far more worryingly, some critics have suggested that darker-skinned pupils are 'viewed' differently to their lighter-skinned companions (Staudenmaier 2008).

The world of the early 1900s did not embrace Steiner's philosophy in the way he had anticipated, apart from a dedicated band of anthroposophical followers who considered him to be a true mystic and polymath. Disappointed that others did not share his vision, he turned his attention to the somewhat chaotic material world. By 1918, World War I was nearing its end, with the consequent societal disruption that war on such a grand scale inevitably brings, and the pain of individual families who were coping with the premature death or permanent disability of one of their members, most often the husband and father. In the aftermath of such destruction, western capitalism was being challenged by revolution in Russia and socialist movements across Europe. Steiner began a lecture tour at this time, delivering his solution for transforming society. This solution became known as Social Three Folding. It principally focuses upon three important areas of human activity: the economic sphere, the legal domain and culture, which includes education. Steiner felt these three areas should work independently, as a 'third way' of organising society, a middle path between socialism and communism (Lindenberg 2012). Steiner now believed that the 'middle path' moral imperative at which he had finally arrived placed him as the person who would lead the way to a society in which humankind could live together in a balanced and fair way, while aspiring to a spiritual domain. In Social Three Folding, none of the domains he describes had dominance over the others and this equality was to be maintained in any bartering or interaction between them. These ideas later became the basis of a book Steiner published under the title *The Three Fold State* (Steiner 1972). In spite of an exhausting lecture tour to promote his ideas, including meetings with high-ranking German government officers, Social Three Folding was eventually rejected by the mainstream (Lindenberg 2012).

Steiner's anthroposophical ideas did, however, attract the interest of Emil Molt, the owner of the Waldorf cigarette factory in Stuttgart, Germany. After Steiner had delivered a lecture on his ideas to the factory's workforce, Molt, inspired by Steiner's views on an independent education system, asked Steiner to create a school for the children of his factory workers. Steiner saw this as an opportunity to put into practice ideas that linked a programme of education with his anthroposophical beliefs of three folding. His school, he determined, would espouse children's rights (legal), provide independent choices and a non-hierarchal structure (culture), and be self-sustaining and self-governing (economic). Steiner saw this as a way of 'spreading the word' and creating a practical reality for his ideas. Against prevailing orthodoxies, this first Steiner school was co-educational, inclusive (open to children from any background) and comprehensive, taking children from the preschool level through to high school.

Initially the Waldorf/Steiner schools, as they became known, were accepted by the prevailing political elite after Germany's defeat in World War I. Some critics suggest this was due in no small measure to Steiner's relationship with a general in the German High Command, Helmuth von Moltke. Indeed, after the General's death, he corresponded with Moltke's wife, Elizabeth von Moltke, relaying messages to her from her deceased husband through his alleged clairvoyant powers (Ullrich 1994).

However, with the growth of the National Socialist movement in Germany, Waldorf/Steiner schools were eventually closed, the reason given that Steiner's

Social Three Folding ideas for reforming society were not in accord with Hitler's National Socialist perspectives, and the schools stayed closed until the end of the war. Steiner experienced another blow to his mission when the 'Goetheanum', his architectural statement piece, was burned down in 1922 by arsonists. Undefeated, Steiner began a reconstruction of the school, this time in concrete. He did not live to see its completion in 1928, but the building remains the cultural centre and head-quarters of anthroposophy and its school of spiritual science, reflecting the very specific design seen in Steiner schools today (Dugan and Daar 1994).

That Steiner died in Dornach on 30th March 1925 is not in doubt, but the reasons for his demise are varied, again depending upon which biographer is consulted. Never having had a robust constitution from childhood (Lindenberg 2012), there is some suggestion that the pressure of writing and lecturing to the extent he did, and his fall from favour with the rising National Socialist party, may all have con-tributed to Steiner's death at age 64 from an 'unknown stomach illness'. Very little is written about the actual manner of his death, but its suddenness gave rise to the suspicion he may have been poisoned. Others around him at the time tell of his frequent statements regarding his increasing 'estrangement' from his own body, which suggests a natural ending of life that would fit with his anthroposophical beliefs (Ullrich 1994).

How far Steiner schools in the twenty-first century still adhere to Steiner's anthroposophical approach to teaching is still something of an unknown. However, with the potential for expansion under state funding within the Government's Free Schools and Academies programme in England, more questions are now being asked about the Steiner schools' approach.

Theoretical and practical legacy: anthroposophical education – a credible contemporary alternative?

To answer the above question, we need to clarify (a) what the main tenets of anthroposophical education are and (b) what is known about the effects of Steiner's anthroposophical beliefs on the practices not only within Steiner schools, but also those settings that adopt a 'Steiner-like' approach.

If we begin to consider some of the central tenets of anthroposophy, we can begin to understand Steiner's concept of 'human development', and why he insisted that all Steiner teachers must have a clear understanding of this to support and enhance a child's holistic learning and development. It needs to be remembered that Steiner's approach is unlike that of other pioneers. It is not an ethical/philo-sophical approach such as that of Kant or Herbart, or a socio/cultural approach like that of Durkheim. There is no empirical rationale underlying Steiner's theory of child development; he could not look to psychology for support; indeed his theory did not even have the internal integrity of Freud's non-empirical theory that you will read about in Chapter 9. Steiner himself proposed, with typical mysticism, that children's development consisted of successive phases of vegetative, animal and intellectual forces and that education was principally about facilitating the spiritual personality's integration within his/her new corporeal body (Steiner 1948).

Here we see a clear focus on the importance of the spiritual dimension of the newborn; there is no attempt to view the infant as a product of biological evolution. Steiner believed in a unity between spirit, soul and body and saw good education as a means of restoring balance between thinking, willing and feeling. For Steiner, child development does not follow the social constructivist ideas of Vygotsky, or the staged theory put forward by cognitive constructivists like Piaget; instead he describes three seven-year cycles, each with their own discrete and distinctive learning needs that move in an ascending spiral of knowledge. However, unlike Bruner's spiral curriculum, Steiner's spiral has a spiritual and cosmic dimension at its centre.

At the end of the first seven years (the Steiner nursery phase is from three to seven), the physical structure of the child has been completed by what Steiner calls the 'ethereal forces of growth from the tips of the toes to the new teeth' (Ullrich 1994). Steiner sees these as external signs that children are ready to enter the next phase, having learned to use their 'inner senses'. Steiner emphasised imitation and active learning in young children, viewing imaginary play during this period as the most important 'work' of the young child. There is a focus at this stage on bodily exploration and constructive and creative play, and oral language is developed through stories and songs. Children are not encouraged to engage in reading at this stage, and there is consequently little print in the environment. The teacher in the nursery will have 'objects' to feel like puppets, artefacts and three-dimensional characters to support her telling of the myth or fable. The morning routine will consist of singing songs, painting with water colours or colouring with beeswax crayons. There will also be an adult-led activity like baking bread, as well as going on a nature walk, working in the garden, building with wooden blocks and making houses out of play stands and cloth. Children during this time are encouraged to become deeply engaged, developing powers of concentration and motivation during an uninterrupted imaginary play period each day. Steiner's approach here recognises the importance of 'rhythm' and a need for balance between energetic and restful play. This rhythmic cycle is seen throughout the yearly, monthly, weekly and daily activities and is reinforced by the celebration of seasonal festivals and food.

The second seven-year cycle is seven to fourteen years, which is spent with the same teacher. Now the teaching becomes more didactic, with the children using what Steiner called epoch notebooks to copy what the teacher writes on the board. The delivery period is two hours long and consists of an introduction, extension and plenary. This is one rare similarity with contemporary teaching in the English National Curriculum. The extension not only consists of writing but may also include the telling of stories, often traditional, and eurhythmics. The idea is that children immerse themselves in specific 'epochs' (topics) for the period of the lesson. The third seven-year cycle moves into specialised subject teaching. By this point, Steiner proposed, the reincarnated spirit had settled into the corporeal body and was ready to assert ego forces (a term reminiscent of Freudian psychology) to support the development of a mature intellectual and social orientation to the world (Ullrich 1994).

As well as his ideas on child development standing in opposition to contemporary psychological research and empirical trends, Steiner's views on personality or 'temperament' are also at odds with contemporary thinking. In his eclectic philosophy, Steiner borrowed from the old medieval concept of the four humours or temperaments: melancholic, phlegmatic, choleric and sanguine. These were envisioned as follows:

- Melancholic: Attention not easily aroused but strong quality present.
- Choleric: The greatest amount of attention and strength most easily aroused.
- Sanguine: Attention easily aroused but little strength present.
- Phlegmatic: The least amount of attention and strength the least easily aroused.

Steiner proposed that in each personality, one of these humours dominated, with the phlegmatic and choleric characters at the extremes and the melancholic and sanguine characters in the middle. He believed that teachers should be aware of the orientations of their students and respond to them as such (Steiner 2014). Although the underpinning theory is nowadays discounted, there is certainly an element here that contemporary teachers might recognise as responding to the individual needs of the learner, although other schools of thought might be wary of 'labelling'.

Teaching and curriculum

Steiner proposed that teaching was a moral and spiritual endeavour, comparing the teacher to a gardener who nurtures his plants to maturity. He felt that there should also be an element of recognition of all human beings of whatever age having a spiritual life, and that there should be some celebration of this as a group phenomenon in which pupils and teachers meet as equals. Steiner headteacher Betty Staley states it is the importance of the teacher's working on his/her inner life through group exercise which supports the processes of transformation of the self through the arts (Dugan and Daar 1994). This mission to continually self-assess and transform then leads their teaching of children, in their own individual 'transformations' through their school years. This has some similarities to the Reggio Emilia practice of acting as a co-researcher with their pupils that you will meet in Chapter 10.

Courses open to those wanting to train as teachers in Steiner/Waldorf schools, or trained teachers who want to gain knowledge of Steiner's methods as part of their own continuing professional development, show a clear focus on the arts, connection with nature and the spiritual dimension. An example of the course content for potential trainee teachers usually includes three main strands: artistic (which includes modelling), music and speech. All of these skills Steiner felt were essential for a Steiner teacher, followed by anthroposophical studies, to provide a deeper understanding of Steiner's philosophy, and Steinerian concepts of child development. All students on Steiner training courses are expected to show a willingness to study anthroposophy. This causes some critics to question why, when asked about the influence of his anthroposophical views, Steiner teachers tend to deny that his philosophical works are taught in their schools.

What is clear from those working within Steiner schools is the interdependency of staff in their daily lives, which fosters self-reflection, meditation and a spiritual aspect to their teaching, as well as other duties. In Steiner schools there is no clear hierarchy of headteacher or deputy with defined roles; rather, the expectation is that each teacher will take some responsibility for the smooth running of the school community, including the involvement of parents. What is also clear is their commitment to children's holistic development. Steiner's most vocal critics have suggested such an organisation has elements of a 'cult' (Staudenmaier 2008). You can view a BBC programme discussing this accusation at http://youtu.be/WpOXitdxzk4.

The lack of focus on standard scientific theory is a concern for many, as is the twice-weekly teaching of eurhythmics, which traditional Steinerians propose is 'curative'. Historical teaching also contains references to post-Atlantis epochs and to the signs of the Zodiac (Lachman 2012). However, the areas of the early years Steiner curriculum have some similarity to those specified by the English EYFS in that they cover the following aspects:

- practical and social;
- artistic;
- oracy and pre-literacy skills;
- numeracy;
- technology (which does not involve information technology but using traditional tools to construct simple artefacts);
- nature study.

However, key differences include no reference to literacy and there are strictly no targets or goals.

Relevance to contemporary practice in the twenty-first century

Of course, in any discussion of early education, an important partner in the debate is the parent/carer. With the increasing numbers of parents wanting to place their children in Steiner schools, we need to ask why. What quality is it about Steiner education that appeals more than state-run settings? In England, successful Steiner schools are frequently placed in prosperous, middle-class areas.

To begin with, parents in Steiner schools are invited to become an integral part of the school, more so than within the mainstream. From the earliest baby and toddler sessions, parents are invited to spend time in the school with other parents on a regular basis. Special days for families are held so induction to school is not traumatic; children and parents get to know the kindergarten teacher who will be with their child for many years, supporting their child's development. There are clear expectations too from the staff, for example the request for parents not to allow their children too much exposure to 'technologies', especially with the younger age range. It is as if such exposure would somehow interfere with or dilute the school's influence through popular culture.

What the parents see are dedicated teachers who carefully prepare work that is individualised for their child. They enter an aesthetically pleasing environment, which is designed to be pedagogically and spiritually enabling. This provides strong messages about the curriculum and respect for children. Assessment is not carried out along traditional lines of tests and grade boundaries, but detailed narrative assessments are undertaken by a teacher who clearly knows their child. A visitor sees beauty everywhere: colours, lighting, artwork carefully chosen with loving attention to human feelings. Walls are painted in blended pastels, using a special wet-layered technique that yields a shimmer effect. Prints of great works of art are displayed, alongside student art and collections of beautiful natural objects which are changed to reflect the seasons. The arts of storytelling, drawing, music and drama are incorporated into lessons in all subjects. Parents who embrace the spiritual aspects of their child's growth are encouraged by teachers, working in partnership to support what is defined as the 'soul's journey'.

Resources in kindergarten are age appropriate; there is a lack of plastic toys, replaced instead by natural resources that have multiple, flexible uses. An emphasis on an ordered day gives children the time to explore and create. Parents see in this unhurried and creative learning environment that children are not subject to academic hot-housing or testing regimes. Children's emotional and creative needs receive as much focus as literacy and numeracy. Teachers greet each student with a handshake and eye contact every morning, emphasising each child's uniqueness.

Critics of the Waldorf approach point to the predominance of middle-class professional parents who choose Steiner schools, thereby creating a homogenous, close-knit school community of like-minded families and professionals. This is a milieu that larger, more anonymous and socially diverse state schools cannot provide; instead they must organise their practice to cope with a diverse array of families, a range of social-economic classes – and must additionally be routinely equipped to provide education and care for children with a range of disabilities. Steiner apologists point to 'special schools' that have adopted a 'Steiner perspective', and the off-shoot organisations of Campill, the community for disabled adults in Scotland founded by Karl Kornig who held similar views of reincarnation and karma to Steiner (see http://www.camphill.org.uk). But this again poses the question of whether Steiner schools are able to offer the genuine 'inclusivity' that state schools are charged with achieving.

In the kindergarten, much praise is given to the freedom from tests and 'outcomes'-driven frameworks, and the custom of putting children in the nurturing care of one adult who considers the needs of the whole child and not primarily the cognitive domain. There is also the key point that Steiner teachers are not dependent upon test results to ensure their next salary raise. The pace of learning is relaxed and this can particularly be seen in the later introduction of reading and writing activities, after the seventh birthday. This can also be seen in Scandinavian countries, as well as the Reggio Emilia schools in Northern Italy, where formal schooling often does not begin until the year of the child's seventh birthday.

Currently, the British 'Too Much, Too Soon' campaign is raising serious opposition to the state drive towards 'school readiness' in four-year-olds, with its intense focus on early literacy and numeracy training. They point to research over time and the latest findings in neuroscience supporting their view that the young brain is not sufficiently mature to deal with such a focus, and that children need to be holistically educated in ways more commensurate with natural human development, based upon a psychobiological model of the child. This differs from the theoretical underpinning of the Steiner framework, which places its emphasis upon the spiritual domain and the idea of reincarnation. They propose that exposure to the mechanics of reading and writing too early, before seven, would frustrate a child's progress from the spiritual to the physical realm (Gray 2011). However, while Steiner pupils may be more comfortable with books, traditional crafts and musical instruments in later childhood than pupils educated in the mainstream, some ex-Steiner pupils, particularly in recent years via internet discussion sites, have complained that they were not sufficiently stretched by the Steiner process; for example, see http://skepdic.com/steiner.html.

The Steiner tradition thus continues to face charges of occult neo-mythology, racist perspectives and a world view that refutes much of contemporary empirical and scientific research that has informed theories of child development. At the same time, however, through its rhythms, rituals, symbols and ceremony, its focus on the environment, crafts and the natural world and its objections to early exposure to television, information technology and junk food, for some it provides a quiet space. It helps to soothe, if not extinguish, some of the deep contemporary anxieties about childhood. Many parents fear that the accelerated learning children experience in Anglo-American state education may result in children being too directed by adults, with too much expected from them at too young an age, and a negative impact upon the depth and richness of skill and knowledge as the child is rushed along a trajectory dominated by targets and testing.

Steiner, in common with the other pioneers featured within in this book, was searching for answers within a particular place and time. His solutions involved turning away from war and violence and attempting to build a vision of an alternative way for humankind to live in harmony. He began with the education of children. Again, like other pioneers, he saw young children as whole and full of creative energy, if given the time and nurture to develop. His own childhood had been very ordinary in many ways, but his description of it paints a picture of being grounded in the rural village life of his early years nurtured first by his parents and then other significant adults on his way to adulthood; a similarity to Pestalozzi (see Chapter 2). His thirst for knowledge, struggles with learning to read and write and difficulties with transmission teaching are all reflected to some degree in his views on education. This is particularly clear in his insistence on waiting until the seventh birthday before more formal learning begins, which, as we learned in Chapter 1, was very much in keeping with the ancient European view of early childhood.

The central figure of the familiar and trusted teacher and a sceptical approach to prevailing orthodoxies underpinned Steiner's alternative view to education and practice, but have left him somewhat open to accusations to the setting up of a 'cult' where the impressionable minds of children are conditioned by a quasi-religious philosophy. Steiner's critics are as vocal today as they have always been, insisting that his views are too rigidly adhered to by his followers, added to the more contemporary criticism that the Steinerian approach to education is no longer fit for purpose in the twenty-first century. However, Steiner advocates counter that current Anglo-American state education is dangerously dominated by rapidly changing policy initiatives based within the agenda of the prevailing political party, which is even less compatible with the ideal of a considered, mature, developmentally informed practice with very young children.

Student integration tasks

- Compare the roles of the teacher in Steiner's world view with that of 'the directress' in Montessori's method and the 'educator' in Malaguzzi's approach. Which of these do you feel is the best 'fit' in today's practice and provision in early childhood education in the UK?

- Steiner/Waldorf is sometimes critiqued as a 'religion'. Look at the system of beliefs in Steiner's anthroposophy and discuss how far this may or may not be a fair criticism.

- How does Steiner's view of child development compare with present-day knowledge and understanding of how children develop and learn?

- What, if any, aspect of Steiner's philosophy has the potential to helpfully inform current early years education in your nation, in your opinion?

References

Clouder, C. and Rawson, M. (2003) *Waldorf Education.* Edinburgh: Floris Books.

Cook, C. (2014) *Why Are Steiner Schools so Controversial?* BBC News, 4 August 2014. Available at: http://www.bbc.co.uk/news/education-28646118 [accessed 14 February 2015].

Curtis, P. (2009) Plymouth University closes Steiner teacher training course. 5th November 2009. *Guardian* online. Available at: http://www.theguardian.com/education/2009/nov/05/steiner-training-courses-university-tuition-fees [accessed 1 June 2016].

Dugan, D. and Daar, J. (1994) *Are Rudolf Steiner's Waldorf Schools 'non-sectarian?'* Free Inquire. 14:2. Available at: http://www.waldorfcritics.org/articles/Free_Inquiry.html [accessed 12 January 2015].

DfE (2013) *Development Matters.* London: DfE Publications.

DfE (2012) *The Early Years Foundation Stage Statutory Framework.* London: DfE Publications.

DfE (2014) *The Early Years Foundation Stage Statutory Framework.* London: DfE Publications.

DfES (2007) *The Early Years Foundation Stage Framework.* Nottingham: DfES Publications.

Grey, J. (2011) *Free Schools and the Steiner School Debate.* Available at: http://www.james-gray.org/times-free-schools-steiner-school-debate [accessed 19 February 2015].

Jarvis, P. and Whitebread, D. (2013) *Too Much Too Soon?* Available at: www.savechildhood.net [accessed 1 June 2016].

Jensen, E. (2008) *Brain-Based Learning: The New Paradigm of Teaching.* London: Sage.

Klocek, D. (2014) *Rudolf Steiner College.* Available at: http://rscfeb.com.#keynote https://t.co/oXm4Afp7KW [accessed 12 January 2016].

Lachman, G. (2012) *Rudolf Steiner: An Introduction to His Life and Work.* Edinburgh: Floris Books.

Lee, J. (2016) We're not doing anything that's massively wacky. *TES*, 8th January 2016, No. 5179.

Lindenberg, C. (2012) *Rudolf Steiner: A Biography.* Great Barrington, MA: Steiner Books.

Nielson, T.W. (2008) *Rudolf Steiner's Pedagogy of Imagination: A Case Study of Holistic Education.* Bern, Oxford, New York: Peter Lang.

Restivo, S. (1985) *The Social Relations of Physics, Mysticism and Mathematics.* Lancaster: D. Reidel Publishing Co.

Sklan, S. (2014) Extremists? Steiner schools are no such thing. *Guardian* online. 22 July 2014. Available at: http://www.theguardian.com/commentisfree/2014/jul/22/extremist-criticism-steiner-schools [accessed 1 June 2016].

Staudenmaier, P. (2008) Race and redemption: racial and ethnic evolution in Rudolf Steiner's anthroposophy. *Nova Religio* 11:3 P.4-36 [accessed 15 December 2015].

Steiner, R. (1919) *Discussions with Teachers: Foundations of Waldorf Education* Series, vol. 3. New York: Anthroposophic Press.

Steiner, R. (1928) *Story of My Life*. London: Anthroposophical Publishing Co.

Steiner, R. (1948) *The Study of Man: Child and Man*. Vol. 2, January. Waldorf Library online [accessed 1 December 2015].

Steiner, R. (1972) *The Three Fold Social Order*. New York: Anthroposophic Press.

Steiner, R. (1996) *The Education of the Child and Early Lectures on Education*. London: Anthroposophical Publishing Co.

Steiner, R. (1997) *Christianity as Mystical Fact*. New York: Anthroposophic Press.

Steiner, R. (2013). *The Four Temperaments*, 4th ed. Forest Row: Steiner Press.

Ullrich, H. (1994) *Rudolf Steiner*. UNESCO: International Bureau of Education, vol. XXIV, no. 3/4, 1994, pp. 555–572.

Waldorf Steiner School Fellowship (2016) www.steinerwaldorf.org [accessed 15 December 2015].

Margaret McMillan (1860–1931)

The original 'liberatory pedagogue'

Pam Jarvis and Betty Liebovich

Introduction

This chapter will explore the work of early twentieth-century Christian Socialist reformer Margaret McMillan as a 'liberatory pedagogue', focusing on her work with disadvantaged children and their families in the nursery she established in Deptford, South London. It will take as its core her remark to a group of her children, 'you may be poor now, but there is nothing to stop you sitting in the Houses of Parliament one day', and how she worked tirelessly to make this a reality.

The chapter will draw on archival data collected by Pam Jarvis relating to feedback given by the children, parents and colleagues with whom McMillan worked. McMillan's respectful work with children from economically deprived backgrounds and their families pioneered a practice which, in the late twentieth century, became world famous as 'liberatory pedagogy' and informed many initiatives focused upon reducing social disadvantage, for example the UK framework 'Every Child Matters' (DFES 2003). The chapter will follow McMillan's journey towards her pioneering nursery, through her children's 'night camp' to the 'baby camp' she set up to 'plan the right kind of environment for (children) and give them sunshine, fresh air and good food *before* they become rickety and diseased'. It will focus on the following concepts:

- the genesis of 'educare': McMillan's life and work;
- the concept of 'liberatory pedagogy' and its relevance to McMillan's work;
- the impact of McMillan's work and its relevance to contemporary practice.

The genesis of educare and the case for outdoor play: McMillan's life and work

The district of Deptford is positioned on the South Eastern Bank of the River Thames, bordered by Bermondsey to the west, Lewisham to the south and Greenwich to the east. It derives its name from being the place of a 'deep ford' over the little Ravensbourne River, known locally as 'Deptford Creek'; a tributary of the Thames. It became part of the County of London in 1889. Deptford can boast a grand history of ship building dating back to Tudor times, when it became the first Royal Dockyard.[1] However, by the turn of the nineteenth century, the requirement for larger ships that were not able to negotiate the Thames meant that most ship building had moved to coastal dockyards, and Deptford fell on less prosperous times.

The school master at the Board School in Regent Street, Mr Farthing, told Charles Booth, the famous documenter of poverty in London at the turn of the nineteenth century, that children were sent to his school hungry, filthy and infested, sometimes suffering from infectious diseases. He reported that the parents had 'a most loathsome dread of the RSPCC [here he means the NSPCC, National Society for the Prevention of Cruelty to Children, established in 1884] whose officers are much more feared than the police'.[2] Booth concluded that Mr Farthing felt that the families in the area were 'practically untouched' by any charitable agencies, proposing that the 'church [was] utterly futile'.[3] The new vicar at St Nicholas, after complaining voraciously about his inebriate predecessor, told Booth that the local police were unable to deal with the local 'drunken disorder and noise. It is almost impossible to sleep at nights owing to the shouts and singing of the drunken villains . . . it is the worst place I know'.[4] This was, however, the locality selected by the McMillan sisters for their charitable work. Nearly twenty years after Booth's investigation, Margaret McMillan described the area in very similar terms: 'a very poor, very crowded district . . . a dozen public-houses within a stone's throw of the school . . . the streets are quite dark and very noisy after dusk'.[5]

The mass movement of people to cities following the Industrial Revolution in England had brought a raft of (alleged) social 'reforms', the most impactful of which was the 'new poor law' of 1834. Measures taken by successive English monarchs and governments to deal with the effects of poverty have been divided by historians into four periods: before the Old Poor Law (pre-seventeenth century), the Old Poor Law (1795–1834), the New Poor Law (1834–1930) and the modern welfare state.[6] Paul Carter and Katie Thompson proposed that the New Poor Law was principally an administrative measure, creating a standardised national response to poverty, with an emphasis upon curtailing relief for the undeserving poor: 'the twin principles of the New Poor Law were the "workhouse test" and "less eligibility"'.[7] This system was rooted in a process whereby families who could not manage without ongoing financial assistance were not deemed eligible for financial support within their family homes, being instead committed to the complete control of the state in purpose-designed 'workhouses' with separate accommodation for men, women and children. Adults deemed fit to work were set to menial tasks in exchange for very basic food and board: 'a fate worse than death'.[8]

The potential for confusion between the 'deserving' and the 'undeserving', and the consequently devastating effects upon an individual unjustly labelled under the New Poor Law, became a pivotal issue in the poverty debate from the middle of the nineteenth century. In the early twentieth century, Margaret McMillan and her sister Rachel took an unorthodox perspective upon this issue, proposing that all young children, given that they were developmentally unready to be economically active, were automatically 'deserving poor'. The way in which charity workers and 'do-gooders' were typically perceived within poor districts presented the sisters with a set of powerful obstacles to overcome, however. Ruth Livesey commented: 'middle class women . . . frequently misread the survival strategies of the urban poor, in their belief that bourgeois domestic arrangements were the only current standard of home management'.[9] Given this mismatch between the economic, social and cultural worlds of working-class Londoners and their middle-class social workers, it is not surprising that Ellen Ross reported:

> *Representatives of the authority of church or state invading streets and homes met harsh treatment. School Board visitors had trouble getting information about numbers of children and their employment. . . . Even as late as 1900, there were occasional physical attacks on London School Board visitors and other school personnel . . . clericals and missionaries, until they had proved their usefulness to the neighbourhood by exchanging goods and services were objects of constant ridicule, if not physical abuse.[10]*

The McMillans were thus facing a difficult prospect, and Margaret in particular spent two decades honing the ideas that fed into the creation of their world-famous nursery, which was additionally founded upon a unique set of circumstances including the social upheaval surrounding the First World War (1914–18).

The McMillan sisters were born in Westchester County, New York, Rachel in 1859 and Margaret in 1860. They were the daughters of Scottish parents who had recently immigrated to the US in the mid-1850s to take up a business opportunity. However, following the death of the sisters' father and youngest sister in 1865, their mother took them back to her family home in Inverness. By 1888, their mother and both grandparents had died, and the sisters had become immersed in Christian Socialism.[11] By 1889, the sisters had moved to London to engage in a range of activities to promote the Socialist movement.[12] Margaret's activities included voluntary work for the settlement movement, membership of the Fabian Society, teaching young women in the East End, public speaking and investigative journalism.[13] She began to build a reputation as a skilled orator, delivering a series of powerful speeches on the benefits of Socialism at Hyde Park Corner,[14] drawing the attention of influential people within the Socialist movement. Carolyn Steedman reported: 'by early 1893 McMillan had gained a considerable reputation as a propagandist and orator'.[15] During this year, McMillan was offered a salaried position by the Independent Labour Party (ILP) in Bradford;[16] this required an extensive programme of Socialist lectures to audiences across Yorkshire and Lancashire. She was elected to the Bradford School Board as a representative of the ILP in November 1894,[17] swiftly becoming a remarkably active social reformer with a keen interest in child welfare. Her first biographer, Albert Mansbridge, quoted her thus:

> *The state compels the children to work [in school] – it makes the demand for sustenance urgent, intolerable. But it does not compel parents to feed their children. Hence it is certain to some of these hungry little ones, free education is less of a boon than an outrage.*[18]

Margaret McMillan ensured, against much opposition, that Bradford became the first education authority in the country to provide school baths and showers in 1897[19] and free school meals in 1902.[20] However, despite being re-elected to the Bradford School Board in 1900, she was not immediately able to build on these successes. In 1902 a new Education Bill became law, resulting in the abolition of the School Boards, giving control and management of elementary schools to the District and County Councils – to which women could not be elected.[21] Margaret was bitterly disappointed; the *Yorkshire Daily Observer* published an interview with her in which she protested, 'when this bill was passed into law, all women would be put on one side. Their work was mentioned very little at present; but by this bill it was to be wiped out altogether.'[22] In late 1902, disappointed but resilient,[23] she rejoined Rachel who was living and working as a travelling teacher of health and hygiene in Bromley.

The sisters rekindled contacts with political allies in London, and by 1906 they won sufficient support to lead a deputation to Parliament to lobby for the compulsory medical inspection of school children.[24] This aim was subsequently realised in the Education (Administrative Procedures) Bill of 1907, and on the strength of this success, the sisters secured a substantial £5,000 bursary to open a school clinic in a suitably 'needy' area of London. Margaret had previously obtained a job managing a group of elementary schools in Deptford,[25] hence the sisters eventually secured suitable premises at The Old Vestry Hall, 3 Deptford Green. The new clinic opened on 21 June 1910, and the children began to 'arrive in torrents'.[26] Expansion of capacity was swiftly achieved when a Socialist contact arranged for them to have free occupation of a whole house on nearby Evelyn Street.[27] The sisters moved into a few of the rooms in the house, and gave the rest over to the clinic. A comment from one of the clinic staff soon led them to consider a further extension of their mission:

> *Nurse Spiker at the clinic said, 'it's all a waste of time. These children come here, are cured and go but in two weeks, sometimes less, they are back again. All these ailments could be prevented, their cause is dirt, lack of light and sun, fresh air and good food'.*[28]

The McMillans subsequently determined that they would open an experimental overnight 'camp' in the garden at Evelyn Street, for the use of local girls. Camp beds were made from gas piping, trestles and canvas, and shelters were constructed by a local carpenter. Washing facilities for the children were provided, as was a nutritious breakfast in the morning. The daily regime was outlined by Margaret McMillan:

> The camp girls ranged in age from six to fourteen. They arrived early in the evening and had certain camp duties to perform . . . they had plenty of time to play in the garden. . . . Every elder girl had charge of a younger one, looking after her toilet: hair, teeth, nails, bathing. . . . At seven o'clock . . . two girls put out their wooden beds. . . . By eight o'clock all was quiet . . . I laid in a good stock of oatmeal. . . . The breakfast was always porridge and milk, which the girls cooked. . . . They left for school at a quarter to nine.[29]

In 1912, following the success of the Night Camp, Margaret and Rachel managed to initiate an experimental Camp School for boys and girls from six to fourteen years old on a site in nearby Albury Street. Instead of children spending long hours in over-crowded classrooms, Margaret believed she could give them a more healthy, active education in the open air.[30] This she quickly managed to accomplish, engaging three schoolmasters, importing the senior from Bradford, to teach fifty-seven children.[31]

However, Margaret's principal aim was moving towards a 'camp' environment for infants under five. In the early days of the Night Camp initiative, one of the girls begged to be accompanied by her ailing younger sister, in the hope that the experience might improve the infant's rapidly failing health. Despite the McMillans' decision to admit the young child on the proviso that she would be watched over by her older sister, she unfortunately died within the same year. On hearing the sad news, Margaret decreed: 'We must open our doors to the toddlers, Rachel . . . we must plan the right kind of environment for them and give them sunshine, fresh air and good food *before* they become rickety and diseased.'[32] The sisters had now arrived at the fully formed incarnation of their concept of 'educare', a way of approaching early years education which presumes that to learn effectively, the physical, social and emotional needs of the child must first be effectively addressed. While McMillan had arrived at this opinion shortly after taking up her role on the Bradford School Board, she had only thus far been able to put her ideas into action in a piecemeal fashion, initially in the curtailed reforms she had introduced into some of the Bradford Schools, followed by the experiments with the Night Camp and Camp School.

The sisters began by setting up a make-shift crèche in the house on Evelyn Street, but they were soon trying to deal with too many infants within the space available. They eventually acquired additional premises on a plot of land known locally as 'the Stowage', based upon local legend that smugglers once used it to hide their treasures. This was owned by the London County Council, who had somewhat vague plans to build an elementary (primary) school there. The McMillans were granted permission to use it free of charge, the agreement being that they would pay £1 per year for the ground rent. The council reserved the right to ask for the land to be returned at any time, but this never happened – the school still stands on the same site today.[33] The move from Evelyn Street to the Stowage was undertaken in late March 1914. The sisters had no help or suitable equipment to accomplish the move and the weather was dismal, rainy and cold. Undaunted, they moved furniture and boxes in wheelbarrows. Such were the inauspicious origins of the nursery that was to later attract national and global attention. The sisters soon established a familiar regime within the nursery: cleanliness, sunshine, fresh air, good food and plenty of time to play in the garden. The 'Baby Camp', which soon became locally known as 'the nursery school', was a great local success during the war years of 1914–18, heavily subscribed by the young children of mothers who had been billeted to employment roles vacated by men conscripted to the armed forces.

The sisters, although delighted by the success of the initiative, nevertheless struggled with the transience of the nursery staff and occasional attacks by German Zeppelins, one of which briefly exposed them to mustard gas. Both were now in their mid-fifties, and both had a range of health problems that, given the war situation and time period, were not being effectively monitored or addressed. Both succumbed to serious illness, from which Margaret eventually recovered. However, Rachel died during early 1917, the last full year of the war.[34] In what Margaret deemed a sad irony, a burgeoning national and international interest arose in the newly christened 'Rachel McMillan Open Air Nursery School' and its holistic 'educare' regime during the period directly following Rachel's death.[35] Through a unique practical demonstration of Christian Socialism, the so-called 'romantic critique of capitalism',[36] Margaret and Rachel had managed to produce healthy, happy slum children who had the potential to become robust, competent workers, mothers and soldiers, and the whole nation was now listening avidly to what the surviving sister had to say. The nursery was visited by a steady stream of dignitaries including Queen Mary, Rudolf Steiner, George Bernard Shaw, many MPs and the Prime Minister Stanley Baldwin, who wrote to Margaret: 'I shall never forget my visit to you and to your children; it was a revelation'.[37] Carolyn Steedman reflected: 'McMillan's reworking of the post-Wordsworthian romantic child into a practical political project is probably her first claim on historical importance'.[38]

During the 1920s, the concept that a range of far-reaching benefits could be achieved through national public health initiatives began to permeate the British national consciousness, and 'in the early 1920s . . . discussions within the Labour Party focused on the public provision of health care, child care and other services by professionals'.[39] The Education Act 1921 made provision for grants to organise nursery schools for children over two years old and under five years old to be disseminated and overseen by Local Education Authorities.[40] The establishment of the Nursery School Association (NSA) soon followed in 1923, with Margaret

McMillan as its first president.[41] Candidate suitability for nursery teacher training became an immediate bone of contention between McMillan and the rank and file of the NSA, most of whom had trained as nursery teachers in a broadly Froebellian tradition. In the UK, this most typically involved preparation for teaching middle-class children aged three to six in conventional classrooms, frequently located within primary schools, in which outdoor activity was just one feature of the 'daily round'. Philip Graham, the biographer of Susan Isaacs, comments that Froebel schools in England were 'mainly for the middle class'.[42] McMillan's rather different focus on educare for disadvantaged children, some of whom were younger than three, had led her along a rather different path, which had resulted in her entrenched opinion that neither teachers nor nurses currently received effective training for practice in a nursery school as she had conceived it:

> *After sad experience we gave up nurses and turned to teachers. Then came new revelations. Even the trained and certified enter school with only three to six weeks in teaching . . . those who came first were shocked; they had never seen the inside of a slum home.*[43]

One of her students reported:

> *[Margaret McMillan] described to me the ideal type of student . . . she said that she had tried nurses and teachers but neither was just what was needed. . . . She had decided that a new type of training was required . . . the contents . . . were rather sparse . . . as one might expect to find at a pioneer training centre. . . . We had constant practice . . . Miss McMillan believed that theory should be put into practice while remembered.*[44]

Here we see the dichotomy between early years *education* and early years *educare* that would still be contentious a century later, with McMillan firmly on the side of the holistic practice represented by educare. She was still following the practical Christian Socialist mission that she began in Bradford, which held far more relevance for her than the more abstract debates focusing upon mainstream early years pedagogy emerging from discussions amongst the nursery teachers who comprised the majority membership of the NSA. McMillan firmly believed that a nursery school should be a self-contained, self-determining institution, rather than a nursery class in a primary school. She felt that the practice in nursery classes would be infiltrated by the type of practices she had abhorred in the primary schools she had observed in Bradford.

It appears that McMillan saw such a development as what we might nowadays term 'schoolification', therefore incompatible with her 'nurture' principles. Her ongoing irritation with her NSA colleagues eventually boiled over into public criticism. Initially McMillan wrote privately to fellow Christian Socialist Robert Blatchford in 1929:

Now I am battling for a nine hour day for nursery school children. We open at a quarter to eight. We close at five thirty. It is not much use to little ones to rattle them in and out of school as they do. They need nurture.[45] You can't give it in five hours. . . . Such humbug. It is such a mean substitute. . . . We can give a happy childhood to all children and solve a good many social problems enroute . . . we must have a new conception of school that it should be a nurture centre as well as a place for lessons.[46]

In early 1930, less than a year before the final illness that would end in her death, McMillan entered the public arena to engage in a heated debate through the letter pages of the *Manchester Guardian*. In response to an accusation in a published letter written by a Manchester member of the NSA: 'although Miss McMillan has never visited one of the Manchester nursery classes, she does not hesitate to attack.'[47] McMillan replied:

What we have got instead of the open air nursery school and its sharp thrust into the nest of evil things that rot and destroy our race is a substitute – that is a nursery class grafted on to an infant school. A diluted new wine safely landed in the new bottle . . . to begin with the 2 year old is dropped altogether . . . also 3 meals have gone. The long nurture day – nine hours – has vanished. The great and powerful services are represented of course: the medical and the teaching services. But they are present under circumstances that make their work barren and fruitless.[48]

McMillan's Christian Socialist mission had focused her sights primarily upon the early years setting as a remedy for social disadvantage, and this agenda became increasingly at odds with much of the teacher 'group think' emanating from the NSA. The *Manchester Guardian* again captured McMillan's outrage on 22 May 1930:

Margaret McMillan addressed an open meeting . . . on the subject of 'Nursery Schools'. . . . Miss McMillan . . . described very trenchantly the nature of the problem [in Manchester] emphasising that the age of 2 was immensely more important than any age that followed it. A child's destiny was practically settled by the age of 5. If you wanted to give nurture you must give it properly or not waste the nation's money.[49]

McMillan's opinionated public announcements were perceived by the teacher-dominated early years establishment as at best well meaning but eccentric and at worst, destructive. Her efforts to establish a teacher training college attached to the Rachel McMillan Nursery were unfortunately impeded by this situation, creating increasing amounts of stress for her, which further impacted upon her health. One of the public officials charged to consider the viability of the teacher training college wrote 'in strictest confidence' to Lady Astor, who had become a benefactor for the initiative:

I have had some difficulty in persuading some of the officials of the board . . . of the possibility of making the McMillan College efficient. . . . Miss McMillan is a genius but an erratic one, and when I have persuaded an official to come to Deptford and have his heart melted by the work done there, Miss McMillan has not always made the situation an easy one; she is inclined to go off the practical side and become rather vague.[50]

McMillan's determination did not, however, fail her, even though she was now moving into her seventies and becoming increasingly frail. Queen Mary opened The Rachel McMillan Teacher Training College on 8 May 1930. Margaret McMillan gave the inaugural speech, characteristically proposing, 'the real object of our work is nurture . . . we are trying to make a place which shall be a training ground for the happier generations of the future'.[51] She died less than a year later, on 29 March 1931. The NSA 'nursery class' strategy went on to dominate the culture of UK nursery education throughout the twentieth century.[52] However, McMillan's educare philosophy was not entirely lost to the world, as we will see in the following section.

Theoretical and practice legacy: the concept of liberatory pedagogy and its relevance to McMillan's work

An interview McMillan gave towards the end of her life recounted that 'she and her sister chose this spot over 20 years ago because in Deptford were the worst slums in London'.[53] Having found the place for their mission, the sisters 'lived above the shop', becoming the neighbours of the people they worked amongst, operating a simple but highly effective regime for local children that could be funded through Margaret's continual canvassing for public funds or charitable donations, including from some of the wealthy visitors to the Deptford nursery. Unlike these more privileged individuals who eventually joined the campaign for nurseries, the sisters 'had [only] a little family money [and] were content to live frugally and trust to providence'.[54] A friend of the sisters later recalled that at times their financial position could not even be described as comfortable; 'they had to struggle to make ends meet'.[55] This appeared to have a positive effect upon their mission, however – it allowed them admittance to the women's survival network in the London of the period described by Ellen Ross, in which 'neighbours and indeed neighbourhoods functioned as auxiliary parents'.[56]

Margaret McMillan in particular was widely remembered as engaging in neighbourly 'give-and-take'. A Deptford resident recalled:

She didn't have very much money and there was a lady I knew along [Evelyn Street], very often used to give her dinner – she's dead now, but this lady very often used to say to Miss McMillan 'well, come on, come in my house, I'll give you a nice dinner', and she used to go in and have dinner with her.[57]

Even those who were children at the time remembered routine reciprocal interactions with their teacher with respect to McMillan's frequently careless personal grooming, one of her older pupils recalling that she 'did [McMillan's hair] up for her and saw to it that she had no slip showing'.[58] Added to her devotion to these children – 'her Dorothy, her Gladys'[59] – and her oft-repeated motto, 'educate every child as if he were your own',[60] it is impossible to construct McMillan in a role that in any way resembles Ruth Livesey's disengaged 'middle class women [charity] visitors'.[61] There is evidence to suggest that instead, the McMillans became key players within the social 'taxation' system[62] underpinning working-class London's sharing culture, giving far more than they received in the process.

To add weight to this analysis, Margaret McMillan consistently demonstrated her belief in the pivotal importance of neighbourly relationships with the families served by the nursery, insisting that her planned teacher training college and its living accommodation be annexed to the nursery. In 1919, she proposed: 'Our students have to know their new neighbours. They have to get some idea of housing, of the cost of food, and the needs of a family who live always on the brink of a financial precipice!'[63] In 1927, she returned to this concept: 'teachers, isolated as a profession . . . do not touch the lives of the mothers in poor streets . . . they do not even live in the neighbourhood . . . they visit it for a few hours every day and see the children in masses'.[64]

It would seem that Deptford children and their families did not become one-dimensional 'client objects' to the McMillans, but real, human neighbours, contradicting the mainstream Labour policy of the time: 'provision of health care, child care and other services . . . from outside the communities'.[65] The historical record indicates that the McMillan sisters, Margaret in particular, had a unique ability to step outside the middle-class charity worker persona through a deep personal immersion within the Deptford community.

In 1970, education academic Paulo Freire, born into a Brazilian middle-class family, outlined his theory of liberatory pedagogy in *Pedagogy of the Oppressed*.[66] His ideas were inspired by his experience of working with a largely illiterate working-class population in the Pernambuco region of Brazil. He became nationally famous for his success in raising literacy levels within such communities, but was eventually driven into exile by the military government instigated in Brazil after a 1964 coup.[67] His theory is now world famous, and although not directly inspired by McMillan's initiatives, appears to stem from almost identical sentiments:

> *Solidarity requires that one enter into the situation of those with whom one is solidary. . . . The oppressor is solidary with the oppressed only when he stops regarding the oppressed as an abstract category and sees them as persons who have been unjustly dealt with, deprived of their voice . . . when he stops making pious, sentimental, and individualistic gestures and risks an act of love . . . to affirm that men and women are persons and as persons should be free.*[68]

So is this how the people of Deptford actually perceived the McMillans? There is no clear evidence that pertains to Rachel, but the University of Greenwich Archive A94/16/A8 is composed of responses to public requests for memories of Margaret McMillan to celebrate her centenary in 1960. Some who had been pupils in the camp school and nursery recalled:

> Margaret McMillan gave her whole life to us children. She was truly a wonderful person in so much that she never thought of herself one bit. . . . Her whole life was centred around us children . . . I can still hear her now saying 'you may be poor now but if you want, there is nothing to stop you sitting in the Houses of Parliament'.[69]

> One cannot think of one's school days and its happy memories without thinking of Miss McMillan . . . she made one see Wordsworth's daffodils fluttering and dancing in the breeze . . . was there ever a school where the children were showered with so much love?[70]

> Miss McMillan came and opened new and wonderful doors for us . . . thank you Miss McMillan.[71]

Some of McMillan's colleagues were also still alive at this time and their comments include:

> [When I visited Deptford] I had to ask my way through smelly streets, but all whom I asked became eager friends as soon as I mentioned Miss McMillan's name. At last I came to a door in the paling and when this was opened I saw a garden full of delphiniums. In among the flowers were many little children, like flowers themselves, with gay overalls and coloured ribbons in their hair.[72]

> I came to the tall wooden gate . . . and passed through it to what seemed to me a veritable paradise.[73]

> The opening of [the garden] door was symbolic of the place her nursery held in the community. Outside all seemed dark and hopeless, but inside there was the promise of fresh growth and beauty.[74]

One contributor to the 1960 McMillan centenary celebrations recalled:

> It was difficult to make people realise what a wonderful person Miss McMillan was unless they knew what Deptford was like many years ago – then they would understand what she was up against . . . the children had no shoes – they played in the streets, sat in the gutter and were very dirty . . . she was stern but when you got to know her she was very kind and gentle . . . in my opinion, there will never be another Margaret McMillan.[75]

The evidence thus suggests that the children, parents and teachers of Deptford did indeed recognise the practice in the Rachel McMillan Nursery as a practical demonstration of liberatory pedagogy, although in 1960, it would be another ten years before Paulo Freire introduced the theory to the world.

The impact of McMillan's work and its relevance to contemporary practice

In the century that followed the inauguration of the Rachel McMillan Open Air Nursery, the fortunes of state-funded early years education and care briefly waxed in the war years of 1939–45, then waned over a period of fifty-two years before moving back onto the agenda of the New Labour government 1997–2010. A new clash of agendas quickly emerged from two different impetuses: the familiar need to provide the type of support McMillan would have termed 'nurture' for the children of socio-economically deprived families, and a new and growing need to meet the increasing demand for affordable daycare for very young children from families in which both parents were working long, 'family unfriendly' hours within the post-modern, service-driven economy of the early twenty-first century. Peter Moss described the resulting confusion:

> *Split between 'childcare' and 'early education', with a fragmented and incoherent patchwork of services, and combining high cost to parents with a poorly paid and poorly qualified workforce: we find ourselves in a hole, and don't seem to know what to do.*[76]

If the McMillan sisters could be reanimated in the twenty-first century, their interest would no doubt be keenly focused upon the children's centres initiative that was piloted within deprived areas by the New Labour Sure Start project in the early 2000s. The provision of childcare services and/or nursery education for middle-class families, regardless of the changing demands that have resulted from a century of economic tumult, is a rather different venture to the core McMillan mission, as demonstrated by Margaret McMillan's interactions with her NSA colleagues. Her trenchant focus upon high adult-child ratios and the need for practitioners to understand the lives of local families not only pre-empted but extended concepts of working in partnership with families that would not resurface on the UK early years stage until nearly a century later, both within the Sure Start concept and the 2003 'Birth to Three Matters' Guidelines.[77] However, a Conservative-led Coalition Government 2010–15, and the election of a Conservative Government in May 2015, has resulted in a significant rolling back of services for children and families in general, and we are again in danger of losing all vestige of 'liberatory pedagogy' from the UK system of early years education and care.

The McMillan sisters' ideals emerged from and remained tightly tied to their deep immersion in Christian Socialism; they never wavered from their fixed focus upon the provision of basic but holistic services for disadvantaged children: clean-liness, sunshine, fresh air, good food and plenty of time to play in the garden, in the care of nurturing adults who were readily available to give children one-to-one attention due to high adult-child ratios. When asked about her philosophy of nurs-ery education in a BBC radio broadcast of 1923, Margaret McMillan said:

> *You may ask, why should we give all this to the children? Because this is nurture, and without it they can never really have education . . . the educational system should grow out of the nursery schools system, not out of a neglected infancy . . . [in the nurs-ery school] everything is planned for life. The shelters are oblong in shape. The air is moving there always . . . healing light falls through the lowered gable and open doors. This world . . . is full of colour and movement . . . the children just emerging from the long sleep of pre-natal life and fitful dream of the first year, waken at last to a kind of paradise. . . . If Great Britain will go forward [with open air nursery schools] . . . she will sweep away the cause of untold suffering, ignorance, waste and failure.[78]*

We still have much to learn from her ethos today, in particular with regard to optimising the potential of children from deprived communities; an endeavour that is still very much required, both with respect to the poverty that blights the lives and futures of so many young children in the developing world, and within west-ern populations living under post-industrial austerity.

Student integration tasks

- Make a list of some of the barriers that Margaret McMillan had to surmount to introduce her initial reforms into schools in Bradford.

- How do you think England would respond to a reformer like Margaret McMillan today? Do you think there might be any parallels with Camila Batmanghelidjh? See http://www.theguardian.com/society/camilabatmang helidjh.

- If you live in a nation other than England, consider what *your* nation would currently make of a reformer like Margaret McMillan.

- Do you think that Margaret McMillan was right to champion the case for nurs-ery schools rather than nursery classes? Give reasons for your answer.

- Does the fact that the reviews on the McMillan nursery collected in 1960 were overwhelmingly positive mean that the sisters were entirely successful in over-turning the stereotype of the 'I know best' middle-class social worker? Give reasons for your answer.

- What advice do you think Margaret would give western early years education and care professionals today, if we could somehow reanimate her?

- Are you a 'liberatory pedagogue'? If not, do you want to become one? If so, how do you think you could pursue this in your current professional situation?

Notes

1 Edward Walford 'Deptford', *Old and New London: Volume 6* (1878), pp. 143–164. http://www.british-history.ac.uk/report.aspx?compid=45272 (accessed 26 July 2011).

2 Charles Booth Archive B290: *Interview with school master Mr Farthing, Regent St Board School Deptford*, ND, pp. 1–11. Presumably the interview was carried out around 1900, in the same batch as the one with the teacher in the nearby ragged school, given the report that attendances had fallen 'since 1898'.

3 Charles Booth Archive B290: *Interview with school master Mr Farthing, Regent St Board School Deptford*, ND, pp. 1–11.

4 Charles Booth Archive B284: *Interview with Rev A. T. Wallis St Nicholas Deptford* 11 June 1900, pp. 116–33.

5 Margaret McMillan, *The Nursery School* (London: J.M. Dent, 1919), p. 24.

6 Paul Carter and Katie Thompson: 'Poverty', OU A825 Block 6 Readings. Source: Chapter 8 in Paul Carter and Kate Thompson, *Sources for Local Historians* (Chichester: Phillimore, 2005), pp. 86–101, 209–11 (p. 37).

7 Carter and Thompson, p. 42.

8 Lynn Hollen Lees, *The Solidarities of Strangers* (Cambridge: Cambridge University Press, 1998).

9 Ruth Livesey: 'Reading for Character: Women Social Reformers and Narratives of the Urban Poor in Late Victorian and Edwardian London'. *Journal of Victorian Culture* 9:1 (2004) 43–68 (p. 55).

10 Ellen Ross, 'Survival Networks: Women's Neighbourhood Sharing in London before World War I'. *History Workshop* 15 (1983) pp. 4–27 (pp. 17–18).

11 Margaret McMillan, *Life of Rachel McMillan* (London: J.M. Dent, 1927), pp. 28–9.

12 Margaret McMillan, *Life of Rachel McMillan*, p. 33.

13 Carolyn Steedman, Margaret McMillan, *Oxford Dictionary of National Biography* http://www.oxforddnb.com/view/printable/34801 (accessed 9 August 2011).

14 Elizabeth Bradburn, *Margaret McMillan: Framework and Expansion of Nursery Education* (Redhill: Denholm House, 1976), p. 32.

15 Carolyn Steedman, *Childhood, Culture and Class in Britain: Margaret McMillan 1860–1931* (New Brunswick: Rutgers University Press, 1990), p. 35.

16 Margaret McMillan, *Life of Rachel McMillan*, p. 29.

17 Margaret McMillan, *Life of Rachel McMillan*, p. 81.

18 Albert Mansbridge, *Margaret McMillan: Prophet and Pioneer* (London: J.M. Dent, 1932), pp. 41–2.

19 V. Celia Lascarides, Blythe F. Hinitz, 'The First School Baths in Britain Were Opened at the Wapping School in Bradford in 1897', *History of Early Childhood Education* (Abingdon: Routledge, 2000), p. 120.

20 John Welshman, 'School Meals and Milk in England and Wales, 1906–45'. *Medical History* 41: 6–29 (1997).

21 Steedman, *Childhood, Culture and Class in Britain*, p. 49.

22 'The Fight for the Schools', *The Yorkshire Daily Observer*, 22 September 1902, quoted in Bradbury, p. 63.

23 Stephen Yeo 'A New Life: The Religion of Socialism in Britain'. *History Workshop* No. 4 (1977) 5–56 (p. 45).

24 Margaret McMillan, *Life of Rachel McMillan*, p. 115.

25 Steedman, 'Margaret McMillan', *Oxford Dictionary of National Biography*.

26 Margaret McMillan, *Life of Rachel McMillan*, p. 120.

27 Margaret McMillan, *Life of Rachel McMillan*, p. 118.

28 University of Greenwich A94/16/A8/34: script of a programme broadcast by the BBC Home Service 27 November 1960. The source for the quote appears to have been Emma Stevinson, the first Principal of the Rachel McMillan Teacher Training College, who died in 1959.

29 Margaret McMillan, *The Camp School* (London: George Allen and Unwin, 1917), pp. 84–5.

30 Bradburn, p. 130.

31 Margaret McMillan, *The Camp School*, p. 111.

32 Emma Stevinson, *Margaret McMillan: Prophet and Pioneer* (London: University of London Press, 1954), p. 8.

33 Margaret McMillan, *The Camp School*, p. 51.

34 Margaret McMillan, *Life of Rachel McMillan*, p. 186.

35 University of Greenwich A94/16/A1/86: letter from Margaret McMillan to 'Mr Mackenzie', 7 July 1930.

36 Chris Waters, *William Morris and the Socialism of Robert Blatchford*. http://www.morrissociety.org/JWMS/W82.5.2.Waters.pdf (accessed 4 January 2011), p. 20.

37 Lewisham Local History Library A94/6/1/69: letter from Stanley Baldwin to Margaret McMillan, 20 December 1928.

38 Steedman, 'Margaret McMillan', *Oxford Dictionary of National Biography*.

39 Ross, p. 20.

40 Board of Education (England) Education Act 1921, 11 & 12 Geo. 5. c. 51. http://www.educationengland.org.uk/documents/acts/1921-education-act.html.

41 Viv Moriarty, *Margaret McMillan: 'I learn, to succor the helpless'* (Nottingham: Educational Heretics Press, 1998), p. 60.

42 Philip Graham, *Susan Isaacs: A Life Freeing the Minds of Children* (London: Karnac 2009), p. xxiii.

43 Lewisham Local History Library A94/2/10A: handwritten A4 sheet by Margaret McMillan, no title, ND, appears to be a fragment from a draft article, refers to 'now in 1924'.

44 University of Greenwich A94/16/A8/28: letter (ND) from Jessie Porter, student teacher at the McMillan Nursery School 1917–20.

45 All underlined in original.

46 University of Greenwich A94/16/A1/74: letter from Margaret McMillan to Robert Blatchford 20 February 1929.

47 ProQuest Historical Newspapers: online, letter from Shena D. Simon to The *Manchester Guardian* letters page 29 January 1930.

48 ProQuest Historical Newspapers: online, letter from Margaret McMillan to The *Manchester Guardian* letters page, 26 February 1930.

49 ProQuest Historical Newspapers: online *Manchester Guardian* 'Miss Margaret McMillan on Old Traditions' 22 May 1930.

50 Reading University Library RUL MS 1416: letter from Henrietta Brown Smith, Inspector (Board of Education) 'in strictest confidence' 14 November 1929.

51 University of Greenwich A94/16/A8/7: extract from Margaret McMillan's speech at the opening of the Rachel McMillan Teacher Training College 8 May 1930.

52 P. Jarvis, and B. Liebovich. 'British Nurseries, Head and Heart: McMillan, Owen and the Genesis of the Education/Care Dichotomy'. *Women's History Review.* (2015). Retrieved from http://www.tandfonline.com/doi/abs/10.1080/096120 25.2015.1025662?journalCode=rwhr20#.VUZripPff4U.

53 Lewisham Local History Library A94/7/29: news cutting from the *London Evening Standard*, '20 years work for children: Woman Pioneer on her work'. 19 April 1929.

54 Bradburn, p. 149.

55 Bradburn, p. 149.

56 Ross, p. 12.

57 BBC London Archive, digital file: BBC Radio broadcast extract *Margaret McMillan: Portrait of a Pioneer*, 27th November 1960, unidentified speaker.

58 University of Greenwich A94/16/A8/35: paragraph in a manuscript marked "Miss Davies' broadcast 7th June 1960".

59 University of Greenwich A94/16/A8/22: letter from F. Hawtry from Darlington, ND.

60 Margaret McMillan, *The Nursery School*, p. 24.

61 Livesey, p. 55.

62 Helen Dendy 'The Industrial Residuum'. *The Economic Journal* 3 (12) (1893) 600–616 (p. 616).

63 Margaret McMillan, *The Nursery School*, p. 109.

64 Margaret McMillan, *Life of Rachel McMillan*, pp. 197–8.

65 Ross, p. 20.

66 P. Freire, *Pedagogy of the Oppressed* (New York: Continuum, 1970).

67 Freire Institute, Paulo Freire Biography: http://www.freire.org/paulo-freire/paulo-freire-biography.

68 Freire, pp. 49–50.

69 University of Greenwich A94/16/A8/35: in a manuscript marked 'Miss Davies broadcast 7th June 1960'. These paragraphs are circled, with a handwritten note 'omit'. Comparing the contents of Archives A8/24 and A8/16 with information contained in *Margaret McMillan: The Children's Champion* (London: Museum Press, 1960), pp. 71–3 (where the comments are presented anonymously) indicates that either Dorothy Lob or Gladys Woodhams may have contributed this paragraph. Miss Mary Davies was principal of the Rachel McMillan Teacher Training College in 1960, following Emma Stevinson's retirement.

70 University of Greenwich A94/16/A8/24: letter from Dorothy Lob, Camp School.
71 University of Greenwich A94/16/A8/16: letter from Gladys Woodhams, Camp School.
72 University of Greenwich A94/16/A8/22: letter from F. Hawtry from Darlington.
73 University of Greenwich A94/16/A8/18: letter from Helen Edwards, Bradford, student 1923–6.
74 University of Greenwich A94/16/A8/28: letter from Jessie Porter, Dundee, student 1917–20.
75 University of Greenwich A94/16/A8/30: handwritten note, ND or address, signed 'Mrs Stiggear'.
76 Peter Moss (2014) 'Our Youngest Children Deserve Better Than a Fragmented Patchwork of Services.' IOE London Blog: http://ioelondonblog.wordpress.com/category/peter-moss/.
77 See http://webarchive.nationalarchives.gov.uk/20130401151715/https://www.education.gov.uk/publications/eOrderingDownload/BIRTHCD-PDF1.pdf.
78 Mansbridge: full text of a broadcast given by MM on BBC radio, on 17 November 1927, pp. 104–6.

References

Primary sources

Archival material

Lewisham Local History Library: the Margaret McMillan Archive

A13: Honour to a Brave Woman, East Ward Advertiser and City Reporter, Bradford; September 1903 (date handwritten).
A94/2/10A: handwritten A4 sheet by Margaret McMillan.
A94/6/1/69: letter from Stanley Baldwin to Margaret McMillan, 20 December 1928.
A94/7/4: Bradford School Board: Resignation of a member, *Bradford Telegraph*, 22 October 1902.
A94/7/8: news cutting from the *Bradford Telegraph*, 12 June 1903.
A94/7/8: news cutting from the *Yorkshire Daily Observer*, 12 June 1903.
A94/7/29: news cutting from the *London Evening Standard* '20 years work for children: Woman Pioneer on her work', 19 April 1929.
A94/16/A7/69: Article, 'The Nuisance who Worked Miracles', by J.B. Priestley. Newspaper cutting with no attribution to publication. 27 June 1947.
A94/16/12/107: Margaret McMillan with the Queen and students at the opening of the Rachel McMillan Teacher Training College, 8 May 1930.

London School of Economics: the Charles Booth Archive

Charles Booth Online Archive, *Map of London* http://booth.lse.ac.uk/cgi-bin/do.pl?sub=view_booth_and_barth&args=531000,180400,6,large,5 (accessed 26 July 2011).

Charles Booth Archive B89: *Interview with Amalgamated Brass Workers London Society Representative, Manganese Bronze and Brass Company, St George's Wharf Deptford*, ND, pp. 46–8.

Charles Booth Archive B284: *Interview with Rev A. T. Wallis St Nicholas Deptford*, pp. 116–33, 11 June 1900.

Charles Booth Archive B285: *Interview with Mr Dodd Hon Sec Deptford Ragged School Giffin Street*, 21 May 1900, pp. 72–89.

Charles Booth Archive B290: *Interview with school master Mr Farthing, Regent St Board School Deptford*, ND, pp. 1–11.

Charles Booth Online Archive B368: *Walk with Inspector Gummer* 18 July 1899, pp. 6–25 http://booth.lse.ac.uk/ (accessed 30 May 2011).

Nursery School Association Archive (1924). The Nursery School Association letter to the Rt. Hon. Charles P. Trevelyan – Minister of Education Spring 1924. BAECE 13/4 (accessed 25 April 2014).

The Nursery School Association Archive

Nursery School Association Archive (1925). Ward, H. (1925) Official letter written to Grace Owen by member of the Board of Education. BAECE 13/5 (accessed 25 April 2014).

Nursery School Association Archive (1925). Summary of meeting of the Nursery School Association, Saturday 3 January 1925. BAECE 13/4 (accessed 25 April 2014).

Reading University: the Nancy Astor Archive

RUL MS 1416: letter from Henrietta Brown Smith, Inspector (Board of Education) to Lady Astor, 14 November 1929.

University of Greenwich: the Margaret McMillan Archive

(A94/3): 'The Schools of Tomorrow' pamphlet written by Margaret McMillan dated 1918.

A94/16/A1/11: handwritten letter from Robert Morant to Margaret McMillan 28 October 1907.

A94/16/A1/14: handwritten letter from Robert Morant to Margaret McMillan, 4 September 1910.

A94/16/A1/45: handwritten note 'strictly private' from George Newman, Chief Medical Officer to the UK Government's Board of Education 5 December 1918.

A94/16/A1/53: letter from Margaret McMillan to Margaret Sutclifffe, 1922.

A94/16/A1/55: from Margaret McMillan, letter to her publisher, 28 December 1925.

A94/16/A1/72: letter from Margaret McMillan to Robert Blatchford, 15 February 1929.

A94/16/A1/73: letter from Margaret McMillan to Robert Blatchford, 18 February 1929.

A94/16/A1/74: letter from Margaret McMillan to Robert Blatchford, 20 February 1929.

A94/16/A1/75: document in Margaret McMillan's handwriting, dated 29 April 1929.

A94/16/A1/83: letter from Margaret McMillan to Robert Blatchford, Christmas Morning 1929.

A94/16/ A1/86: letter from Margaret McMillan to 'Mr Mackenzie', written 7 July 1930.

A94/16/A1/92: handwritten letter on paper headed 11 Downing Street Whitehall, ND, signed Mrs Ethel Snowden.

A94/16/A1/ 98: letter from Mrs A. Abbott 92, Rectory Buildings Crossfield Street, Deptford, ND.

A94/16/A8/7: extract from Margaret McMillan's speech at the opening of the Rachel McMillan Teacher Training College, 8 May 1930.

A94/16/A8/16: letter from Gladys Woodhams, Camp School.

A94/16/A8/18: letter from Helen Edwards, Bradford, student 1923–6.

A94/16/A8/19: letter from Miss Abigail Eliot, Brooks School, Concord, MA, USA, ND.

A94/16/A 8/22: letter from F. Hawtry from Darlington, ND.

A94/16/A8//23: typewritten document attributed to Lillian de Lissa, ND.

A94/16/A8/24: letter from Dorothy Lob, Camp School.

A94/16/A8/28: letter from Jessie Porter, Dundee, student 1917–20.

A94/16/A8/30: handwritten note, no date or address, signed 'Mrs Stiggear'.

A94/16/A8/34: script of a programme broadcast by the BBC Home Service, 27 November 1960.

A94/16/A8/35: a manuscript marked 'Miss Davies', broadcast 7 June 1960.

A94/16/A8/95: handwritten manuscript entitled 'Rachel MacMillan College: Yesterday, Today and Tomorrow', dated 1949.

A94/16/B7/5: *The Dentist at Work in the Deptford Clinic.*

A94/16/B7/8: *The Boys' Camp.*

A94/16/B7/12: *The Girls' Camp.*

A94/16/B7/?: Margaret McMillan with a child in the Rachel McMillan Open Air Nursery Garden, circa 1930.

Books

Booth, C. *Life and Labour of the People in London* (London: Bibliolife, 1902).

Mansbridge, A. *Margaret McMillan: Prophet and Pioneer* (London: J.M. Dent, 1932).

Mayhew, H. *London Labour and the London Poor* (First published in weekly editions over 1851–2; republished London: Wordsworth Classics, 2008).

McMillan, M. *The Camp School* (London: George Allen and Unwin, 1917).

McMillan, M. *Early Childhood* (London: Swan Sonnenschein, 1900).

McMillan, M. *Education Through the Imagination* (London: Swan Sonnenschein, 1904).

McMillan, M. *Labour and Childhood* (London: Swan Sonnenschein, 1907).

McMillan, M. *The Child and the State* (Manchester: The National Labour Press, 1911).

McMillan, M. *The Nursery School* (London: J.M. Dent, 1919).

McMillan, M. *The Life of Rachel McMillan* (London: J.M. Dent, 1927).

Owen, R. *A New View of Society and other Writings* (London: Penguin, 1991).

Pease, E. *History of the Fabian Society* (St Petersburg: Red and Black Publishers, 1916).

Pember Reeves, M. *Round About a Pound a Week* (London: G. Bell and Sons, 1913).

Sims, G. *How the Poor Live* (London: Dodo Press, 1893).

Smith, N. A. and Douglas Wiggin, K. *Children's Rights* (London: Dodo Press, 1892).

Stevinson, E. *Margaret McMillan: Prophet and Pioneer* (London: University of London Press, 1954).

Woodward, K. *Jipping Street* (London: Virago, 1928).

Journal articles

Dendy, H. 'The Industrial Residuum'. *The Economic Journal* 3 (12) (1893), 600–16.

McMillan, M. 'After the Echoes of the Congress of School Hygiene'. *The Labour Leader*, 30 August 1907.

Walford, E. 'Deptford', *Old and New London* 6 (1878), 143–164. http://www.british-history.ac.uk/report.aspx?compid=45272 (accessed 26 July 2011).

Acts of Parliament

Board of Education (England) Education Act 1918, 8 & 9 Geo.5. Ch. 39. http://www.educationengland.org.uk/documents/pdfs/1918-education-act.pdf.

Board of Education (England) Education Act 1921, 11 & 12 Geo. 5. c. 51. http://www.educationengland.org.uk/documents/acts/1921-education-act.html.

Multimedia sources

BBC London Archive, digital audio file: BBC Radio broadcast extract *Margaret McMillan: Portrait of a Pioneer*, 27 November 1960.

British Pathé Archive, video file: *Nursery Days!* Video Newsreel Film, 21 August 1939. http://www.britishpathe.com/record.php?id=11403 (accessed 5 August 2011).

British Pathé Archive, video file: *Her Majesty the Queen opens the Rachel McMillan Teacher Training College*. Video Newsreel Film, 12 May 1930. http://www.british pathe.com/record.php?id=8281 (accessed 7 August 2011).

Newspaper articles

Guardian Archive '*Independent Labour Party Conference*', first published 14 January 1893. http://www.guardian.co.uk/politics/2010/jan/14/archive-independent-labour-party-conference (accessed 4 January 2011).

ProQuest Historical Newspapers: online, letter from Shena D. Simon to the *Manchester Guardian* letters page, 29 January 1930.

ProQuest Historical Newspapers: online, letter from Margaret McMillan to The *Manchester Guardian* letters page, 26 February 1930.

ProQuest Historical Newspapers: online, *Manchester Guardian* 'Miss Margaret McMillan on Old Traditions', 22 May 1930.

Miscellaneous

Anonymous: *The Weavers Song* – from Deptford and Lewisham Women's Labour pageant 'Out of Bondage' performed 16 November 1950 (from author's family – private collection).

Secondary sources

Books

Bradburn, E. *Margaret McMillan: Framework and Expansion of Nursery Education* (Redhill: Denholm House, 1976).

Bradburn, E. *Margaret McMillan: Portrait of a Pioneer* (London: Routledge, 1989).

Davin, A. *Growing Up Poor: Home, School and Street in London 1870–1914* (London: Rivers Oram, 1996).

Fort, A. *Nancy: The Story of Lady Astor* (London: Vintage, 2013).

Freire, P. *Pedagogy of the Oppressed* (New York: Continuum, 1970).

Graham, P. *Susan Isaacs: A Life Freeing the Minds of Children* (London: Karnac, 2009).

Hollen Lees, L. *The Solidarities of Strangers* (Cambridge: Cambridge University Press, 1998).

Lascarides, V. C. and Hinitz, B. *History of Early Childhood Education* (Abingdon: Routledge, 2000), p. 120.

Lowndes, G. A. N. *Margaret McMillan: The Children's Champion* (London: Museum Press, 1960).

McPhillips, K. *Joseph Burgess 1833–1934 and the Founding of the Independent Labour Party* (Lampeter: Edward Mellen Press, Studies in British History Vol. 78, 2005).

Moriarty, V. *Margaret McMillan: 'I learn, to succor the helpless'* (Nottingham: Educational Heretics Press, 1998).

Paterson, M. *Voices from Dickens' London* (Cincinnati: David and Charles, 2006).

Steedman, C. *Childhood, Culture and Class in Britain: Margaret McMillan 1860–1931* (New Brunswick: Rutgers University Press, 1990).

Steedman, C. *Oxford Dictionary of National Biography* (Oxford: Oxford University Press, 2004–14).

Stevinson, E. *Margaret McMillan: Prophet and Pioneer* (London: University of London Press, 1954).

Thane, P. *Happy Families? History and Family Policy* (London: British Academy Policy Centre, 2010).

Journal articles

Backstrom, P. N. 'The Practical Side of Christian Socialism in Victorian England'. *Victorian Studies* 6:4 (1963) 305–24.

Briggs, A. 'The Welfare State in Historical Perspective'. *European Journal of Sociology* 2:2 (1961) 221–58.

Brebony, K. J. 'Lady Astor's Campaign for Nursery Schools in Britain 1930–1939: Attempting to Valorize Culture Capital in a Male-Dominated Field'. *History of Education Quarterly* 49:2 (2009) 196–210.

Davin, A. 'Imperialism and Motherhood'. *History Workshop* 5 (1978) 9–65.

Gazeley, I. and Newell, A. 'Poverty in Britain in 1904: An Early Social Survey Rediscovered', *PRUS working paper no. 38* (2007). http://www.sussex.ac.uk/Units/PRU/wps/wp38.pdf (accessed 26 July 2011).

Hennock, E. P. 'The Measurement of Urban Poverty: From the Metropolis to the Nation, 1880–1920'. *Economic History Review*, 2nd ser. XL, 2 (1987) 208–27.

Henriques, U. 'How Cruel Was the Victorian Poor Law'? *The Historical Journal* 11:2 (1968) 365–71.

Herberg, W. 'The Christian Mythology of Socialism'. *The Antioch Review* 3 (1) (1943) 125–32.

Hirst, J. 'The Growth of Treatment Through the School Medical Service 1908–18'. *Medical History* 33 (1989) 318–42.

Jarvis, P. and Liebovich, B. 'British Nurseries, Head and Heart: McMillan, Owen and the Genesis of the Education/Care Dichotomy'. *Women's History Review* (2015) Retrieved from http://www.tandfonline.com/doi/abs/10.1080/09612025.2015.1025662?journalCode=rwhr20#.VUZripPff4U.

Kidd, A. J. 'Historians or Polemicists? How the Webbs Wrote Their History'. *The Economic History Review* 40:3 (1987) 400–17.

Kirk, N. 'Traditional Working Class Culture and the Rise of Labour: Some Preliminary Questions and Observations'. *Social History* 16:2 (1991) 203–16.

Koven, S. and Michel, S. 'Womanly Duties: Maternalist Policies and the Origins of Welfare States in France, Germany, Great Britain and the United States 1880–1920'. *American Historical Review* 95:4 (1990) 1076–108.

Lewis, M. 'Impact of Industrialisation: Comparative Study of Child Health in Four Sites from Medieval and Postmedieval England'. *American Journal of Physical Anthropology* 119 (2002) 211–33.

Lipset, S. M. 'Radicalism or Reformism: The Sources of Working-Class Politics'. *The American Political Science Review* 77:1 (1983) 1–18.

Livesey, R. 'Reading for Character: Women Social Reformers and Narratives of the Urban Poor in Late Victorian and Edwardian London'. *Journal of Victorian Culture* 9:1 (2004) 43–68.

Mandler, P. 'The Making of the New Poor Law Redivivus'. *Past and Present* 117:1 (1987) 131–57.

MacRae Campbell, L. 'Whole Person Education', *Transforming Education*. http://www.context.org/ICLIB/IC18/MacRae.htm (accessed 13 August 2011).

Moss, P. 'We Cannot Continue As We Are: The Educator in an Education for Survival'. *Contemporary Issues in Childhood* 11:1 (2010) 8–19.

Munro, O. 'Our Maggie'. *The British Medical Journal* (International Edition) 299:6706 (1989) 1048.

Perkin, H. 'The Condescension of Posterity: The Recent Historiography of the English Working Class'. *Social Science History* 3:1 (1978) 87–101.

Ross, E. 'Survival Networks: Women's Neighbourhood Sharing in London before World War I'. *History Workshop* 15 (1983) 4–27.

Rowan, C. 'Women in the Labour Party 1906–1920'. *Feminist Review* 12 (1982) 74–91.

Thompson, E. P. 'The Political Education of Henry Mayhew'. *Victorian Studies* 11:1 (1967) 41–62.

Ward, D. 'The Victorian Slum: An Enduring Myth?' *Annals of the Association of American Geographers* 66:2 (1976) 323–36.

Waters, C. 'William Morris and the Socialism of Robert Blatchford'. http://www.morrissociety.org/JWMS/W82.5.2.Waters.pdf (accessed 4 January 2011).

Welshman, J. 'School Meals and Milk in England and Wales, 1906–45'. *Medical History* 41: (1997) 6–29.

Yeo, S. 'A New Life: The Religion of Socialism in Britain'. *History Workshop* 4 (1977) 5–56.

Websites

Davis, M. Socialism. *TUC History Online* http://www.unionhistory.info/timeline/1880_14_Narr_Display.php?Where=NarTitle+contains+%27Socialism%27+AND+DesPurpose+contains+%27WebDisplay%27 (accessed 28 July 2011).

DFES (2003) *Every Child Matters,* Green Paper. London: The Stationery Office. https://www.education.gov.uk/consultations/downloadableDocs/EveryChildMatters.pdf (accessed 25 February 2016).

Early Education: Our History. http://www.early-education.org.uk/about-us/our-history (accessed 29 April 2014).

Freire Institute, Paulo Freire Biography: http://www.freire.org/paulo-freire/paulo-freire-biography (accessed 15 August 2015).

Moss, P. (2014) Our Youngest Children Deserve Better Than a Fragmented Patchwork of Services. IOE London Blog: http://ioelondonblog.wordpress.com/category/peter-moss/ (accessed 13 March 2014).

Rachel McMillan Open Air Nursery, *Picture of the Margaret McMillan Memorial.* http://www.rachelmcmillannursery.co.uk/ (accessed 5 August 2011).

Rachel McMillan Open Air Nursery, *Pictures of Rachel and Margaret McMillan.* http://www.rachelmcmillannursery.co.uk/about/ (accessed 31 July 2011).

Steedman, C. Margaret McMillan, *Oxford Dictionary of National Biography.* http://www.oxforddnb.com/view/printable/34801 (accessed 9 August 2011).

Maria Montessori (1870–1952)

Scientific pedagogy

Wendy Holland

Introduction

This chapter will focus on Maria Montessori (1870–1952), the first female doctor of medicine in Italy, who later became a pioneering educator. It will consider the influences of her early life and education, exploring the subsequent success of her pedagogical method, which included multiple nominations for the Nobel Peace Prize, first in 1949, again in 1950 and then posthumously in 1951. It will explore her 'scientific pedagogical' approach to early childhood education, focusing on her project with the 'Children's House' (Casa dei Bambini) and her application of this pedagogical regime to children with additional learning needs, following her journey from medical practice to teaching. The chapter will also consider her influences: Sigmund Freud (1856–1939) in terms of the child's psyche, Jean Itard (1775–1838) who studied deaf mutes and feral children, and Edouard Seguin (1812–80) who worked with children with learning difficulties, using a physiological method. Montessori's own later methods show influences from the work of these men, particularly in her insistence that children first learn through their senses, followed by their intellect. The chapter will also consider the impact of her theories on contemporary practice, both in terms of teacher training in Montessori methods and their implementation in Montessori schools.

> *Education must no longer be based upon a syllabus but upon the knowledge of human life.*
>
> *(Montessori 1967, p. 11)*

Early life and education: the young feminist

Born in Chiaravalle, Italy in August 1870, Montessori was the only child of a middle-class, well-educated family who were devout Roman Catholics. Her mother,

Renilde Stoppani, was related to a renowned philosopher-scientist priest, Antonio Stoppani, and was reportedly 'a lady of singular piety and charm' (Standing 1984, p. 21). Renilde's insistence that the young Maria knit garments for the poor every week is an illustration of her belief in practical charity. Montessori seemed quite happy with this task, even imposing tasks of her own such as scrubbing a section of the kitchen floor. Both activities found their way into the pedagogical method she was later to devise, which specified practical tasks for the infants and young children. Her father, Alessandro Montessori, was described by her two main biographers, Standing (1984) and Kramer (1988), as a former soldier who had received a commendation for bravery: 'an old fashioned gentleman of conservative behaviour and military habits' (Kramer, p. 23). By the time Montessori was born, her father was employed by the government as a financial officer whose duties included overseeing the management of the tobacco industry, which was a state-run concern. His conservative personality contrasted with that of Montessori's mother, whose upbringing had been strongly influenced by Antonio Stoppani's liberal philosophy, embracing the changing world and the promises it held, which she strongly communicated to her daughter. This impacted upon the family dynamic as Montessori grew older, with Renilde giving much support to her fiercely stubborn and passionate daughter's ambitions, while Alessandro's plans for his daughter were far more traditional. This led to family disagreements, with the young Montessori sometimes acting as peace maker between her parents; a role she would later attempt to extend to the world stage (Standing 1984).

Montessori's strong mindedness and ambition began to show itself at the young age of twelve, when she elected to go to the technical school, dismissing the usual route of classical studies that was specified for girls entering the public system. Kramer (1988) gives an insight into the type of education Montessori would have had to endure at this time at the technical school. Physical immobility was enforced, everyone moved at the same pace, studying the same material at the same time, and knowledge was something to be passively ingested. From this description, it would be easy to understand Montessori's later aversion to the process of 'transmission' teaching.

Having completed her technical school education very successfully by 1886, Montessori decided she wanted to become an engineer, much to her father's disapproval, particularly as he had already begun to come around to her decision to become a teacher, one of the few acceptable professions for a woman in Italy at that time. Montessori quickly accepted that she could not become an engineer, but decided to flout convention through an alternative choice – reading medicine at university. At that time, medicine was seen as strictly a male preserve; a highly unsuitable career choice for a lady. Against strong opposition from her father, but with support and encouragement from her mother, Montessori got her way, unlike Susan Isaacs who did not have a mother to support her efforts to break free from the limitations placed on her by a domineering, patriarchal father (see Chapter 9). In 1890, Montessori enrolled at the University of Rome. Her father then capitulated, but insisted upon escorting her to and from class in keeping with the nineteenth-century convention of ladies being accompanied at all times in public. This drive and perseverance in the face of strong opposition was to become a trademark of her later life and career. From the brief information about her father in the literature, it would seem that he was a strict, somewhat difficult man, who did not countenance Montessori's choices or her developing feminist leanings. She herself admitted a stronger attachment to her mother. Standing (1984) describes Montessori's relationship with her parents as affectionate and understanding, but events that at this point lay in the future, in the birth of an illegitimate son and Montessori's failure to acknowledge him as her own child until just before her own death, suggest that there were limits to such understanding, even with respect to her mother's liberal views.

Montessori's independence of mind and spirit served her well during her university medical training, where she was continuously exposed to discrimination. Standing gives an almost Gothic picture of the trials that Montessori faced:

> *It was not considered proper that a girl should dissect dead bodies in the presence of male students. So her practical work in the dissecting room had to be done by herself; and this meant that she was obliged to pass many hours alone amongst the corpses, very often in the evening after darkness had set in.*

> *(Standing 1984, p. 25)*

Montessori completed her studies with her characteristic passion and determination, finally achieving the accolade of an honours degree in medicine from the University of Rome in 1896. Uniquely, her degree was in both medicine and surgery, making her the first woman in Italy to achieve this accolade; surgery was still considered the exclusive domain of men (Shannon Helfrich 2011, O'Donnell 2013). In August of the same year, Montessori was asked to represent Italy at the International Congress of Women in Berlin, where subjects for discussion included the plight of working women and the education of women. Montessori spoke with particular passion on the right of women to be granted equal pay for equal work; an issue that is still to be fully resolved in the twenty-first century (Ball 2010).

Her first appointment after qualifying was as an assistant doctor at the psychiatric clinic at Rome University. As a clinical paediatrician, her main interest was mental health and part of her job entailed visiting the local asylums to find children suitable for treatment at the clinic. The children were termed 'mental defectives' (today these children would be described as having learning difficulties/disabilities or special educational needs). Montessori began a series of systematic observations of her patients' behaviours. Such close and detailed observations brought her to the conclusion that the children's conditions were the result of social or environmental experiences and were not medical in origin. She determined that the answer to a 'cure' lay in pedagogical and environmental 'stimulation' (O'Donnell 2013). 'Mental deficiency presented chiefly a pedagogical, rather than mainly a medical problem' (Montessori 1964, p. 31).

Theoretical and practical legacy: pedagogic anthropology

On making such a discovery, Montessori felt the need to consult with others working in the field of pedagogic anthropology. This led her to the work of Jean Marc Itard (1775–1838), who had worked in Paris at the Institute for Deaf Mutes (O'Donnell 2013). Most famous amongst his cases was the 'feral' child, Aveyron, who walked on all fours, 'a creature more like an animal than a man, expressionless, rocking back and forth, locked in his own world' (Kramer 1988, p. 59). Montessori was drawn to the scientific method of close observation that Itard used in his attempt to 'civilise' the boy. She was also interested in Itard's development of specific resources which he used to support and develop the boy's cognitive, linguistic and social skills. Itard's methodology focused on developing the young boy's mind through the use of all his senses. Montessori, ever the perfectionist, travelled to Paris and London to collect and document Itard's work for herself, returning to Rome with the intention of using his methods with her young 'defectives' in the clinic.

Another important influence was that of Itard's student, Edouard Seguin (1812–80), a teacher and physician who believed in emphasising the skills and aptitudes of the individual child. He taught his students, some of whom were bedridden, to walk through a carefully planned programme of physical exercises over a long period of time. He also designed individual resources to support differing individual needs. This focus on individual need was in complete agreement with Montessori's thinking at the time and laid the groundwork for many of the painstakingly designed trademark resources she began to create, which are now used internationally in all Montessori settings as early sensory and manipulative materials (O'Donnell 2013).

Seguin's philosophy of education also reflected Montessori's own thinking, centred as it was on the balance between nature (the genetic construction of the individual) and nurture (the individual responding to the environment). Another aspect of Seguin's philosophy that Montessori co-opted into her own pedagogical system was the practice of democracy within the classroom, removing the authoritarian nature of the teacher–pupil relationship, which Seguin proposed would permeate into the student consciousness, consequently influencing wider society for good. It can be argued that this concept was in turn drawn from Pestalozzi's original ideas of this nature (see Chapter 2). Montessori enthusiastically took Seguin's approach on board, and through her pedagogical method, bequeathed it to a global perspective of democratic pedagogical practice; hence her later work in helping found UNESCO and ongoing support for world peace initiatives (O'Donnell 2013).

Another influence came indirectly from the work of Freud who wrote a letter to Montessori expressing his interest in her work on the 'inner child' (cited in Kramer 1976). Montessori's ideas on the young child's psyche, and the importance of internal self-direction within the first five years, linked with similar views being formulated by Freud at the time. The need for self-discovery and self-direction within the young child also links to Montessori's rejection of punishment as an aid to instilling discipline and eliciting moral behaviour. She believed instead in providing an environment where a child could resolve conflict within themselves without any extrinsic reward or punishment (Kramer 1976, p. 74).

In 1890, Montessori became co-director of the Orthophrenic School in Rome, a new institution that took in children with a range of disorders, alongside Giuseppe Montesano. The professional partnership developed into a romantic relationship and a son, Mario, was born to the couple in 1898. There are differing views on why they did not marry. Some sources suggest it was the refusal of both families, particularly the mothers, to countenance a marriage; others suggest it was Montessori's own unwillingness to stop working, which at that time would have been the inevitable outcome of marriage and motherhood (Ball 2010). Whatever the reason, the couple came to a highly unorthodox arrangement whereby their son would be sent to the country to be wet nursed, and they would not marry, but would agree never to marry anyone else. Mario did eventually come to live with his mother from the age of fifteen, but she introduced him in public as her 'adopted' son. It was suggested by some sources that Giuseppe Montesano was 'not in robust good health, but elegantly handsome', and was dominated by his mother, 'a very severe dowager' who could trace the family line back to Old Italian aristocracy (Gardner 2012). What is clear, however, is that within a year of Mario's birth, Montesano met and married another woman. Montessori's biographers suggest that she took this betrayal in her stride, but nevertheless took the step of putting distance between herself and Montesano by leaving the Orthophrenic School, ostensibly to immerse herself in further study (Kramer 1988, O'Donnell 2013).

It is mooted that Montessori spent some time in meditation at a convent during this period of her life (Gardner 2012), and given her family's deeply held Catholicism, it is quite possible. She was to emerge from her contemplation and solitude a different woman, one who had decided to give up medicine, the career she had so determinedly fought for, to concentrate on her 'scientific pedagogy'. Ironically, teaching had been one of the very few avenues open to professional women before Montessori had paved the way in medicine, but one that she had previously shunned. Now it was to become the whole focus of her life. When she was thirty, her father, perhaps finally acknowledging his daughter's gifts and determination, presented her with a book he had created; a collection of over 200 articles, newspaper clippings and reports of conferences all celebrating Montessori's achievements (Standing 1984). Perhaps, too, this was an affirmation of his love for his strong-minded daughter, who had recently given birth and subsequently been rejected and betrayed by the man she had loved; although it is unknown how much Montessori's father knew about these events. Mario did live with his grandparents for some time following his infancy, but it is unknown whether they were led to believe that he was Montessori's adopted rather than natural son.

It is clearly documented that Montessori now began to immerse herself in the works of Rousseau, Pestalozzi and Froebel. At the University of Rome she enrolled on courses of study in anthropology, psychology and philosophy, the ideas of her tutors also influencing her thinking at this time. She wrote about the anthropologist Giuseppe Sergi (1841–1936) as a teacher whose passionate beliefs mirrored her own; that a new kind of education based on 'scientific pedagogy' rooted in close observation of the individual child must be developed (O'Donnell 2013). In refining her 'scientific pedagogy', Montessori came to theorise the child's development through a series of 'planes', each lasting six years (O'Donnell 2013, p. 13). There are clear similarities with the Piagetian stages in this respect and with Steiner's theory, although some obvious differences exist in the underpinning concepts behind each stage. In this sense, Montessori was clearly a constructivist, viewing the child as capable, active and eager to construct meaning from their experiences. In establishing her first 'Casa dei Bambini', she created groups of children in narrower three-year age bands, and began to theorise a strong teacher role, reflecting the more knowledgeable 'other' embedded in Vygotsky's social constructivism.

In 1904 she accepted a post as a lecturer at the Pedagogic School in the University of Rome and may well have stayed there for some years, helping in the training of teachers, if in 1906 she had not been approached by a group of developers who were trying to rebuild some of the slum tenements in Rome. They were encountering difficulties with vandalism enacted by groups of slum children who were running wild, damaging the newly refurbished dwellings. The problem was that the requirement for parents to work long hours had left the children of the area to their own devices and their consequent destructive behaviour was working against the improvement the builders were hoping to accomplish (Kramer 1988). Montessori saw this as an opportunity to put into practice some of her developing ideas around 'scientific pedagogy', and she wasted no time in opening her first Casa dei Bambini in 1907 for the children of Rome's slums. The focus on 'slum children' mirrors the McMillan sisters' work in England at the very same time (see Chapter 7), and you will find in a later chapter that Malaguzzi experienced a very similar event that placed him on the road to the development of his pedagogical framework (see Chapter 10), a set of intriguing parallels between the pioneers in terms of underpinning events that spurred their initial efforts.

In the following year, 1908, Montessori opened another Casa dei Bambini in Milan. Her influence and reputation were, however, reaching much further than Italy itself. Following a very successful visit to America, the first American Montessori school opened in New York in 1911. In 1916, Acton Borough Council in England made the decision to base all its provision for young children on Montessori's principles and practice, a testament to how well her methods were being received. Montessori's own developing ideas around 'scientific pedagogy' at this time included:

- the importance of close observation of children;
- the need for a structured environment;
- the role of the 'directress' in supporting children's learning;
- positive behaviour management;
- sensitive periods of development;
- the 'absorbent mind';

■ the child's need for freedom;

■ processes, not results.

These successes led to the establishment in 1909 of the first Montessori training course for teachers. Teacher training remained an important part of Montessori's expanding educational empire, with its stringent application of rules for the newly trained teachers (directresses) to follow; indeed, Montessori would continually return to this topic in international lectures throughout the remainder of her life. During an intense period between 1911 and 1915 Montessori showed her immense stamina and passion for the education of young children through her global travels, delivering lectures on her philosophy and setting up teacher training courses in the Montessori method. Kramer informs us that:

> By 1911, the Montessori system had been officially adopted in the public schools of Italy and of Switzerland; two model schools had been established in Paris . . . official preparations were under way to introduce the method in England; and plans were being made for opening Montessori schools in India, China, Mexico, Korea, Argentina and Hawaii.
>
> (Kramer 1988, p. 155)

All of this was achieved through Montessori's ability to energise and inspire those who came to listen to her lectures or attend her training courses, or who read her writings on pedagogy. Kramer tells us how Leo Tolstoy's daughter, Countess Tatiana Tolstoy, read of the Casa dei Bambini in a Russian educational magazine and later spoke about Montessori's methods at a teacher's conference in Moscow, which in turn led to classes in Montessori pedagogy being set up in Russia (Kramer 1988).

In conjunction with this heavy workload, Montessori still found time to publish several works, which were quickly translated into other languages, including English. Montessori published *Il Metodo della Pedagogia Scientifica* in 1909, in an attempt to provide a more detailed description of her 'scientific pedagogy'. The book was then translated and published in the United States as *The Montessori Method: Scientific Pedagogy as Applied to Child Education in the Children's Houses. Doctor Montessori's Own Handbook* followed in 1914, a practical guide to help with the exact and proper use of the specially designed auto-didactic materials that Montessori had developed to enable children to regulate their own learning (Moretti 2011).

Montessori's ideas were swiftly disseminated worldwide; however, her attempts to explain her theory to an international audience were viewed as a blatant programme of self-publicisation by some observers (Kramer 1988); a form of 'hubris'. A kinder interpretation would be that Montessori had a passionate belief in what she was doing, and was attempting to ensure that real changes could be made through her scientific pedagogy. This, she hoped, would result in a population who better understood the processes of democracy, and ultimately, a world more at peace with itself. Becoming a recognised figure worldwide had its privileges. As a result of her methods being embraced in America, she was praised by President Woodrow Wilson and inventor Alexander Graham Bell, and in 1912 she received funding for opening further Montessori schools in the USA. Montessori was so confident of her methods that she agreed to teach in a glass classroom at the International Exposition in San Francisco in 1915, where thousands of visitors flocked to see for themselves the 'calm and purposeful' environment in which twenty-one children aged three to six years moved about 'gracefully and freely, accessing resources when needed' (Standing 1984, pp. 63–4). It was observed that even the youngest children could remain absorbed with a task for considerable lengths of time.

By 1915 Montessori's critics began to make themselves heard, possibly the most notable of whom was American William Heard Kilpatrick, an influential figure in the field of child pedagogy, and a sympathiser and interpreter of John Dewey's methods. O'Donnell (2013) states that after studying and observing Montessori's method in action, Kilpatrick published a searing critique of her approach, which damaged her professional reputation, particularly in the US. Kilpatrick's *Montessori System Examined* (1914) claimed that Montessori's approach was 'more than half a century behind the times' and 'to teach the 3Rs before eight years was at best a waste of time, and might possibly be harmful' (Kilpatrick 1914). He disapproved of the structured resources that were so essential to Montessori's approach, proposing that they were too formal, limited and 'very remote from social interests and connections' (Kirkpatrick 1914).

The US at this time favoured more progressive views on education – Froebel's kindergarten approach in particular with its focus on freedom and the importance of play. As such, Kilpatrick's critique was devastating to Montessori's campaign in the US. Nevertheless, Montessori continued to exert tight control over her method, her resources and her teacher training programme, insisting that her method should be applied 'without deviation' (Gutek 2016, p. 24). This led to further disagreements and acrimony, particularly with her initial sponsor, Samuel McClure. Her popularity continued to fade, and her final visit to the US was in 1919. The resurgence of the Montessori method and its eventual widespread popularity did not properly begin until 1952, when Montessori's son Mario and Nancy McCormick Rambush relaunched the Montessori method in the US for a new generation of parents and teachers who would have no memory of Kilpatrick's critique (Rambush 1977). This was not without controversy, as Rambush's attempt to modernise the Montessori method drew criticism from Mario Montessori, who was concerned that she did not stay true to his mother's original scientific pedagogy.

Kramer (1988, p. 250) describes a moment that illustrates the iron will of Montessori. She returned to work almost immediately following the death of her father in 1914. One of her scheduled business appointments was to attend a Christmas Mass with various important officials, which she dutifully did, but 'was unable to stifle her sobs' during the service. Kramer goes on to describe Montessori's dismissal of offers of comfort, insisting on the serious nature of her purpose; to 'seek to discover the man in the child, to see in him the true human spirit, the design of the Creator: the scientific and religious truth' (Homs, cited in Kramer 1988).

Maria Montessori moved to Barcelona in 1915 at the request of the regional Catalonian government. She took up the management of the Laboratori Seminari de Pedagogia, a government-supported training centre and its partner school which had been designed to educate children between three and ten years of age. Montessori began an expansion of her methods, this time for use with secondary-age children. She headed an international training course in Barcelona in 1916 which acted as the showcase for her further developments on her materials and methods which, with the help of Mario, she had developed over the previous five years. These methods and resources were created to support the teaching of grammar, arithmetic and geometry. Montessori had sunk a large proportion of her assets into this venture, and was relying on the conference to open up a market for her auto-didactic resources within public secondary schools. To further support this expansion of her method, in 1917 Montessori published *L'autoeducazionne nelle Scuole Elementari (Self-Education in Elementary School)*, appearing in English translation as *The Advanced Montessori Method*.

In 1920 the Catalan independence movement demanded that Montessori take a political stand and publicly announce her allegiance to Catalan independence. She naturally refused, and as a result her official financial support was withdrawn. Four years later in 1924, with the advent of a new military dictatorship in Spain, Montessori's model school in Barcelona was closed, with a resulting decline in Montessori education within the nation in general. Nevertheless, Barcelona would remain her home for the next twelve years. Montessori's fortunes were revived in 1933 under the Second Spanish Republic; her school reopened with support and sponsorship from the new government and she constructed a new training course on the Montessori method. This was also sponsored by the government, but once again such support was short-lived. With the onset of the Spanish Civil War in 1936, political and social conditions became so difficult that Montessori had no option but to leave Spain permanently (Kramer 1988).

This experience should have forewarned Montessori against placing any reliance upon a national government, particularly given the political volatility in Continental Europe between the two world wars. In this book, we can find a similarity to the fragility of Pestalozzi's initiatives amidst the insecurity created in Switzerland by the Napoleonic wars (see Chapter 2). In what Standing (1984, p. 72) calls Montessori's 'journeyings oft and self-sacrificing labours on behalf of the child – and through him of humanity', she was disappointed time and again both in the lack of recognition of the value of her methods, and with respect to the lack of stability within national public school systems. She had given up well-paid jobs to internationalise her ideas on the education of the young and the training of directresses to relay that message, so convinced was she that her method would provide real liberty for the child and by so doing, eventually advance the potential for world peace. But within the space of a decade she had first been thwarted in the US, and then in Spain.

Montessori visited Italy in 1922 to deliver a government-sponsored programme of lectures on the Montessori method and to inspect the remaining Montessori schools in the country. Yet again she was plunged into a difficult political situation, as in late 1922 Mussolini's Fascist dictatorship was imposed upon the nation (see also Chapter 9 for the effect of this era upon Malaguzzi). Whether or not Montessori actually took tea with Mussolini, as some proposed, it is clear that she did attempt to accommodate some of the demands of the ruling fascist regime. Moretti (2011) describes a remarkable departure from her principles, in that she agreed to remove a section of her method to appease the government in terms of their ideological emphasis upon the traditional role of women with regard to child-bearing and the family. The section was eventually replaced in its original form in 1950. Montessori's collaboration with the Italian government expanded when Mussolini extended his official support for Montessori schools, paving the way for them to become part of the national education programme under the name of Opera Montessori; this was a level of recognition that Montessori had coveted for many years.

However, there were some difficulties between what the government expected and what Montessori wished to deliver (Moretti 2011). Both Montessori and her son Mario tried to negotiate within what Moretti terms 'the grey zone of political neutrality' (Moretti 2011, p. 17), until it became clear to both that Mussolini was using the international reputation of the Montessori method to publicise his attempt to address illiteracy levels amongst the Italian population that had exposed him to public criticism, and moreover, to increase a fascist polemic within Italian education.

There were, however, some short-lived triumphs for Montessori in Italy during this period. In 1927, Mussolini established a Montessori teacher training college, and Montessori received a life-long Catholic benediction from the Vatican. She also continued her international activities with the formation of the Association of the Montessori Internationale (AMI) with help from her son Mario. Such was her international reputation as a pedagogue and scientist that leading figures in the world of child development such as Jean Piaget and Sigmund Freud were early signatories.

However, her relationship with the Mussolini government deteriorated in a process which must have seemed sadly familiar. This disagreement was particularly difficult for her, given that she had to confront a fascist dictatorship to complain about a lack of financial support. She was also brought to task by the Italian government for what she termed 'ideological issues', which she had introduced in her lectures on Peace and Education in France and Geneva in 1932. Her comments elicited an accusation levelled at the Montessori schools in general, that of anti-fascist behaviour on the part of some of her directresses. Montessori and her son Mario were placed under political surveillance (Moretti 2011), and consequently, by 1934, they realised they would be unable to live or work in Italy while Mussolini remained in power. In 1936 the Italian government closed down the Montessori training centre and all Montessori-inspired activity in Italian schools. It was a bitter pill for Montessori to swallow; that her mission had faltered so badly within her own home nation (Kramer 1988).

Montessori and her family, which consisted of the now divorced Mario and his four children, moved to Laren near Amsterdam in 1936, where both Maria and Mario busied themselves with developing and refining the resource materials that are still in use within the Montessori method. It is relatively well known that the most famous of all Holocaust authors, Anne Frank, attended a Montessori school in Amsterdam during the mid-1930s. It is clear from the contents of her diary that she highly valued this experience, particularly given the extent to which the Nazi occupation of Holland between 1940 and 1945 impacted upon her later education (Frank 1947). It was during this period, in 1938, that Montessori was invited by the Theosophical Society of India to provide courses to train teachers in her Montessori methods. She knew her method was well received there after the formation of an Indian Montessori society in 1926. Although settled in Holland with her family with an idyllic small school in which to practise her methods (Kramer 1988), Montessori could not resist the call. So, in 1939, just as World War II was about to begin, and at the age of sixty-nine, she set out for India with Mario, where they would remain until the end of the war.

Montessori was, of course, familiar with issues experienced by the children of the numerous 'slum' districts she found in India; this was very much like the situation in Rome that had triggered the earlier development of her pedagogical method. The plan in moving to India had originally been for Montessori and Mario to travel around the country's universities giving a series of lectures after providing an initial training course at the Theosophical Society's headquarters in Adyar. World events, however, laid waste to their plans. As Italy was allied to Nazi Germany, both Montessori and her son, as Italian citizens, were seen as 'enemy aliens' by the ruling British regime, and in accordance with the rules of internment for the colonies, both Maria and Mario were subsequently interned. Given her age and considering her international status, Montessori was allowed to remain confined to the Theosophical Society's compound. Mario was initially given no such dispensation and was routinely interned. Gardner (1970) refers to Montessori's 'dark days' without her son, in a country where she didn't speak the language. However, the Viceroy of India decided to give her the 'present' of her son on her seventieth birthday, by releasing him from internment. Although neither of the Montessoris were allowed to travel internationally during the war years, they managed to establish a Montessori training centre in Sri Lanka, and Maria travelled throughout India giving lectures. Always the acute observer, she was fascinated by the speed at which even the youngest children in India were able to speak their mother tongue. She put her thoughts into lectures which appeared in book form in 1949 as *What You Should Know About Your Child.* These ideas, created by her observations of very young children, were later to form the basis of her book *The Absorbent Mind*, in which she focused upon child development from the point of birth. She also developed a stage theory she named the 'four planes of development': birth to six, six to twelve, twelve to eighteen and eighteen to twenty-four, which to some degree reflected and extended Piaget's stage theory (Shannon Helfrich 2011).

Montessori never lost the energy to pursue her dream of peace through educating the young; indeed, the war intensified this ideology. In 1950, at the age of eighty, she became one of the founder members of UNESCO (Barres 2004).

Created in order to respond to the firm belief of nations, forged by two world wars in less than a generation, that political and economic agreements are not enough to build a lasting peace. Peace must be established on the basis of humanity's moral and intellectual solidarity.

(UNESCO 2016)

Such passionate commitment resulted in her being nominated three times for the Nobel Peace Prize in 1949, 1950 and finally posthumously in 1951. Throughout his life, her son Mario was her most loyal supporter. When Jerome Bruner introduced the notion of a spiral curriculum that suggested a child could be taught anything at any age given an effective teaching regime by drawing upon the theories of Lev Vygotsky (Bruner 1966), Mario sharply reminded him that Maria Montessori had practised that theory with some success for the past thirty years (Lillard 2008). There are some who might wonder at the irony of such faithful support, given that Montessori had not been available to Mario during those crucial early years of his own life. Indeed, up to the point of her own death on 6 May 1952 she defined him as her *adopted* son. It is ironic that she seemed confident to flout strict nineteenth-century ideology relating to the 'correct' conduct for women in every way, except to acknowledge her status as a single mother to her most constant and loyal companion. Mario died in 1982 (Indian Montessori Centre 2011). His own daughter wrote a short but touching obituary for him, which gives some insight into his gentle personality and his fierce, protective love for his mother (Henny-Montessori 2016).

Teaching and curriculum: 'looking becomes reading: touching becomes writing'

First the education of the senses, then the education of the intellect.
(Montessori 1964, p. 137)

So what was it about Montessori's methods that caught the imagination of educators around the world? The time in which her philosophy and practice emerged was one of social experimentation. In such a zeitgeist, progressive ideas around education flourished, and the unique qualities possessed by the young child were explored and celebrated. No longer was the child viewed as a 'mini adult' waiting for maturation to take place, or as a 'blank slate' for adults to write on, or as an 'empty vessel' waiting to be filled by adult transmission of knowledge. Montessori, with her biological and scientific background, was uniquely placed to explore the impact of nurture upon nature, when observing her 'deficient' children in the Orthophrenic School. There is a clear similarity to Margaret McMillan here, in that the practice in which Montessori initially engaged had one foot in education and the other in health care (see Chapter 7). Taking her lead from mentors such as Itard and Seguin, Montessori managed, through the use of their sensory methods, alongside some of her own adaptations to the environment, to help and direct children who had been labelled educationally 'subnormal' to read and write at a very early age; in Montessori's own words: 'Looking becomes reading: touching becomes writing' (Montessori 1964, p. 185).

Montessori challenged contemporary thinking with her credo: the development of the child's sensory and cognitive skills leading to the formation of 'character'. In particular, this conflicted with the ideas underpinning Froebel's philosophy, in which children of three and four years were not deemed ready or able to learn such skills. With the creation of her first Children's House, Montessori was eager to try out her methods on some of the poorest inhabitants of the city, the children of Rome's slums. The consequent global spread of schools using the Montessori method was testament to its success and to its credibility as an education programme. Montessori's vision of the child as capable and self-educating, given the right resources, was innovative in its time. The expectation that very young children should engage in practical tasks, such as cleaning and helping to prepare meals, had not previously been considered.

The role of the 'directress', as her teachers became known, was critically different to that of the teacher involved in the transmission teaching that typified traditional teaching and learning. In this, she echoed the earlier approach of Pestalozzi (see Chapter 2). Montessori was insistent that the directress should not teach didactically, drawn from her belief that the child, given time, the right self-correcting resources and an enriched environment, would 'discover' for themselves. This was a view that would later be supported by Piaget's psychological theory which introduced a model of the child as a young 'lone scientist', attempting to make sense of the world by trial and error.

If the environment was to act as a teacher, it logically follows that the early years classroom would need careful and detailed preparation by the teacher. Montessori believed that it was important that no elements were distracting or superfluous, that there needed to be order, simplicity and accessibility. This involved innovations that are commonplace in early years settings today, for example the provision of open shelving at child height to enable children to independently access resources. Objects only earned their place on these shelves if they provided sensory interest and stimulation for the child. Child-sized furniture that was so light it could be moved around by a child was another innovation, freeing children from rows of heavy, cumbersome overlarge tables and chairs. Children were grouped in quite narrow age cohorts, birth to three years and three to six years, which Montessori proposed would lead to mutual cooperation and learning. This evokes the concept of the Vygotskian Zone of Proximal Development. Such an environment, Montessori believed, created independent, autonomous, self-regulating, free young individuals, who in collaboration with others like themselves would grow up to create effective democratic societies.

The directress was seen not as the director of the *children*, but as the facilitator of the environment. Her role was to observe and intervene from the periphery (O'Donnell 2013). Only when children showed by their actions and knowledge that they were ready for the next stage or next set of resources would the directress appear by their side to support them. This did not mean the directress's role was a passive one. On the contrary, she was expected to be ever-vigilant, closely observing the child's actions and struggles. If an individual child was having difficulty in using one of her carefully prepared resources, Montessori would expect the directress to adapt the resource or situation to remove any barriers to the child's independent learning. The directress would also be expected to continually adapt the environment in new and exciting ways to facilitate the child's fulfilment of their potential – physically, cognitively, emotionally and spiritually, with growing degrees of complexity. Montessori saw the directress as more the 'interpreter' of the child's inner potential than as the outside controller of the child's behaviour. The directress's principal role was as an unobtrusive, highly focused observer in the classroom as children engaged in self-directed activity, individually or in small groups. This detailed, systematic observation of children results in a unique set of personalised data for each child, which can be used to further adapt the environment for individual needs. Montessori found that this way of working provided an atmosphere of productive calm as children smoothly moved along in their learning, sometimes for long uninterrupted periods of time (Montessori 1964). This was not to deny that the directress would, on occasion, need to deal with disruptive behaviour, but Montessori was insistent that reliance on external punishments or withdrawal of privileges was not the correct way to deal with such a situation. Montessori proposed that 'liberty', by which she meant a child's freedom to act, allowed them to exercise an emerging self-discipline; the child 'advancing indefinitely towards perfect self mastery' (Montessori 1964, p. 86). It was the role of the directress to develop special, trusting and respectful relationships not only between teacher and child but also between child and child within a 'social contract, that helps develop the relationship between freedom and discipline' (Montessori 1964, p. 86).

Structure is clearly shown in the Montessori curriculum. There is a set of lessons with materials for each classroom level and subject area. These are presented in an ordered sequence and a clear emphasis is placed on the need for such structure in Montessori teacher training courses. If a child chooses to wash a table (part of the practical life skills), there are specific steps that must be followed, even down to wiping the table from left to right (a mix of the gross and fine motor skills that will be needed in writing). Some links could be made here to Piaget's concepts of schema development. In an odd mixture of freedom and direction, children can choose freely what to do, who to do it with, for how long, and how many times they repeat an activity. However, this choice is located within precisely planned lessons using highly specific materials. Lillard (2008) proposes that the system of children handling specific objects that is deeply embedded in the Montessori method has been securely researched as an effective method of enhancing learning. Perhaps one of the most generally recognised Montessori resources is the wooden cylinder, colourful and smooth to handle. A set of cylinders of different sizes support the development of early mathematical concepts, of width, height and volume, as a three-year-old focuses on where to place each cylinder in its appropriate slot on a long wooden base. This resource is typical of Montessori's learning resources in that it is self-correcting and so consequently gives children continuous feedback as they engage in investigative play.

In *The Absorbent Mind* (1967) Montessori is very clear about the importance of birth and even pre-birth, ascribing an unconscious ability of cultural absorption to children between birth and three. The skills and knowledge constructed by this process result in the ability of the three-year-old child to think and understand; to use language and to recall memories. Gotek and Gotek (2016) suggest that the esoteric, almost spiritual language Montessori uses in this book could be related to her prolonged stay in India. When talking of the acquisition of language during the period of unconscious absorption, she proposes that 'the child knows to perfection the name of things, he knows the verbs, the adjectives etc. If anyone studies the phenomenon he will find it marvellous to follow the development of language. . . . It is as if he had a particular timetable' (Montessori 1967, p. 5).

Montessori (1967) goes on to express her belief in 'sensitive periods': windows of opportunity which, if not taken, create difficulties for the older child and adult in learning a new skill. The concept of sensitive periods fit into modern 'nature via nurture' theories, particularly in the area of linguistic development, where human neurophysiology gives rise to symbolic language, but a child has to be exposed to adult speech in early childhood to fully develop human linguistic competence.

Montessori also refers to the child becoming 'normalised'. In *The Montessori Method*, this relates to a child being calm, happy and self-disciplined. Montessori proposed that such a state can only be achieved when a child is free to choose, and becomes totally absorbed in a task as a result of their own choice. The experience of this absorption can thence develop the child's potential for internal behaviour management, creating a virtuous circle of learning and emotion regulation.

Montessori insisted that her directresses must develop the ability to undertake close, detailed, non-participant observations of the children in the setting. These create a holistic profile of each child. For Montessori, observation was the skill through which the teacher could turn theory into practice. It is important to remember that focused observation of children was not an activity routinely undertaken by teachers at the beginning of the twentieth century. However, this became embedded in everyday practice through the Montessori method and the practice of psychologist-educators such as Susan Isaacs (see Chapter 9). O'Donnell (2013) claims that Piaget, who had studied the practice of both Montessori and Isaacs, decided to change his research focus to children rather than animals after attending one of Montessori's lectures. However, he was to develop a very different research method, constructing experiments to test the limits of children's knowledge, and using these to propose universal stages of development rather than compiling records on individual children's learning and development.

Relevance to contemporary practice in the twenty-first century

There are currently approximately 20,000 Montessori schools in the world, with 4,500 of these in the USA (North American Montessori Teachers Association 2016) and 700 in the UK (Montessori Media Centre 2016). But Montessori's practice is still not without controversy in the twenty-first century, much of which centres on her reported rejection of fantasy and imaginative play. Based upon her own words, quoted in O'Donnell (2013, p. 124), Montessori clearly did not encourage 'free drawing' by her pupils. She also did not regard fantasy play as a suitable or productive use of children's time (Montessori 2009). However, a body of research undertaken after Montessori's death links the development of problem-solving skills to children's opportunities to be creative (Robinson 2001). Fisher et al. (2011) propose that learning in free play is far more developmentally appropriate for children under seven than the employment of didactic approaches drawn from practices with older children. This is a debate which raises questions about the continuation of classical Montessori practices in the twenty-first century. Montessori's method is a combination of freedom to construct, but within the boundaries and constraints provided by the resources and activities themselves. If there was a hypothetical line between creativity in free play at one extreme and didactic 'transmission' teaching at the other, Montessori's method would sit in the middle.

Montessori's theories linking movement to brain development (Montessori 1967) are now beginning to accord with the findings of neuroscience which suggests a much firmer link between hand movements and neuronal growth than was previously thought, particularly in the area of language development (Iverson 2010, Isaacs 2012). Her kinaesthetic approach, involving the use of practical tasks, and the tactile resources she designed (sandpaper letters and numbers or the child polishing a table from left to right) have the potential to promote neuronal connections. The idea that a child should be encouraged to develop self-discipline is becoming more embedded within positive behaviour policies used in many contemporary early years settings. Montessori's insistence on the need to give children ample time and to allow them to engage in repeated behaviours clearly links with the model of schema theory presented by Cathy Nutbrown in 1994 in her well-known book *Threads of Thinking*. It also has parallels with the Reggio Emilia approach (see Chapter 10).

We come back, however, to the distinction that Montessori makes between 'work' and 'play', and as ever with the pioneers, to consider her statements in the light of the cultural context in which they were made. The unchecked free play of the slum children in Rome had led to vandalism and anarchic behaviour, with all the potential dangers of children running wild in slum clearances. In the first Casa dei Bambini, Montessori knew she needed to establish some rules, order and a place of safety and the children responded positively when they realised that the core goal of the adult was to address their individual needs. Montessori was careful to introduce simple practical tasks before more complex activities, mindful that one of the most important facilitators of a child's learning is their sense of self-confidence in their own problem-solving abilities. This perspective also underpins Montessori's auto-didactic materials, designed to enable children to self-correct/problem solve in their own time until they are successful. It is clear that Montessori embedded the requirement to ensure that the child is supported to feel secure, happy and confident within the learning environment. She also believed that each child should feel they had contributed something to the environment of the Casa dei Bambini. The insistence on quiet surroundings and 'gracious' movement provided another tempering of the environment from which the slum children came, providing order out of chaos.

English Montessori practitioners point to the parallels between the Montessori approach and some of the main themes of the early years foundation stage (EYFS) (DFE 2014): the recognition of the unique child concept, the need for positive relationships and the ongoing development and resourcing of enabling environments, all of which fit within the Montessori approach. The famed ability of her method to enable children as young as three and four to read and write again fits with contemporary views on promoting readiness for formal schooling; however, this is more controversial. There is clearly some similarity between Montessori's controlled resources and modern target-led planning, which leads to increasing levels of adult-led practice. With conscientious application, young children may certainly be trained to 'perform'; the question is whether it is beneficial to shallowly programme them in this way during a period in which the young brain is so plastic. The other pioneers in this book would all have seen something rather problematic in this facet of Montessori's pedagogy, albeit from different perspectives and to different degrees. However, Montessori's method demands its 'directresses' to demonstrate a love and respect for all the young children in their care along with a tremendous dedication to the individual needs of each child, and the value of these elements of her 'scientific method' is not in doubt. There is also no doubt that former Montessori pupils have gone on to be highly original trailblazers in adult life, for example Larry Page and Serg Brin, co-founders of Google, and Jeff Bezos, the founder of Amazon. Montessori will always have her critics, but the fact that she is still causing controversy some seventy-four years after her death demonstrates her continuing importance as a pioneer of early years education.

Student integration tasks

- Consider this chapter alongside those on Froebel, Steiner and Malaguzzi, focusing upon the function of the child's environment in each. What are the similarities and differences, and which elements of each are reflected in the English early years foundation stage 'enabling environments' concept today? (See http://www.optimus-education.com/sites/optimus-education.com/files/attachments/articles/environment_3-5_yr_olds.pdf.)

- Within the Montessori method there is a particular view of how children learn and develop; to what extent is this view still relevant to our twenty-first century understanding of the child?

- Montessori held very firm convictions regarding the role of the educator. How do her views compare with teachers in the Reggio Emilia framework?

- To what extent does Montessori's method to promote early reading and writing 'fit' with current theories of cognitive and neuronal development in young children?

References

American Montessori Society (2016) The Glass Classroom. http://amshq.org/Montessori-Education/History-of-Montessori-Education/the_glass_classroom (Accessed 11 November 2015).

Ball, L. (2010) *Psychology's Feminist Voices.* http://www.feministvoices.com/about/ (Accessed 3 November 2015).

Barres, V. (2004) Maria Montessori and UNESCO. http://montessoricentenary.org/srunescoarticle.htm (Accessed 23 February 2016).

Bruner, J. S. (1966) *Toward a Theory of Instruction.* Cambridge, MA: Belknap Press.

DFE (2014) Early Years Foundation Stage. London: DFE. https://www.gov.uk/government/uploads/system/uploads/attachment_data/file/335504/EYFS_framework_from_1_September_2014__with_clarification_note.pdf (Accessed 24 February 2016).

Fisher, K., Hirsh-Pasek, K., Golinkoff, R. M., Singer, D. and Berk, L. E. (2011). Playing Around in School: Implications for Learning and Educational Policy. In A. Pellegrini (Ed.), *The Oxford Handbook of Play.* New York: Oxford University Press, 341–363.

Frank, A. (1947) *The Diary of Anne Frank*; English translation edn 1954. London: Pan.

Gardner, R. (2012) The Maria Montessori No One Knows: A Heartbreaking Betrayal. http://www.clanmore.ca/2012/08/31/the-maria-montessori-no-one-knows-a-heartbreaking-betrayal-part-1-of-2/ (Accessed 24 February 2016).

Gardner, R. (1970) The Maria Montessori No One Knows: Enemy Alien in India. http://www.ourkids.net/school/the-maria-montessori-no-one-knows-language (Accessed 24 February 2016).

Gutek, G. and Gutek, P. (2016) *Bringing Montessori to America.* Tuscaloosa, AL: University of Alabama Press.

Henny-Montessori, M. (2016) Mario Montessori. http://ami-global.org/montessori/mario-montessori (Accessed 23 February 2016).

Indian Montessori Centre (2011) Mario Montessori. http://www.indianmontessoricentre.org/mario-montessori-sr (Accessed 22 February 2016).

Issacs, B. (2012) *Understanding the Montessori Approach: Early Years Education in Practice.* Abingdon: Routledge.

Iverson, J. (2010) Developing Language in a Developing Body: The Relationship Between Motor Development and Language Development. *Journal of Child Language* 37 (2), 229–261. http://www.ncbi.nlm.nih.gov/pmc/articles/PMC2833284/ (Accessed 24 February 2016). doi: 10.1017/S0305000909990432.

Kilpatrick, W. H. (1914) The Montessori System Examined. https://archive.org/stream/montessorisystem00kilprich/montessorisystem00kilprich_djvu.txt (Accessed 23 February 2016).

Kramer, R. (1988) *Maria Montessori: A Biography.* Chicago: University of Chicago Press.

Lillard, A. S. (2008) *Montessori: The Science Behind the Genius.* Oxford: Oxford University Press.

Lillard, A. S. (2013) Playful Learning and Montessori Education. *American Journal of Play* 5 (2), 157–186.

Montessori, M. (1912) *The Montessori Method: Scientific Pedagogy as Applied to Child Education in the Children's Houses.* New York: Stokes and Co.

Montessori, M. (1967) *The Absorbent Mind.* New York: Delta.

Montessori, M. (1964) *The Montessori Method.* New York: Schocken Books.

Montessori Media Centre (2016) MSA & Schools. http://www.montessori.org.uk/msa (Accessed 24 February 2016).

Moretti, E. (2011) Recasting Il Metodo: Maria Montessori and Early Childhood Education in Italy. *Cromohs* 16, 1–19 http://www.cromohs.unifi.it/16_2011/moretti_montessori.ht (Accessed 3 November 2015).

North American Montessori Teachers Association (2016) How Many Montessori Schools Are There? http://www.montessori-namta.org/FAQ/Montessori-Education/How-many-Montessori-schools-are-there (Accessed 24 February 2016).

Nutbrown, C. (1994) *Threads of Thinking.* London: Sage.

O'Donnell, M. (2013) *Maria Montessori: A Critical Introduction to Key Themes and Debates.* London: Bloomsbury.

Rambush, N. (1977) The American Montessori Experience. *American Montessori Society Bulletin* 5 (2), 1–27.

Robinson, K. (2001) *Out of Our Minds: Learning to be Creative.* Oxford: Capstone Publishing.

Shannon Helfrich, M. (2011) *Montessori Learning in the 21st Century.* Troutdale: New Sage Press.

Standing, E. M. (1984) *Maria Montessori: Her Life and Work.* New York: Plume.

UNESCO (2016) Introducing UNESCO. http://en.unesco.org/about-us/introducing-unesco (Accessed 23 February 2016).

Wylie, W. (2008) Montessori and the Theosophical Society. *Quest* 96.2 (March–April 2008), pp. 53–55.

Susan Isaacs (1885–1948)

A message in a bottle

Pam Jarvis

Introduction

This chapter will focus on the mid-twentieth-century psychoanalyst and educator Susan Isaacs (1885–1948). She will be rather unconventionally referred to as 'Susan' throughout to aid clarity, as she operated under three different surnames at different times of her life, her maiden name Fairhurst, and the names of her first and second husbands, Brierley and Isaacs respectively. The chapter will track the formation of Susan's theoretical position, investigating the complexity of its roots in the theory of Sigmund Freud, Susan's alliance with the Freudian apostate, Melanie Klein and the tendrils that connect Kleinian theory with early feminism. Although this led to Susan becoming quite deeply involved in the dramatic schisms that fragmented Freudian theory, she nevertheless managed to bring some amount of order to her own conceptualisation of psychoanalysis. This gave some underpinning to her creation of a more comprehensively theorised, mature concept of the process of 'educare', initially piloted by Margaret McMillan (see Chapter 7). Susan not only managed to root this concept more firmly in research through her practice of naturalistic child observation, she was also able to apply theory, drawn from one of the most prestigious psychological paradigms of the era, to everyday practice in the early years setting. Whitbread (1972, p. 70) proposes that Susan Isaacs extended 'the theoretical basis of nursery education beyond the point reached by Margaret McMillan'. Susan was also a talented author, whose production of exceptionally clear texts permitted her to communicate her ideas of theory-informed practice to a wide audience which included academics, teachers, nannies and parents. Like Margaret McMillan, Susan developed her theories of practice in one particular setting, The Malting House School, and the chapter will explore the somewhat controversial history of this experimental nursery. It will focus on the following concepts:

- early life and education: a troubled childhood;
- the psychoanalytic connection: the underpinning theory;

- the Malting House School: the practical demonstration;
- writing, academia and legacy: a message to the twenty-first century.

Early life and education: a troubled childhood?

Susan Isaacs attained qualifications as both a school teacher and a psychoanalyst. She was born Susan Sutherland Fairhurst on 24 May 1885, and lived with her family in Bolton, Lancashire until she was twenty-three years old. Bolton was a northern manufacturing town on the west side of the Pennines, not dissimilar to the neighbouring town of Bradford, to the east. Bradford was of course the city in which Margaret McMillan carried out her initial 'educare' experiments (see Chapter 7), during the period in which Susan was at primary school. Unfortunately, Susan and her peers did not have the benefit of such a fiery advocate on the board that governed the state primary school they attended, and records indicate that during this stage of her life, she received quite a poor education; this makes her eventual achievements even more remarkable. Graham (2009) speculates that Susan may have been a victim of the Victorian 'payment by results' system of education, which instigated a vicious circle by depriving schools with poor results of funds, thus further depressing the teachers' pay and making it less likely that the school could attract competent staff. This system unfortunately endured for three and a half decades from its inception in 1862, a 'narrow, restrictive system of educational accountability' (Glass 1994, p. 1).

Susan's family were from the financially secure Victorian middle class, although her parents originated from working-class stock. Her mother was a painter and decorator's daughter and her father, William, started his working life in a saddlery firm before teaching himself shorthand to enter journalism. By the time of Susan's birth, he was a sub-editor on the *Bolton Evening News* with a specialism in sports reporting. The family lived in a large, comfortable house in Bolton, but perhaps because William Fairhurst had achieved so much despite his working-class origins, added to the narrow gender constructions of the era, he saw no problems inherent in the lacklustre education his daughters received at the local state school. Birch (2008, p. 78) proposed that 'education is a political process . . . and this is sharply true of its consequences for women'. Susan would have found this to be a highly salient insight at many points within her educational and professional experience.

Susan was the seventh and penultimate child in the Fairhurst family. William Fairhurst was an enthusiastic Methodist, and a lay preacher. He had a keen interest in literature, art and music, and the house was full of books, which the Fairhurst children (the three oldest boys and the four youngest girls) grew up to read and discuss enthusiastically. When Susan was four, her mother became ill, following the birth of the youngest Fairhurst sister, Alice. Mrs Fairhurst remained an invalid for two years, probably suffering from septic arthritis, and died when Susan was six. Graham (2009, p. 14) suggests that there is evidence that Susan thereafter 'idealised' her mother. After eighteen months had passed, William Fairhurst married the housekeeper he had engaged shortly after his wife became ill. This was not to the liking of Susan and Alice, and they were frequently in trouble with their father and stepmother.

Susan passed the exam to enter secondary school at twelve (the equivalent of a contemporary English grammar school); at around the same time, Bessie, one of her older sisters, won a scholarship to a teacher training college. While Susan was allowed to attend secondary school, William Fairhurst did not allow his older daughter to take up her scholarship, as he felt it was inappropriate for girls to receive a college education. When Susan declared she was an atheist at fourteen, following a similar declaration by one of her older brothers, her father made her leave the secondary school because 'if education makes women godless they are better at home' (Graham 2009, p. 22). It was not unusual for children to leave school at fourteen during this time (education was compulsory until only twelve years of age); however, Susan remembered being an angry adolescent from this point onwards. So, like Maria Montessori (see Chapter 8), Susan experienced opposition to advancing her education from a strict, overbearing father, but unlike Montessori, she was unable to access support from a liberal mother to overcome such a barrier.

At eighteen, she was finally allowed the freedom to travel to Morocco to be a governess to an English family living in Casablanca, which she enjoyed. When she returned to England she found work as a teacher at Heaton Village Club School in a deprived area of Bradford. By this time, William Fairhurst had allowed Alice to attend teacher training college, and he subsequently allowed Susan to enrol at Manchester University in 1908 to train as an infant teacher; a two-year, sub-degree course. This brought her into contact with Grace Owen (1873–1965) who became the first Honorary Secretary to the Nursery School Association (NSA); a national leader in the field of early years education.

Owen is described as 'a pivotal figure . . . [who] also played a key role in designing the NSA's "suggested scheme of training" for teachers' (New and Cochran 2007, pp. 576–577). Owen had trained in Froebelian methods at the Blackheath Kindergarten Training College in London, later taking a degree at the University of Columbia in the US, graduating in 1905. On her return to England, she joined the staff of the University of Manchester (Jarvis and Liebovich 2015). So, at the age of twenty-three, Susan entered one of the most prestigious teacher training programmes in the country, opening the door to opportunities she had been denied in her previously restricted education.

She quickly became quite a favourite with Owen, who encouraged her to apply for a full degree course. To Susan's surprise, her father agreed, principally because, on the basis of Owen's recommendation, John Joseph Findlay, one of the nation's leading educational scholars, wrote to him to request Susan's admission to the course. Susan was given a small grant, which was then unexpectedly supplemented by a legacy that she received following her father's death in 1909. At the end of this academic year, she received an award for most outstanding woman student. The evidence suggests that she was probably the most outstanding student in the group, male or female (Graham 2009). She joined the Fabian and Sociological societies and became renowned for her feminist views. She invited Margaret McMillan, fellow suffragist and professional associate of Grace Owen, to speak to the Manchester University Sociological Society. In June 1912, Susan was awarded a first-class degree in philosophy.

Susan then transferred to Cambridge to study for a PhD with Charles Myers, an anthropologist and psychologist. They agreed that her thesis would focus upon the development of spelling ability in children, in particular the function of visual and auditory memory. She eventually published a paper on this topic in 1918; however, she discontinued her PhD studies in 1913. Graham (2009) suggests that Susan was not happy at Cambridge, and became short of money when she did not receive a fellowship at the end of her first year. It is unclear whether she ever applied for this, however. Susan was subsequently employed as head of teacher training at Darlington College.

In 1914, Susan married her first husband, William Brierley, who had been a fellow student in Manchester. Britain entered World War I three weeks after their marriage and Brierley joined the army. He was invalided out in 1916, and eventually returned to his job as a research scientist, studying fungi at Kew Gardens. Susan had left her job to get married, as was the custom at the time, and she now found herself in London. The concept of a married woman seeking paid work became less unusual due to the absence of men during the war, and she soon became a part-time lecturer in psychology, teaching adults at the University of London and the Workers Educational Association. She also wrote up the results of her spelling research during this time, bringing her into contact with others who had credentials in psychology. She separated from Brierley in 1918, the reasons for which are not entirely clear, and in 1919, possibly as a reaction to this separation, she sought psychoanalytic treatment.

The psychoanalytic connection: the underpinning theory

In 1919, Susan began psychoanalytic treatment in London, and became so interested in the process she went to Vienna for three months in 1920 to continue her analysis with Otto Rank, one of Sigmund Freud's associates. The process of psychoanalysis was becoming popular with the European middle classes at this time. The treatment works by exploring early relationships with parents. This then implies that it may not just have been the failure of Susan's marriage that led her along this pathway; she may have also felt that she had unresolved issues stemming from the early death of her mother and the subsequent difficulties in her relationship with her father and stepmother.

Psychoanalysis is still a specialist branch of psychology today, but it does not hold such a central position within the discipline as it did in the first three decades of the twentieth century. The key issue is that although Sigmund Freud's concepts tend to appeal to human emotional sense, there is no scientific evidence that our minds are in fact organised in the fashion that he suggested, and those who work in increasingly biologically informed twenty-first-century psychological research tend to be uneasy with such an inconsistency. Psychoanalysis is, however, rooted in carefully listening to the patient's account of their feelings, a premise that Susan would later introduce into early years education, which Graham (2009) comments was one of her most important contributions to the profession. Rather more problematically, however, psychoanalysis additionally requires that the analyst constructs their own analyses of the issues underlying 'neurotic' behaviour and emotions which, Graham suggests, led Susan to some 'outlandish' interpretations of the data she collected (p. 326).

Susan already had credentials in psychology from her degree in education and her PhD studies. To become a psychoanalyst, one first has to undergo psychoanalysis. The British Psychoanalytical Society was satisfied that Susan's own psychoanalysis record supported her admission as a full member by December 1921. Susan published a text book entitled *Introduction to Psychology* in 1921 (as Susan Brierley), which introduced Freudian theory as an extension of biology. This was not an unusual orientation at the time, but it would be very heavily frowned upon by twenty-first-century psychology.

Classical psychoanalysis is based upon Sigmund Freud's theory that children move through a set of 'psychosexual' stages to full emotional competence. Freud believed that people were born with an internal energy he called libido, which was focused upon different behaviours over the course of development, finally ending up as the energy behind the adult sex drive. Before this happens, however, the libido underpins the energy that babies between birth and eighteen months focus upon feeding (the oral stage), then upon controlling their bladder and bowels (or choosing not to) between the age of eighteen months and approximately three years, the typical age of toilet training in western society (the anal stage). Classical Freudian theory suggests that children under three are dominated by unchecked libido, which drives them to seek out immediate gratification for their basic needs, principally focused upon nutrition, comfort and company. He proposed that this libido lives on inside the adult, naming it 'the id', the part of the personality that drives us to seek satisfaction for our wants and needs. Another entity he named 'the ego' develops in parallel with the child's growing understanding of the concrete world of inanimate objects; the ego provides our understanding that some of our wants are ultimately unobtainable (for example, a desire to grow wings and fly like a bird).

Once toilet training is completed, Freud believed that the child developed a romantic fixation upon the parent of the opposite sex, resulting in a jealousy of the parent of the same sex, combined with a wish to replace him/her. Freud's theories were relentlessly male oriented; this being so, he called this fixation 'the Oedipus Complex' after an ancient Greek legend about a man who fell in love with his mother, and killed his father. The child moves through this stage over the next two to four years, and by so doing, psychologically internalises the parent of the same sex by striving to become him/her. Again, with a male orientation, Freud named this period of development 'the phallic stage'.

The Freudian position is that we internalise both gender-appropriate behaviour and all the values and morals of our same-sex parent by striving to be him/her; thence an 'inner parent' (which Freud called 'the superego') emerges into our psyche from this experience, which remains with us for the rest of our lives, allowing us to 'police' ourselves by the instigation of guilt for moral lapses. Freud also claimed that there were major differences between the consciences of men and women, because boys internalised the disciplinary aspect of the father's role, so moral lapses could induce real fear, rather than only a concern relating to disapproval and withdrawal of affection. He also proposed that girls suffer from something called 'penis envy' during the phallic stage; however, this is one of the most contentious parts of his theory and has been called both misguided and sexist. Karen Horney, a mid-twentieth-century Freudian theorist, commented that it is not the penis that girls envy, but the social advantages that are given to the male (Feminist Voices 2015).

Children resolve the Oedipus Complex by eventual acceptance that they can never become the same-sex parent, reluctantly letting the opposite-sex parent 'go'; the first romantic disappointment. Once this resolution is reached, the seeds of the adult personality have become embedded in the psyche. Psychoanalysis therefore involves an in-depth investigation of the way that the patient was parented before the age of seven, with a view to the analyst 're-parenting' in problematic areas. It is not hard to intuit the issues that might have been raised in Susan's analysis, given that she was six when her mother died. In the psychoanalytic frame, overwhelming guilt may have followed the 'granting' of the unconscious wish to be rid of the mother, and a devastating rejection experienced when the father married another woman not long afterwards.

Classical Freudianism sees the adult as having three parts to the personality – the id, which drives us to seek out gratification, the superego which stops us behaving in an immoral fashion, and the ego, which negotiates between both entities and keeps the personality 'whole'. The issue that arises in neurosis is an unequal balance between id and superego urges, which can result in an over-stressed ego. For example, the ego will be constantly under attack from the id if the superego is too weak to support the ego to check unreasonable and immoral demands; but if the superego demands over-suppression of the id, the id will become 'squashed', and the person will become consumed with guilt and resentment.

As she emerged from her own psychoanalysis, Susan became attracted to the theories of neo-Freudian Melanie Klein, who was advocating 'a very different psychoanalysis, one increasingly focused on the mother' (Zaretsky 2004, p. 249). Born in Austria in 1882, Klein arrived in London in 1926, and remained there until her death in 1960. She became a leading member of the British Psychoanalytical Society, taking the position that very young children were not as psychologically unsophisticated as Freud had proposed. She posited that children were quite capable of feeling the full range of emotions that adults felt, but that their lack of understanding of the world led them to see their environment as a series of part-objects, for example the breast of the mother that feeds them as being completely separate from the arms that comfort them. This she called 'the paranoid position' in which feelings were experienced as fragmentary and discontinuous, leaving the child to feel that they have no control over their emotional experiences. To achieve psychological integration, Klein proposed, children needed to enter the 'depressive position'; to integrate whole objects and understand that other people, the mother in particular, are separate and potentially subject to the self, that they can also be hurt and rejected. She believed that children's complex inner psychology could be analysed through their play activities, which allowed analysis to occur before an individual reached an age at which they could verbally introspect on internal feelings and thereby engage in the classical Freudian 'talking therapy'.

Klein thus 'emphasis(ed) the social over the individual, the external over the internal' (Zaretsky 2004, p. 253). Moreover, the mother rather than the father becomes central to psychological development, given that psychological separation from the mother has to be achieved to reach the depressive position. At this point, the person accepts responsibility for the 'separate' self, in particular the distress that we are able to cause to others, who they now realise are separate from the self; they now have an effective grasp of what Klein termed 'object relations'. Zaretsky (2004, p. 253) comments that female analysts attracted to this version of psychoanalytic theory consequently 'had a strong emphasis on early childhood . . . the reorientation to the mother'. For Freud, then, the relationship with the father's authority sits at the heart of the superego, but for Klein, this is replaced by the way we orient to the love of the mother. In the Freudian world-picture, the individual seeks control and autonomy through the ability to manage one's own morally acceptable behaviour, 'finding one's place in the world' (Zaretsky 2004, p. 259); for Klein, individuals are 'dominated by responsibility to others' (Zaretsky 2004, p. 259). Freud focused on strengthening the ego to avoid it becoming battered between the demands of the id and the superego, shoring up its ability to become logical and impersonal from the basis of a secure grasp of culturally imposed moral imperatives; Klein insisted that people could have 'no independent or impersonal viewpoint' (Zaretsky 2004, p. 236); that their decisions would always be driven by their obligations to others.

Similar gender debates were to rise again in psychology a century later from different theoretical orientations; writing from the position of evolutionary psychology, Jarvis (2006, p. 335) described gendered play in children aged four to six: 'girls creating imaginary narratives where good relationships are maintained, compared to the male-generated scenarios in which boys explored status and dominance'. Feminist psychologist Carol Gilligan had previously argued that the genders approach moral decisions differently, with women putting more emphasis on caring, going on to propose that women of all cultures are more inclined than men to consider the motivations and circumstances of others before making judgements about other people's behaviour (1993). This is further supported by Marder's (1987) review of empirical courtroom-based research which found male jurors to be 'verdict driven', and female jurors to be 'evidence driven'; that women were more likely than men to carefully consider different points of view contributed by different members of the jury, in particular why the defendant may have behaved in the way they did, before coming to a decision on guilt or innocence.

The differences between classical Freudian and Kleinian psychoanalytical theory were never fully resolved, and this created a schism within psychoanalysis, under which a fire was ignited when the Freudian contingent arrived in London in the mid-1930s, fleeing Nazi-occupied Vienna. By this time, Sigmund Freud was in the last stages of his final illness, dying in 1939, but his daughter Anna Freud, who specialised in work with children from the premise of classic Freudian theory, engaged in a pitched battle with Melanie Klein within the British Psychoanalytical Society. Susan was at root a Kleinian – it is easy to understand how as a feminist who had lost her mother in early childhood she oriented to this position – but nevertheless, she attempted to bridge the gap between the two sides, which is demonstrated in her article 'The Nature and Function of Phantasy' (Isaacs 1948). However, most importantly for early years practice, Susan had thoroughly absorbed the Kleinian principle that children's emotions could be analysed through the careful observation of their play activities, and it was this impetus that led to her next major project.

The Malting House School: the practical demonstration

Susan remarried in 1922, to a man ten years younger than herself, who she met through her Workers Educational Association teaching. Nathan Isaacs came from a Russian-Polish background, and had arrived in England in 1907 at the age of twelve. His family were Jewish, and emigrated to escape the persecution that Jews experienced in central Europe at this time. Nathan had followed a similar path to William Fairhurst, through the recognition of his potential in the world of work, despite having very little formal education. When he enrolled for Susan's class, he was a manager in a company trading in metals. He spoke English, French and Spanish fluently, and had some competence in Hebrew and Italian. In his spare time he enjoyed reading psychology and philosophy, and the economist Lionel Robbins described him as 'an intellectual' (Graham 2009, p. 76) despite the fact he never attended university. John Rickman wrote of Susan and Nathan that 'the movement of their minds was in such close touch it seemed as if a single figure moved in the intellectual scene' (Graham 2009, p. 77). They also shared a commitment to atheism, despite both having been raised in devoutly religious families, Susan's Methodist and Nathan's Jewish.

Nathan's influence can be seen in two papers that Susan published around this time, focusing upon the incompatibility of human psychology with the processes of industry. In one she comments that people 'have rarely considered whether the new world of great factories in crowded cities was really satisfactory to human beings . . . fitting the human being to the machine and neglecting the needs of human nature in industry' (Graham 2009, pp. 84–85). She questioned whether people could be both 'docile and externally controlled' and 'free, intelligent and responsible' (Graham 2009, p. 86). Her interests remained principally within child development, however, and in 1923 she published a paper discussing differences between girls and boys in sexual development (Brierley 1923).

In 1924, Susan answered an advertisement for a young woman with a first-class honours degree to head a small school for children aged two and a half to seven, both to lead the delivery of education and to undertake research on the provision. It had been placed by ex-public schoolboy, war hero and entrepreneur Geoffrey Pyke, who sought an education for his three-year-old son that would be 'free from trauma and repression' (Graham 2009, p. 98). It turned out that Pyke had a keen interest in psychoanalysis and he and Susan had an acquaintance in common, James Glover, who was a member of the British Psychoanalytic Society. Glover arranged a meeting with Pyke, which was attended by both Susan and Nathan. At this time, it was unusual for English middle-class children to start school before they were six or seven, but once they entered mid-childhood they were typically sent, sometimes as boarders, to strict preparatory schools which operated regimes of rote learning and corporal punishment.

Mainstream Freudian psychology eschewed corporal punishment; however, Melanie Klein went further, advocating highly permissive practices, both within the school and the home. She believed that psychoanalysis should be the theory at the root of all educational practices and that female psychoanalysts should be in charge of education within the kindergarten environment. Susan was in agreement, and relished the opportunity to 'observe what children do under free conditions' (Graham 2009, p. 106). Pyke believed that the way British children were schooled squashed curiosity, and that teachers should be co-investigators rather than dictators.

Pyke and the Isaacs agreed employment terms, after which Pyke rented the Malting House in Cambridge as the site for the school. He moved into it with his wife and son. The other rooms were converted for the school, but it contained no classrooms. There were reading and writing rooms for older and younger children, but most of the activity took place in a carpentry room/laboratory, a kitchen and an art room. There was a large garden with a water tap, a summerhouse, a see-saw (with movable weights), boards, ladders and a jungle gym. There were also many pet animals; mice, rabbits, guinea pigs, hens, chickens, snakes, salamanders, a wormery, an aquarium, two cats and a dog. The school opened in October 1924 with ten boys from two years eight months to four years ten months (Graham 2009, p. 110).

There were never more than twenty children in the school, the oldest within the three years that it remained open being eight years six months. There were a few girls admitted over this time, but they were always outnumbered at least four to one by boys. The Malting House children were principally from academic, middle-class families, many of whom were connected to Cambridge University. Some were quite academically gifted, and when the cohort's IQs were tested, they were found on average to be within the top 5 per cent. Many of the Malting House children were, however, difficult and aggressive. Some modern writers (e.g., Graham 2009) have suggested that a high proportion of the children may have had high-functioning autism syndrome disorders, although this is impossible to investigate further, as the condition was not recognised in the 1920s.

Graham (2009, pp. 113–114) states that the Malting House School was very different from other schools because 'there were no lessons . . . there was an emphasis on activity undertaken spontaneously'. This led to some amount of independent learning; for example, Susan helped but did not instruct the children to put together a map of Cambridge in response to some questions that they posed. Each child had his/her own small allotment in the garden and was allowed to freely experiment with it to discover how to best care for plants. For example, if plants were not watered, the children found out that they would die; the adults did not step in to prevent this. Susan also tried to ensure that the children's reading and writing emerged from 'real-life' applications such as lists and menus; there were no formal literacy lessons.

There were also no formal rules, although adults would physically remove children creating danger to themselves or others. The children were also supposed to order the food they wanted and to contribute to the preparation of meals, which did not always work out well (Graham 2009, p. 116). The lack of formal discipline led to controversy, even amongst Susan's fellow psychoanalysts, who were concerned that there was unchecked aggression and bullying occurring within the school. After a visit during which Melanie Klein herself passed the opinion that Susan should be more proactive in checking the children's verbal aggression (Graham 2009, p. 120), Susan exerted more control over the children's behaviour, particularly towards each other. She later reflected 'in the first few days of the school . . . I was far too passive in my treatment of cruelty and bullying' (Isaacs 1933, p. 422).

The reports of experiences at the school that the children gave in later life were mixed. Some reported enjoying their time at the school, while others felt that they had been very distressed by some of the events that occurred due to the permissive regime, and that the adults had not picked up on these. One who was later given the observation notes that Susan had compiled on him complained that she clearly lacked any insight into his unhappiness. He reported that as an adult, he had been medically treated for depression (Graham 2009, p. 122). A film was made of life at the school that led to a glowing report appearing in *The Spectator* magazine. The producer of the film was, however, more ambivalent, later commenting that the extent of the children's freedom was problematic, giving an example of a bonfire started by the children that spread to the trees in the garden – which had not been recorded on film (Graham, p. 129).

Jean Piaget, the creator of the first and most comprehensive theory of human cognitive development, visited the school in March 1927 and was generally impressed with its regime, particularly Susan's meticulous observations. Susan and Piaget reviewed one another's research and generally produced complimentary reports, although they differed on some points. In *The Intellectual Growth of Young Children* (Isaacs 1930) Susan commented that Piaget was over-pessimistic about what children were able to do due to the experimental method he used to carry out his research, and that her naturalistic observation method was superior. This was a point that would much later be more powerfully made by experimental psychologist Margaret Donaldson in her now classic critique of Piaget's theory, *Children's Minds* (1978). Susan also made the point that cognitive development cannot be as neatly divided into stages as Piaget suggested, another point that was to be more effectively and empirically demonstrated by Donaldson and her associates forty-eight years later. Piaget answered Susan's criticism by proposing that they focused on different aspects of development – while he was interested in the limits of children's competence, Susan's observations focused upon how children acquired knowledge. What they shared, he suggested, was the conviction that children learn by doing rather than by being 'told' (Graham 2009, p. 163).

The Malting House School experiment was curtailed by the sudden failure of all of Geoffrey Pyke's business interests, in mid-1927. The Isaacs left Cambridge and returned to London, where Nathan was swiftly re-employed as a manager in the metals trading industry, and Susan focused on writing up the observations she had carried out in the Malting House School, which were to form the basis for her two most famous academic books, *The Intellectual Growth of Young Children* (1930) and *Social Development in Young Children* (1933). Susan's biographer, Philip Graham, comments: 'an experiment . . . that only lasted five years . . . and that had never involved more than twenty most unusual children at any one time made an impact far greater than Susan Isaacs herself can have expected' (Graham 2009, p. 141). He further suggests that Susan took some time to recover from the failure of the Malting House, and that there is some evidence to suggest that she had become romantically involved with Geoffrey Pyke during her time at the school. There was also far more conclusive evidence, in the form of correspondence, that by the time the Isaacs arrived back in London Nathan had become involved in a long-term affair with one of Susan's colleagues, Evelyn Lawrence, and that Susan was fully aware of this (Graham 2009). The Isaacs marriage did not dissolve, however, and Susan turned her attention back to psychoanalysis, receiving her licence to practise as a psychoanalyst in 1933.

Writing, academia and legacy: a message to the twenty-first century

The failure of the Malting House School had left the Isaacs somewhat short of funds, inspiring Susan to write a mainstream book for mothers and nannies, providing easily accessible child development advice. In 1929, she published *The Nursery Years*, which became a classic 'kitchen shelf' parental advisory book, remaining in print until 1971. She had a great talent for presenting complex ideas in very clear prose, and effectively crafting her communication for a particular audience; she had previously honed this skill in her academic writing, and now she demonstrated that she was able to speak just as clearly to a lay audience. For example, she advises 'there could not be a more cruel or a more stupid thing said to little children than "don't touch". It simply means "don't learn, don't grow, don't be intelligent"'

(p. 73) and 'we have to be ready to share [the child's] interests . . . and not to feel his questions and his efforts . . . [are] just an interference with our serious pursuits' (p. 78). She also advocates 'patient friendliness and steady love' (p. 83). She clearly outlines the open-ended play materials with which she resourced the Malting House, and concludes her book with a very clear list of 'dos and don'ts' for child-care. She also disseminates some highly complex psychoanalytic concepts in an accessible fashion, advising parents that very young children have to learn how to comprehend their mother as a person 'not just as a breast to feed him and arms to serve him' (p. 81). Writing for a more academic audience in *Social Development in Young Children*, she makes similar points: 'if we try to cramp and control [the child] with our own notions of what he ought to do we may close up the very channels which bring him value and safety' (p. 427). She also emphasises the fundamental relevance of theory to practice, quite a novel message for an academic book to trans-mit at that time: 'psychological fact . . . has to be translated into *usable* educational theory (1933, p. 415, italics in original).

In the same year *The Nursery Years* was published, Susan was invited to write a column in *The Nursery World* magazine, which was aimed at mothers and nan-nies. In this, she answered problems submitted by readers under the pen name of 'Ursula Wise'. Some of the problems she dealt with in this column were subse-quently used as case examples in *Social Development in Young Children*. This was well-paid work, which brought in quite a significant salary for the time, around £300 a year (Graham 2009, p. 208). *The Nursery Years* was subsequently published in the US, and in 1937 Susan won the US *Parents' Magazine* award for the best advi-sory book for parents.

Susan was still a committed psychoanalyst, and regularly gave public lectures on this topic. Her psychoanalytic approach to the analysis of her observations in *Social Development in Young Children* led to some quite critical reviews (Graham 2009, p. 236). However, in May 1933, she became the part-time head of a new depart-ment of child development at the Institute of Education (IOE), a division of the University of London – which was allocated just one room within the building! Despite undergoing the first of several regimes of treatment for breast cancer in 1935 which included surgery and radiation treatment, she managed to visit the US, Australia and New Zealand in 1937 to meet child development experts in these nations, and to give a programme of lectures.

When war broke out in 1939, Susan moved to Cambridge and subsequently worked on a study of evacuated children, which became known as 'The Cambridge Evacuation Study'. This discovered that the separation from fam-ily had caused great trauma to children, far more than had been expected by those who had advocated the mass evacuation programme at the beginning of World War II. Susan commented strongly in the study write-up upon the advisability of keeping families together whenever and wherever possible. The report was studied by the young John Bowlby who would go on to conduct his own research project in the early post-war period, focusing upon children who had been separated from their mothers through the wartime evacuation programme. His seminal theory of human attachment underpinned the United Nations Declaration of the Rights of the Child in 1959, and still informs theories of emotional development in the early twenty-first century. We are currently discovering neuronal evidence providing strong support for Bowlby's insistence that separation from principal carers causes enduring damage to children's emotional functioning (Jarvis and George 2016). This is just one powerful reason to include Susan Isaacs in a book that outlines the work and influence of the most prominent early years pioneers.

Bowlby reported finding that Isaacs was very interested in his early work, even though Melanie Klein had been dismissive of his theories (Graham 2009, p. 262). Bowlby's theories mixed ethology and anthropology with Freudianism, which appeared not to be to Klein's liking. Although she had, in her time, been an apostate to classical Freudianism, she clearly did not welcome an apostate to her own theory *and* Freud's. Bowlby sardonically commented that Melanie Klein was 'a frightfully vain old woman who manipulated people' and that 'Anna Freud worshipped at the shrine of St Sigmund [her father, Sigmund Freud] while Melanie Klein worshipped at the shrine of St Melanie' (Issroff et al. 2005, p. 57). World War II was over, but the battle between the Freudians still raged, with a new generation of psychoanalysts joining the melee.

In 1941, Susan had a recurrence of breast cancer and was again treated with surgery and radiation. Again, she made a recovery, and in 1943, resigned from the IOE, to focus on her psychoanalytic practice. In 1945, she gave evidence to the Curtis Committee, which was investigating practice in children's homes. Again, Susan emphasised children's vital need for love and attention, and the damage caused by harsh punishment. This was taken on board to some extent by the committee, whose eventual report advised banning physical punishment in children's homes (Graham 2009, p. 303). In 1946, Susan again became ill, and this time her cancer was not treatable. She became housebound, and in the two years before her death prepared two collections of her writing, *Childhood and After* and *Children and Parents: Their Problems and Difficulties*, which were published posthumously. She died on 12 October 1948.

Graham (2009) comments that Susan Isaacs does not always get the credit she deserves for introducing naturalistic observation into early years practice, and that this is sometimes proposed to have originated with the ethological methods introduced into psychology in the 1960s (p. 318). It is certainly the case that I was taught about the ethologists in my own undergraduate psychology degree, but not about Susan Isaacs. Within the sphere of early years education, she was more appreciated. Writing in 1972, Nanette Whitbread commented that Susan's 'observational method . . . led to an appreciation of the value of individual records in nursery and infant schools' (p. 70). This endures to some extent today, for example in the existence of the early years foundation stage (EYFS) profile that plays such an important role in English national summative assessment as children transfer into Key Stage 1 and the mainstream National Curriculum; although it is fairly certain that Susan would have not been at all impressed by the advent of the brief post-it observation (Tassoni 2012, p. 244) that plays such a large part in this documentation. However, she would have been even more displeased with recent suggestions to drop the EYFS profile altogether and replace it with formal assessments of children which would dramatically curtail the role that ongoing naturalistic observation plays within contemporary early years education.

In 1941, Susan commented that the government's post-war aim should be 'humanising our town schools . . . [in] the full knowledge and understanding of human nature as a whole' (Giardiello 2013, p. 120). This is a poignant quote for two of the authors of this book, who recently commented on British and American education in the early twenty-first century:

> *Rather than continuing to be developmentally constricted in such an unbalanced fashion by the traditional model of school/school-oriented environments dominated by highly directive, target-driven adults as the answer to all children's development needs, we should instead be considering how to create 'policies . . . grounded on the best available evidence of what human beings are like' (Singer 1999, p. 61).*

Compare also our comment that:

> *It is only the recognition of the need for flexible, authentic and collaborative play-based and open 'discovery' learning activities that will help us create a modern developmental environment that can holistically nurture children's socio-cognitive capacity.*
>
> *(Jarvis, Newman and Swiniarski 2014, p. 63)*

Compare this with Susan's avocation to 'give [the child] material and opportunity and leave him free to his own creative spirit' (Isaacs 1933, p. 426) and her emphasis on 'the value of play, play with companions, free imaginative play as well as play leading to ordered skill and knowledge' (Isaacs 1933, p. 428).

It is sobering to think that Susan would have been bitterly disappointed to learn that researchers who had not even been born at the time she published *Social Development in Young Children* would be making such similar representations to policy makers nearly a century later. Her enduring legacy lies in her clear prose, still centrally relevant to educators and policy makers in the contemporary field of early years practice. It is her voice; her 'message in a bottle' from 1933, that now brings this chapter to a close:

> *What the child actually needs is that the parents and the adults who make up his social world should represent to him a stable and ordered world of values, values closely related to the child's real abilities at any given age, and based upon an understanding of his psychological needs . . . the child can bring out the good that is in him, provided he is given support against his fears of the bad.*
>
> *(Isaacs 1933, pp. 420–21)*

Student integration tasks

- Read the short book *Our Victorian Education* by Dinah Birch, and consider how Susan must have felt when she emerged from such a culture to commence her studies at the University of Manchester at the age of twenty-three.

- Consider this chapter alongside the chapter on Margaret McMillan. What are the similarities and differences between these two pioneers?

- What do you think psychoanalytic concepts have to offer children with emotional and behavioural disorders (EBD)? To focus effectively on this question, you might find it useful to google the term 'play therapy', which is still providing support for troubled children in the twenty-first century.

- Do you think psychoanalysis has anything to offer *mainstream* practice in early years education and care, as Melanie Klein proposed?

- What were the problems with the data and data analysis techniques with which Susan underpinned her academic conclusions and her advice to parents? Do you think that any problems you have identified make her conclusions and suggestions less valid?

- Applying theory to practice is hugely important for leaders of early years practice. What did Susan Isaacs contribute to this endeavour? You will find this question much easier to answer if you read some of her writing. *The Nursery Years* in particular is easy to obtain at a very low price from online used books websites, and some of her articles are available online.

References

Birch, D. (2008) *Our Victorian Education*. Oxford: Blackwell.

Brierley, S. (1923) A note on sex differences from the psychoanalytical point of view. *British Journal of Medical Psychology* 3, pp. 288–308.

Donaldson, M. (1978) *Children's Minds*. London: Fontana.

Feminist Voices (2015) *Karen Horney*. Available at: http://www.feministvoices. com/karen-horney. Accessed 28 July 2015.

Giardiello, P. (2013) *Pioneers in Early Childhood Education: The Roots and Legacies of Rachel and Margaret McMillan, Maria Montessori and Susan Isaacs*. London: Routledge.

Gilligan, C. (1993) *In a Different Voice* (second edition). Cambridge, MA: Harvard University Press.

Glass, G. (1994) Payment by results: An example of assessment in elementary education from nineteenth century Britain. *Education Policy Analysis Archives* 2: 1. Available at: http://epaa.asu.edu/ojs/article/view/664/786. Accessed 27 August 2015.

Graham, P. (2009) *Susan Isaacs: A Life Freeing the Minds of Children*. London: Karnac.

Isaacs, S. (1929) *The Nursery Years* (edition published by Shocken, 1968). New York: Shocken.

Isaacs, S. (1930) *Intellectual Growth in Young Children*. London: Routledge and Kegan Paul.

Isaacs, S. (1933) *Social Development in Young Children*. London: Routledge and Kegan Paul.

Isaacs, S. (1948) The nature and function of phantasy. *International Journal of Psychoanalysis* 29, pp. 73–97.

Issroff, J., Reeves, C. and Hauptman, B. (2005) *Donald Winnicott and John Bowlby: Personal and Professional Perspectives*. London: Karnac.

Jarvis, P. (2006) Rough and tumble play, lessons in life. *Evolutionary Psychology* 4, pp. 268–286.

Jarvis, P. and George, J. (2016) Principles in childcare and education. In P. Jarvis, J. George, W. Holland and J. Doherty, *The Complete Companion for Teaching and Leading Practice in the Early Years*. Abingdon: Routledge.

Jarvis, P. and Liebovich, B. (2015) British nurseries, head and heart: McMillan, Owen and the genesis of the education/care dichotomy. *Women's History Review*. Available at: http://www.tandfonline.com/doi/abs/10.1080/09612025.2015.10 25662?journalCode=rwhr20#.VUZripPff4U. Accessed 1 June 2016.

Jarvis, P., Newman, S. and Swiniarski, L. (2014) On 'becoming social': the importance of collaborative free play in childhood. *International Journal of Play* 3, 1, pp. 53–68. Available at: http://www.tandfonline.com/doi/pdf/10.1080/215949 37.2013.863440. Accessed 1 June 2016.

Marder, N. (1987) Gender dynamics and jury deliberations. *Yale Law Journal* 96, 3, pp. 593–612.

New, R. and Cochran, M. (2007) *Early Childhood Education: An International Encyclopaedia*. Westport, CT: Praeger, pp. 576–577.

Tassoni, P. (2012) *Practical EYFS Handbook*. Harlow: Pearson.

Whitbread, N. (1972) *The Evolution of the Nursery-Infant School: A History of Infant and Nursery Education in Britain 1800–1970*. London: Routledge.

Zaretsky, E. (2005) *Secrets of the Soul: A Social and Cultural History of Psychoanalysis*. New York: Vintage.

10

Loris Malaguzzi (1920–94)

Liberatory pedagogy for democracy

Wendy Holland

Introduction

This chapter will begin by exploring the origins of the preschools in the town of Reggio Emilia in Northern Italy. These first nurseries, built brick by brick in 1945, were subsidised by money acquired from the sale of left-over German tanks and military hardware from World War II; a more recent demonstration of the drive for individual rights and democracy that originates from the philosophy of Rousseau and the spirit of Pestalozzi (see Chapter 2). Such events can also be seen as a reaction to the formal, church-dominated and state-funded early years provision available at the relevant time and place: war-weary Italy in the late 1940s. Building upon the work originally carried out by the women of Reggio Emilia, and their need to engage in paid labour, Loris Malaguzzi (1920–94), at that time a young teacher, later psychologist and philosopher, helped to create and coordinate a world-renowned approach to early childhood education. The Reggio Emilia project began with preschools and was later extended to include infant/toddler centres in 1970.

This chapter will reflect on Malaguzzi's social constructivist perspective with its unique emphasis on the rights and responsibilities of its three main co-constructors of the Reggio Emilia early years education framework: children, parents and teachers. The influence of such an approach on contemporary ideas and practice within international constructions of early childhood education will be explored and the democracy of the Reggio Emilia approach will also be compared with the revised English early years foundation stage (EYFS) (DFE 2014a) and its emphasis on 'school readiness' for four to five-year-olds. The chapter will additionally consider the concept of the 'rich' child and childhood embedded in the Reggio Emilia approach, opening the way for parents, teachers and children to become equal partners and co-constructors. The unique role of the teacher in the Reggio Emilia framework will also be explored, as researcher, facilitator and pedagogue. The Reggio development of detailed documentation as a resource to track the learning of both the child and the teacher will be outlined, alongside the concept of the learning environment as a 'third teacher' and the unique orientation to time that exists in the Reggio Emilia setting.

> *Our image of children no longer considers them as isolated and egocentric, does not only see them as engaged in action with objects, does not emphasise only the cognitive aspects, does not belittle feelings or what is not logical and does not consider with ambiguity the role of the reflective domain. It has an image of the child as rich in potential, strong, powerful, competent, and most of all, connected to adults and children.*
>
> *(Loris Malaguzzi cited in Penn 1997, p. 117)*

Life and work

Post war in Reggio Emilia

There is an element of romanticism in the way this story is told, many years after the events of those traumatic days after the end of World War II, when a community of women gathered together to build a preschool from the rubble of war. Some short time afterwards, they encountered a young primary school teacher almost by chance, who agreed to forsake his job to help them run a school for their youngest children. Achtner (1994) outlines the remarkable set of occurrences that led Malaguzzi to his life's work. Only five days after the end of the war, rumours had started to spread in the Reggio area about some peasant women attempting to build a school. On hearing this, Malaguzzi, a twenty-year-old primary school teacher at the time, apparently jumped on his bicycle and rode out to see for himself. He found the women cleaning bricks by the river. When they realised that he was a teacher, they immediately made a fervent request for his help to 'look after' their children, emphatic that they were 'just as intelligent as the rich people's children' (Achtner 1994). Malaguzzi agreed that was undoubtedly so, but admitted he had no experience of working with such young children. When they redoubled their request, he finally acquiesced, commenting that he would do his best. He determined at this point that he would only take on the role with the proviso that he would continue to learn as he was teaching the children, and that this would be a reciprocal situation, in that the children would learn as he worked alongside, rather than 'in charge' of them. This idea of the reflective, lifelong learner-teacher in the Reggio Emilia framework went on to become a tradition.

Malaguzzi was a very private person and little is known of his personal life, other than he was born in Coreggio in Italy in 1920 (Brunson Day 2001) and all of his childhood memories were rooted within fascist Italy, as the government headed by the fascist war leader Mussolini was set up in 1922 (BBC History 2016). Brunson Day quotes Malaguzzi as reflecting that the six years of World War II 'gobbled up my youth' (2016). He also commented:

War, in its tragic absurdity, is the kind of experience that pushes a person toward
the job of educating, as a way to start anew and live and work for the future. This
desire strikes a person, as the war finally ends and the symbols of life reappear with a
violence equal to that of the time of destruction.

(LeBlanc 2006)

Malaguzzi felt that he recognised the role of fate in his meeting with the women of Reggio Emilia, telling Lella Gandini that 'destiny must have wanted me to be part of an extraordinary event' (Gandini 2011, p. 49). Whether he was aware of it at the time, his promise to these working mothers became the basis of his educational philosophy and 'doing his best' eventually led to the internationally renowned preschools and infant and toddler centres of the Reggio Emilia region.

A more pragmatic historical view would take into account the fact that the 'peasant women' were members of two associations, the Union of Italian Women (UDI), an anti-fascist association founded in 1944 and the Catholic Italian Women's Centre, created in 1945 (de Haan et al. 2013). The need for the preschools may well have been founded on the wish to have the young children of Reggio Emilia educated, but it was also part of the women's pressing need to earn money.

The Reggio Emilia region was suffering a serious economic crisis in the mid-1940s, hence the women Malaguzzi spoke with were in desperate need of paid work. The preschool was necessary, as it provided somewhere safe for them to leave their children, allowing the women to be available to engage in the seasonal work available in the region, winnowing, threshing and grape harvesting. As early as 1945, the UDI had set up seven preschools, which they autonomously managed without state intervention. This had expanded by the 1950s to sixty preschools run by women's associations and trade unions to cope with the needs of seasonal workers (Wortham 2013).

Alongside this economic drive, the women were adamant they wanted a different type of education for their children than the traditional education they had received, delivered by the public schools under the direction of the Catholic Church, which focused above all upon instilling obedience and respect for authority. Given the disaster that had unfolded in Italy under a fascist dictator who had demanded exactly these very qualities from their citizens, the women were insistent that they wanted their children to be educated in a manner that would nurture them to become non-conformist, critical young thinkers who were self-aware and intolerant of inequality and injustice (Wortham 2013).

Loris Malaguzzi continued to support the Reggio Emilia preschools throughout the next twenty years, learning as he went, gradually introducing his own distinctive philosophy of education. In 1950, he qualified as an educational psychologist, setting up the Reggio Emilia Municipal Psycho-Pedagogical Centre (Reggio Children 2016). In the 1960s the women's groups in Reggio Emilia petitioned the Municipality to take responsibility for funding the preschools, with Malaguzzi's support, and this was agreed. The first preschool set-up still exists, located a short distance from the city of Reggio Emilia (Brunson Day 2001). Malaguzzi also supported the women's campaign for an additional initiative to set up and fund infant and toddler centres funded by the Municipality, with the first one opening in 1970 (New 2000). During the two last decades of the twentieth century, the Reggio Emilia preschools began to gather national and international fame for their innovative and highly effective preschool practice.

Malaguzzi's portfolio of work expanded to include being an adviser to the Ministry of Education, director of several journals, including *Bambini*, setting up the Nidi Infanzia (a research and support base for families and children in preschool Reggio settings) and becoming the inspiration for the touring Reggio exhibitions such as *The Hundred Languages of Children*. He also won numerous awards including the prestigious Lego award in 1992 for making an extraordinary contribution to improve the lives of children and pedagogical development. He retired in 1985, but remained involved in the schools until his death in 1994 (Brunson Day 2016). Wolfgang Achtner, who wrote Malaguzzi's obituary in the London *Independent* newspaper, contributed the information that Malaguzzi was married with one son, and that his wife had died in 1993, preceding his own death by only a few weeks. Achtner further commented:

> *Loris Malaguzzi was greatly respected and even venerated by all who worked with him. He embodied the best of Italian virtues: commitment, creativity and that uncanny ingenuity that permits his countrymen to make do in any situation, even with the least of materials.*

> *(Achtner 1994)*

The community of Reggio Emilia resolved to carry on and implement his dream to fulfil the Reggio mission 'to enhance the potential of all children'. A foundation named Reggio Children was established and named as the International Centre for the Defence and Promotion of the Rights and Potential of All Children in 1995 (Thornton and Brunton 2015).

Theoretical and practical legacy

Much has been written about the theory and philosophy underpinning what has come to be known as the Reggio Emilia approach, and Malaguzzi is often seen as the creator and driving force of this unique method. There is, however, no book that clearly details Malaguzzi's theory, as he was very clear that pedagogy should be fluid and open to change and continually informed by practice. He admitted some hesitation in publishing a theory of any kind, because he so highly valued questioning, reflection, research and adaptation. And indeed, this is how his theory and philosophy emerged, through direct practice in schools for infants, toddlers and preschoolers over a thirty-year period. One of his co-workers, American Lilian Katz (Katz et al. 2014), observed that in Reggio Emilia, practice tends to drive theory, rather than the opposite, and sometimes may be ahead of it; hence the 'fluidity' Malaguzzi preferred. He often described himself as being 'stubborn' and wanting to carry everyone along with him. His colleagues speak of him as strong willed, but collaborative at heart, with a deep sense of respect for children and all their capabilities (Edwards et al. 1993).

Malaguzzi made good his initial promise to the working women of Reggio, to learn as he went. Travelling to Rome to study psychology, he took inspiration from reading theorists such as Vygotsky, whose ideas on social constructivism he took to heart. He was also deeply interested in Piaget's belief in the richness of children's innate curiosity, leading to a constant striving to find answers to unfolding intellectual problems and the value of environment as 'teacher' in this respect. Malaguzzi also took from Dewey a concept of the responsibility of being a social being, aware of the welfare of others, and from Bruner's ideas on how children learn, through ever-complex spirals of knowledge and experience. Malaguzzi always kept the children of Reggio Emilia at the centre of his thinking, with a core focus upon how their needs could best be met, even travelling to the Rousseau Institute and the Ecole des Petits of Piaget in Geneva (Malaguzzi 1993). He studied the works of Erikson and his views on the child's inner psyche and Bronfenbrenner's entwined psychological and sociological nests of experience and spoke admiringly of Maria Montessori's belief in the great capabilities of the individual child, to develop self-dependence. Malaguzzi's model of the child includes the following key components:

- 'rich' in potential;
- able to co-construct their world;
- strong, powerful and competent;
- able to develop their own theories about the world and how it works;
- able to explore such ideas in collaboration with other children and adults;
- able to use 'a hundred languages' with which to express themselves, which should all be equally valued;
- the potential to become a self-confident explorer/investigator with a sense of curiosity and the freedom of spirit to venture beyond the known/given.

All else stems from this central image that Malaguzzi constructed of the child in his environment (Malaguzzi 1993).

Environment is viewed as crucially important. Here Malaguzzi looks to Montessori for inspiration, in the way that she studied the ergonomics of the Casa dei Bambini, realising the need for the space and resources to be accessible and suitable for the young child's needs (see Chapter 8). Malaguzzi goes further in constructing the environment as a 'third teacher'. Students who travel to any of the Reggio preschools will see immediately how this is interpreted, through the child-sized furniture, the use of natural and artificial light, with windows that reach from floor to ceiling, pale walls, so children's art work is not 'drowned' out, but framed and offset, hanging textiles that provide temporary, secret spaces, mirrors that catch the light and reflect back to the child their own self-image and myriad natural resources for children to explore with their senses. Every preschool has an art studio (atelier) managed by a professional artist (atelierista). The atelierista's role is to encourage and facilitate the ability of children and staff to 'see' in new ways, and to provide resources for the children to communicate in the 'hundred languages' that Malaguzzi proposed were at the heart of every child's ability to communicate and be self-expressive. This might, for example, involve art, music and movement or shadow puppet shows (Edwards 1993). 'We shape the room, and the room shapes us' (Rinaldi 2006, p. 64).

Documentation panels line the walls of the setting, illustrating projects in which the centre has engaged over time, providing a historical timeline of ideas visited year on year which gives staff, parents and visitors an insight into the depth and variety of experiences the children have had. It shows the children that their work is valued. As well as a place for exploration and research, the environment is purposefully designed like a mini town, with an indoor piazza or meeting place, similar to a town square. Malaguzzi considered this to be one of the most important areas where children can gather in small or large groups. The piazza leads directly into the classrooms and kitchen/dining areas, with no narrow connecting corridors. To encourage friendships and communication among even the youngest children, the setting provides each child with a box, on which their name is clearly printed, which is fixed to a wall at child height. Children can use these to send messages to each other. Children who cannot yet write are encouraged to wrap a special stone in paper and to place it in a friend's box as the next best thing to a letter.

This leads on to the point that relationships form a central tenet of Malaguzzi's philosophy. He put great emphasis on adults and children learning together, valuing others' opinions, viewpoints and interpretations. In all his writings and lectures a key emphasis is not only put upon the rights of the child within the learning community, but also the rights of parents and staff; it was his policy that each Reggio setting should prominently display such a Charter of Rights. In Malaguzzi's view adults are co-constructors of knowledge, researchers and facilitators working with the children. Within the preschools, two teachers work together as equals, supporting the learning of twenty children (Edwards 1993).

Parents were particularly important to Malaguzzi. From the very beginning of his involvement with the Reggio centres, parents played an important part. His admiration for the original group of mothers working to build their own school was heartfelt. Time and again in his writings he refers to his respect for their mission to create a safe and nurturing place for their children; one that would help them become independent young people capable of critical thinking and of challenging injustice. The initial preschools lacked funding from the Municipality, and were not prepared to become beholden to the Roman Catholic Church, so they had no other option but to work together as a community to survive; Malaguzzi was very aware of this. Consequently he was in no doubt that parents were important; without their input and support, the first Reggio centres would never have been created. But it is more than this in Malaguzzi's vision. The dyad that is the partnership between the educator and the child is not sufficient in itself. The triad, however, that is between staff, children and parents has strength and vision. He was insistent that it was communities rather than parents or teachers alone who raise the children, so close did he see the relationship between the setting, the children, staff and parents (Hall et al. 2010). It is not uncommon in Reggio preschools to see parents helping out with projects or just generally giving support throughout the school. There is a relaxed and trusting feel to the relationships between teachers and parents, who are continually kept in the loop about any decisions affecting their child, or just exchanging the latest news. It is essential to the Reggio approach that the welfare of the child is seen as a collective responsibility and that all parties concerned experience a deep feeling of belonging.

How time is spent and used is also a key factor in supporting the child's learning within Malaguzzi's philosophy. In terms of a 'sense' of time, children are encouraged to be aware of the present, build on the past (the latter is evidenced all around them through their work and projects that are displayed on panels for them to see) and also look to the future. Priority is given to setting aside the necessary time for children and adults to discuss, debate and reflect. Revision and reflection are considered central to a child's learning. Projects meander at the child's pace as children are encouraged and expected to concentrate for long periods of time from a very young age, to solve problems both independently and collaboratively. Time is also set aside daily for teachers to complete documentation and for interpretation and sharing of information between colleagues and parents.

Teaching and curriculum

As has been outlined above, the role of the teacher in the Reggio approach is multi-faceted. Reggio teachers fill simultaneous roles of partner in learning, nurturer, guide and researcher. Malaguzzi was clear in his view that teachers must have a positive image of children and their vast capabilities, and that the teacher constructs their role as a genuine partner with children in the co-construction of knowledge. Like Pestalozzi, he utterly dismissed the idea of the didactic or 'transmission' teacher, standing in front of the children and directing them. Malaguzzi also dismissed the construction of the quiet facilitator that is reminiscent of Montessori's directress. In Malaguzzi's approach, teachers must be constantly *with* rather than directing the children: discovering, exploring and learning together. The whole group or class community understand that each person's contribution is valued and there is very little concept of differential status, either between teacher and pupil, or between the pupils themselves in terms of being 'smarter' or 'less able'. This, Malaguzzi suggests, makes children more willing and powerful contributors in their own learning.

Through genuinely eliciting children's thoughts and ideas, thereby creating an environment which genuinely supports the interests of the children, Reggio teachers are able to provide provocations which develop children's learning through their own interests rather than those of the teacher, the parent or (in terms of fixed national curriculums) the government. By embedding the 'curriculum' in children's own interests in this way, there is a much greater chance that they will develop a deeper and more complex understanding of the area of study. Reggio teachers are additionally expected to work in creative collaboration with one another towards original agreed goals, which may be established or transitional. This is supported by a lack of externally imposed policies, manuals and curriculum guidelines. The teacher is expected to be a continually reflective researcher in this way, reviewing their own responses and ideas. In this sense, then, the Anglo-American concept of teacher professional development is turned on its head; teachers are not expected to develop skills of transmitting knowledge to children through 'curriculum content', but to enhance their understanding of how children learn. Reggio teachers' research activities are supported by regular visits by and talks with people working outside the boundaries of education, for example scientists, musicians, writers and architects (Thornton and Brunton 2015).

In place of the concept of a curriculum, Malaguzzi substituted the term *progettazione*, which means the staff gathering together with the children, parents and community to discuss how a particular project might evolve. Topics for study are retrieved from the conversations of the children, family and the wider community, for example family events and celebrations, and the expressed interests of children. These could be as diverse as wondering where the sun goes; what makes a rainbow; where water comes from (not simply 'out of the tap'), what makes a shadow, or more tangible things, like dinosaurs, steam engines and super heroes. It is the flexibility and fluidity of this process that prevents the Reggio teaching and learning process becoming a formulaic and impersonal 'off-the-shelf' curriculum. Through such discussion, the original project might change direction and/or focus, which is nevertheless scrupulously resourced, documented and flexibly planned. Teaching and learning thus becomes a creative, fluid art form that is expressed through the use of *progettazione* (Rinaldi 1998).

The documentation that is created as a result of this initial process then becomes part of the process itself, which in turn changes as dialogues develop in an ongoing fashion between educators, children and parents. The process results in projects supporting a truly emerging curriculum, which clearly documents the authentic development and learning that has taken place, through genuine dialogue and listening between all parties concerned; in the Reggio approach, everyone has an equal right to be heard (Learning and Teaching Scotland 2006). Maintaining a cohesive structure within the pedagogic documentation, given there is no pre-set curriculum, is an essential part of the Reggio teacher's role. Its main features can be seen as:

- documentation that involves a specific question that guides the process, often with an epistemological focus (focus on questions of learning);

- documentation that involves collectively analysing, interpreting and evaluating individual and group observations which is strengthened by multiple perspectives;

- documentation that makes use of multiple 'languages' (different ways of representing and expressing thinking in various media and symbol systems) – here the atelierista (resident artist) plays an important role, collaborating with the class teachers in planning and documentation;

- documentation that makes learning transparent and visible rather than private. Documentation becomes public when it is shared equally with children, parents and teachers, who are all viewed as learners;

- documentation that is not only retrospective, but also prospective, shaping the design of future contexts for learning.

(Based on Rinaldi 2006)

Hall et al. (2010, p. 61) quote Filippini's idea of such documentation as a 'second skin' giving the adults conceptual tools with which to 'make visible the values of the group' and to create a permanent record that can stand as an assessment. To support cohesion and what Anglo-American culture would construct as 'accountability', the Municipality of Reggio Emilia appoints a head administrator who reports to the town council and works with a group of *pedagogista*, who are team leaders for teachers of five to six centres.

With this degree of documentation, an assessment of each child is undertaken and shared with the child, parent and other educators (see above the 'visibility' of the documentation panels). But there is no formalised framework against which a child is measured and given a level or grade. Likewise, no empirical research has ever been carried out to formally 'measure' the impact of the Reggio approach, either nationally or internationally; however, numerous narrative accounts have been produced. Indeed, it would be difficult to create an account dominated by facts and figures around the Reggio approach, given that the framework is grounded in relatively transient data that is gathered around each child, and there is no pre-written curriculum or assessment framework. As such, there could be no conclusive 'reliability and validity', factors which are given primary importance within the Anglo-American culture of early years education. There is, however, a key question around whether we have lost sight of the idiographic 'rich child' in Britain and America, under the nomothetic weight of 'accountability'. We will now move on to consider some reflections on the co-option of the Reggio Emilia approach into the education systems of other nations, and how these might help us to consider potential international ways forward for early years education in the twenty-first century.

What now for Reggio in the twenty-first century?

Many countries have taken aspects of Malaguzzi's vision and attempted to replicate them with varying degrees of success. The Reggio Emilia framework has many enthusiastic Anglo-American supporters; for example, Tess Bennett from the University of Illinois commented:

> *I believe that we can learn from Reggio Emilia. Such important basic ideas as taking time to listen to and observe children, valuing and respecting children, involving families, valuing differences rather than perpetuating stigma, and being open as a teacher to learn along with the children as they investigate real-life questions through projects are worthy of our consideration. Building strong community educational networks that are supportive and nurturing for all children and families, regardless of social class or cultural and linguistic background, are possible and desirable. But, first, children and families must become a priority.*
>
> *(Bennett 2001)*

Perhaps it is the Anglo-American emphasis on the child as human resource rather than the child as holistic being that has prevented the Reggio Emilia approach being wholly 'cargoed' over to English and American early years practice. However, Reggio Emilia centres have been set up in many other nations, for example Scotland and Sweden and also the USA. In considering the adoption of a Reggio approach in a Scottish early years framework, Learning and Teaching Scotland reflected:

> *Undoubtedly, there is much that we can learn from Reggio educators: in particular, true collaboration between all parties involved in the children's learning and in the life of the schools; detailed documentation of children's learning processes; the importance of the environment in learning; the unique way in which expressive arts are used as a stimulus for all areas of learning; excellent professional development. All of these deserve careful consideration in our early years classrooms. However . . . we need to be cautious in attempting to replicate the Reggio Approach in our own early years settings. . . . The values and beliefs intrinsic to the pedagogical approach are so much a part of the wider cultural context that is the town of Reggio Emilia and its people that to attempt somehow to drop the educational approach into a very different social and cultural setting would be damaging to the new culture's existing good practice and to the integrity of the Reggio Approach itself.*
>
> *(Learning and Teaching Scotland 2006, p. 23)*

Taken together, these transatlantic reflections illustrate why non-Italian Reggio enterprises have had to compromise on some elements of Malaguzzi's vision. A school within a cohesive community that supports the rich child, where teachers are not overly concerned about status, and engage in constant collaborative ventures with children, parents and other staff, with no pre-set curriculum or assessment framework to 'guide' them, may be viewed as 'not achieving' in cultures that espouse a very different socio-political ideology. The Anglo-American neo-liberal context tends towards the analytical, reductionist and decontextualised (Jarvis 2016) compared to the holistic, dynamic and relational world view of the inhabitants of the Reggio Centres.

In England, as early years practice becomes increasingly more target orientated and outcome driven, Malaguzzi's vision seems to be moving ever further beyond the reach of the early years education agenda. The EYFS (DFE 2014a) in its revised form has increased the early learning goals for mathematics and literacy by almost 100 per cent, the inference being that early years practitioners have been at least misguided since 2007, or at worst, poorly performing. The supportive, trusting, cooperative relationship between the Reggio Schools and their Municipality seems a far cry from this. The USA's initiatives of No Child Left Behind and Race to the Top pose similar problems for their early years education culture (Jarvis et al. 2014).

Questions of fitness for purpose need to be explored. Research is continuing on both sides of the Atlantic to consider whether highly structured curriculum models improve the quality of outcomes or merely diminish the professional responsibilities of early childhood teachers and their ability to address the individual needs of the child.

In the meantime, is there something positive we can take from visits to the centres in Reggio Emilia? We can certainly contemplate a fresh conception of the child as a rich and capable co-constructor of their own reality, and reflect upon a reassessment of priorities in terms of the development of a more flexible mode of thinking about early years practice and a willingness to share and collaborate with children, other professionals and parents. We can also take a more creative look at the environment, which, as Katz reminds us, is a very powerful 'shaping' force; this element of the Reggio framework might be aligned with the 'enabling environments' concept in the English EYFS (see http://earlyyearsmatters.co.uk/index.php/eyfs/enabling-environments/). Perhaps, too, we can engage in some lateral thinking when it comes to interpreting current English statutory frameworks, which, despite being dominated by targets and testing, are conceptually moving towards a more individual and inclusive view of the child; see, for example, the Children and Families Act 2014 (DFE 2014b).

The key question is: in twenty-first-century Britain and America, should we embrace 'the most exceptional example of the highest quality early education that the world has ever seen' (Dahlberg et al. 2007)? This is Malaguzzi's legacy.

Student integration tasks

- Malaguzzi proposes that it takes a community to raise a child. How do you consider this vision compares with current policies within early years settings in your local/national context?
- Compare the roles of Montessori's 'directress' and that of the 'researcher/facilitator' in the Reggio approach with respect to supporting children's learning and development.

- Compare the use and role of the environment between Steiner, Montessori and Reggio settings.

- What are the similarities/differences between Steiner, Montessori and Malaguzzi in terms of their implicit theories of child development, and which do you think is the most appropriate in terms of current understanding, including neurophysiology, of how human beings develop in early childhood?

References

Achtner, W. (1994) Obituary, Loris Malaguzzi, *The Independent* online. Available at: http://www.independent.co.uk/news/people/obituary-loris-malaguzzi-1367204.html. Accessed 20 February 2016.

BBC History (2016) Benito Mussolini. Available at: www.bbc.co.uk/history/historic_figures/mussolini_benito.shtml. Accessed 20 February 2016.

Bennett, T. (2001) Reactions to Visiting the Infant-Toddler and Preschool Centers in Reggio Emilia. *Italy Early Childhood Research and Practice* 3, 1. Available at: http://ecrp.uiuc.edu/v3n1/bennett.html. Accessed 21 February 2016.

Brunson Day, C. (2001) Pioneers In Our Field: Loris Malaguzzi – Founder of The Reggio Emilia Approach. *Early Childhood Today*. Available at: http://www.scholastic.com/teachers/article/pioneers-our-field-loris-malaguzzi-founder-reggio-emilia-approach. Accessed 20 February 2016.

Dahlberg, G., Moss, P. and Pence, A. (2007) *Beyond Quality in Early Childhood Education and Care: Languages of Evaluation*. London: Routledge.

De Haan, F., Allen, M., Purvis, J. and Daskalova, K. (2013) *Women's Activism: Global Perspectives from the 1890s to the Present*. Abingdon: Routledge.

DFE (2014a) *The Early Years Foundation Stage*. London: DFE. Available at: https://www.gov.uk/government/uploads/system/uploads/attachment_data/file/335504/EYFS_framework_from_1_September_2014__with_clarification_note.pdf. Accessed 21 February 2016.

DFE (2014b) *The Young Person's Guide to the Children and Families Act 2014*. London: DFE. Available at: https://www.gov.uk/government/uploads/system/uploads/attachment_data/file/359681/Young_Person_s_Guide_to_the_Children_and_Families_Act.pdf. Accessed 21 February 2016.

Edwards, C., Gandini, L. and Forman, G. (eds) (1993) *The Hundred Languages of Children*. New York: Ablex Publishing.

Gandini, L. (2011) History, Ideas and Basic Principles, An Interview with Loris Malaguzzi, in Carolyn Edwards, Lella Gandini and George Forman (eds) *The Hundred Languages of Children*, 3rd edn (pp. 27–72). New York: Ablex Publishing.

Hall, K., Horgan, M., Ridgway, A., Murphy, R., Cunneen, M. and Cunningham, D. (2010) *Loris Malaguzzi and the Reggio Emilia Experience*. London: Bloomsbury Academic.

Jarvis, P. (2016) The Child, the Family and the State: International Perspectives, in P. Jarvis, J. George, W. Holland and J. Doherty, *The Complete Companion for Teaching and Leading Practice in the Early Years*. Abingdon: Routledge.

Jarvis, P., Newman, S. and Swiniarski, L. (2014) On 'Becoming Social': The Importance of Collaborative Free Play in Childhood. *International Journal of Play* 3, 1, pp. 53–68. DOI:10.1080/21594937.2013.863440. Available at: http://www.tandfonline.com/doi/pdf/10.1080/21594937.2013.863440. Accessed 21 February 2016.

Katz, L., Chard, S. and Kogan, Y. (2014) *Engaging Children's Minds: The Project Approach, 3rd Edition: The Project*. Westport, CT: Praeger.

Learning and Teaching Scotland (2006) *The Reggio Emilia Approach to Early Years Education*. Available at: http://www.educationscotland.gov.uk/Images/Reggio Aug06_tcm4-393250.pdf. Accessed 21 February 2016.

LeBlanc, M. (2016) *Reggio Emilia, An Innovative Approach to Education*. Available at: http://www.communityplaythings.co.uk/learning-library/articles/reggio-emilia. Accessed 21 February 2016.

Malaguzzi, L. (1994) The Bill of Three Rights Innovations in Early Education. *The International Reggio Exchange*, 2, 1.

New, R. (2000) Reggio Emilia: Catalyst for Change and Conversation. *ERIC Digest*. Available at: http://www.ericdigests.org/2001-3/reggio.htm. Accessed 21 February 2016.

Penn, H. (1997) *Comparing Nurseries: Staff and Children in Italy, Spain and the UK*. London: Paul Chapman Publishing.

Reggio Children (2016) *Loris Malaguzzi*. Available at: http://www.reggiochildren.it/identita/loris-malaguzzi/?lang=en. Accessed 21 February 2016.

Rinaldi, C. (2006) *In Dialogue with Reggio Emilia: Listening, Researching and Learning*. London: Routledge.

Thornton, L. and Brunton, P. (2015) *Understanding the Reggio Approach*. Abingdon: Routledge.

Wortham S.C. (ed.) (2013) *Common Characteristics, and Unique Qualities in Pre-School Programs: Global Perspectives in Early Childhood Education*. London: Springer.

What now for the pioneers?
*Pam Jarvis, Louise Swiniarski and
Wendy Holland*

Introduction: the pioneers in time and place

As we reach the end of our book, we now turn back to view the pioneers from our current vantage point, and consider what they have to bequeath to us at the beginning of the twenty-first century. We must, however, begin with the philosophers, Locke and Rousseau, who questioned the nature of childhood, leading directly to Pestalozzi's quest to create a pedagogy that was worthy of such a positive view of humankind. Ironically, the more negative aspects of human co-existence, war and foreign occupation provided a formidable barrier to his efforts, and he was only able to realise his dream for a very short period, towards the end of his life. His ideas were, however, passed down to subsequent generations, and we can see echoes of Pestalozzi's practice in the spirituality of Froebel, Steiner, Peabody and Blow; in the holistic focus of Owen and McMillan; and in the focus upon democracy and social equality that underpinned the practices of Montessori and Malaguzzi, which was also an important factor in the work of McMillan.

The female pioneers experienced the frustration of the extreme gender discrimination that was a feature of time and place for them all. Blow, Montessori and Isaacs had to struggle to secure the education they needed to enter their chosen professional fields, while unequal suffrage policies acted to thwart McMillan's initial efforts to build a network of services for deprived children. Peabody, who achieved so much in a time when women were seen as inevitably inferior to men, and who was perceived as a feminist by many, has left behind a body of correspondence that indicates her tendency to be highly deferential to men.

Peabody and McMillan both clearly found comfort and resilience in strong, mutually supportive and loving relationships with their respective sisters, Mary and Rachel. Indeed, but for Rachel McMillan's untimely death, it is highly likely that the McMillan sisters would have been equally credited in the historical record for first blazing the 'educare' trail, a point that Margaret frequently made in her writing and speeches. Steedman (1990, p. 32) viewed Margaret's frequent attempts to attribute all her successes to her sister in the years that followed Rachel's death as an attempt 'to have used her dead sister to construct some kind of personal story for herself', thus only through Rachel could she countenance 'a story of political action and political achievement to be related'. It is possible that such apparent modesty sprang from the same source as Peabody's deference to men: an ingrained identification with the designated place of women within the culture of time and place. Perhaps poignantly, it was only with Rachel forever at her side that McMillan felt strong enough to challenge the patriarchal culture in which she was immersed.

Blow's successes were highly dependent upon the close supportive relationships she created with other women, including Peabody, and during the time that Montessori was disseminating her 'scientific pedagogy' she had the staunch and unwavering support of her son Mario, always at her side in a relationship that in many ways resembles the personal and professional collaboration of the McMillan sisters. The personal history of Isaacs suggests strong mentorship from her friend and fellow psychoanalyst Melanie Klein, alongside a quest to find a man who could be a worthy personal *and* professional partner. Sadly, Isaacs was only able to secure this in a temporary and fragmented fashion in the conflicted, triangular relationship between herself, Nathan Isaacs and Geoffrey Pyke in the ill-fated Malting House School experiment, the disappointing culmination of which created a permanent rift within the Isaacs marriage.

Conversely, Malaguzzi's entrance to the set of circumstances that put him on the road to becoming an important pioneer in the early years arena was a request from a group of women to become, in effect, their 'champion', while Steiner explicitly placed himself as the originator and leader of anthroposophy, a philosophy he

FIGURE 11.1 New Lanark site in the early nineteenth century. © New Lanark Trust

believed was going to change the world; a confidence in himself as a pedagogical pioneer that he shared with Pestalozzi and Owen.

Overall, it is clear that the time and place in which the pioneers operated – Western Europe and Europe-influenced America from the early nineteenth to the mid-twentieth century – created very different roles for men and women, and that all of the pioneers were heavily influenced by their milieu in this respect.

Pestalozzi, Steiner, Montessori and Malaguzzi conceived many of their ideas in times of war and violence, and represent a turning away towards peace and reconstruction. They are united in an explicit idealism that advocates a democratic process of education, particularly in the early years, as being at the centre of a rebirth for society as a whole. They all built on coherent visions of how to improve humanity by facilitating young children's realisation of their full potential as intelligent, creative, whole persons. In each approach, children are viewed as active authors of their own development, strongly influenced by natural, dynamic, self-righting forces within themselves, opening the way towards growth and learning.

Teachers within the frameworks created by Steiner, Montessori and Malaguzzi depend on carefully prepared, aesthetically pleasing environments that serve as a pedagogical tool and provide strong messages about a deep, inherent respect for children as people. Partnering with parents is highly valued in all three approaches, and children are evaluated by means other than traditional tests and grades. While Pestalozzi was not able to build such a comprehensive pedagogical framework, he indicates his agreement with the principle of parent and family involvement in his point that 'The school really ought to stand in the closest connection with the life of the home, instead of, as now, in strong contradiction to it' (Pestalozzi 1801).

Montessori and Pestalozzi both experienced the intrusion of political manipulation into their attempts to create a pedagogical method to instil concepts of democracy. Some readings of history might suggest that Montessori was sometimes not as ethical as Pestalozzi in negotiating her way around oppressive regimes, but perhaps the traditional gender roles outlined above did not allow her to be. The example of this episode in Montessori's life and work inevitably leads to the reflection that those currently attempting to embrace liberatory pedagogies in the UK and the US, for example those modelled upon practices in Reggio Emilia, currently meet with formidable barriers. These are erected by the incompatibility of such frameworks with the neo-liberal approach to education, which is at its core immersed within the narrow development of human capital rather than the holistic development of human potential.

In this respect, it can be suggested that those attempting to embrace liberatory pedagogy in contemporary neo-liberal political milieus may in fact be finding themselves in an uncomfortably similar position to Montessori. Whether the UK and US as deeply intertwined neo-liberal Anglophone nations will be able to learn the lessons of history in this respect is still uncertain. It is currently clear that Susan Isaac's 'message in a bottle' that so neatly encapsulates what young children fundamentally need – 'a stable and ordered world of values, values closely related to the child's real abilities at any given age, and based upon an understanding of his psychological needs' (Isaacs 1933, p. 420) – has yet to be embraced by those who make policy for children in families within both nations.

So what are the debates we need to raise to move the situation along, and how can the example of the pioneers help us in this respect? This chapter will attempt to create a succinct summary.

Practical philosophies of early years education

Marshall McLuhan, a Canadian sociologist, predicted the rapid pace of the ever-changing world in the 'global village' that our children now encounter (Swiniarski 2014). New technologies link nations inextricably together, changing the culture and tone of communities worldwide. In the United States, as with other countries, what knowledge is worth promoting is constantly being redefined. Government mandates for educational standards, policies and practices struggle to keep abreast in the competitive race with other nations as to who is first in reaching politically defined goals. While the pundits apply the open-market model to shape school standards and curriculum approaches, the goalposts keep moving. Success is seemingly always eluded. In the United Kingdom, under a more all-encompassing education and care regime, policies have been developed that increasingly put early years practitioners into a 'straitjacket' in this respect.

Despite ongoing accomplishments in technology and ever-expanding pathways to knowledge, schools everywhere remain dissatisfied with their underpinning educational systems and the results of new and ever-changing pedagogies. Today's schools differ significantly from Froebel's and his followers on the notions of what an effective kindergarten needs to achieve for its young children's success in the future. One of the primary goals of this book is to look back at the genesis of early childhood education to explore time-honoured practices and attainments and examine the methodologies deemed most suitable for working with young children. In doing so, readers on both sides of the Atlantic are faced with several dilemmas.

In England in particular, the onerous set of targets and tests that children have to negotiate before their seventh birthday leaves very little room for teachers to embrace holistic or genuinely play-based pedagogical approaches. A head-teacher recently interviewed by Bradbury and Roberts-Holmes vividly illustrates the position in which teachers of five-year-olds are placed by the relentless programme of testing in England:

> *If you have got 60 young people coming in through the door and in six weeks' time you have got to tick 47 boxes about all of them, of course your mind is going to be on that rather than on talking to them about their nice shiny shoes and about their pet rabbit at home and all those things that give young people a sound, secure start to learning.*
>
> *(Bradbury and Roberts-Holmes 2016, p. 16)*

In the USA, both public schools and charter schools are subject to whatever their state mandates for testing. If federal government monies are accepted for the Common Core curriculum for reading and mathematics, the schools must prepare their students for the Partnership for Assessment of Readiness for College and Careers (PARCC), which is based currently on the Common Core for Grades 3 to 8. There is a movement to include preschool and kindergarten years as well. Many families are questioning such practices. To some extent, this echoes the English 'schoolification' of the reception year, and the housing of nursery classes within schools under school management, a practice to which Margaret McMillan was bitterly opposed (Jarvis and Liebovich 2015). In the US, however, there is no consensus amongst states and within the populations on which directives to take.

This book offers a historical basis from which to start a pathway that begins with early childhood education as the foundation for a viable route to success in terms of deeply developing the whole person as an effective independent learner rather than shallowly transmitting skills and knowledge. The pioneers of the early childhood movement present multiple options to consider and apply to the contemporary needs of young children in education and care settings, to liberate their cognition rather than direct it in ways that create a risk it will become 'cramped and paralysed' (Owen 1991, p. 163). It is ironic to consider that an early industrialist attempting to construct a pedagogy for life rather than simply for industry was able to intuit an irony that apparently eludes contemporary neo-liberal policy makers; that children caught in the wheel of a relentless, ultimately *illiberal* 'teaching to test' regime can actually 'never become really useful subjects of the state' (Owen 1991, p. 163). Montessori (1943, p. 23) sums this up in her comment: 'the child who has never learned to act alone, to direct his own actions, to govern his own will grows into an adult who is easily led and must always lean upon others', due to the inculcation of inflexible cognition which in turn depresses the development of independent problem-solving ability.

Setting-based pedagogical considerations

Upon entering many kindergarten/nursery classes throughout the US and the UK respectively, a visitor might find the traditional opening class activities with children seated in circles as prescribed by Froebel, evidence of guided play centres, a display of art experiences, reading groups around a small table, story-telling centres and/or a block corner for hands-on mathematics' activities. However, with the growing dependence on testing at an ever earlier age, early years settings of all varieties in both nations are being pressured to pursue an academic curriculum for reading, writing and mathematics. The notion of preparing children from birth to eight for college and career has altered the climate and tone of early education programmes across both nations. Yet, in the US, and to some extent in preschool settings in the UK, there remain alternative options in both the public and private domains. For example, there is still evidence of Montessori's practices used in private, public and charter schools from kindergarten to Grade 8 in the US and in the preschool years in the UK. A model Montessori charter school for kindergarten to Grade 8 in Newburyport, Massachusetts, USA is offered to its community families as a choice.

The National Association for the Education of Young Children (NAEYC) in the US endorses preschools and child care centres for infants and toddlers that adapt and implement the Italian practices of the Reggio Emilia schools. The opportunity for state-funded early years settings in England to be flexible in this way is rather limited, due to the constraints of the early years foundation stage (EYFS). Over the past few years, schools that have opened as or converted to 'academies' have rather more freedom at the moment, but they are still inspected by Ofsted against criteria drawn up with reference to the EYFS or National Curriculum, so have to comply with national policies and strategies to some extent.

While most Waldorf Schools in America are private, there is always interest in their pedagogy shared for curriculum modification by early childhood educators in the public settings. Some Steiner Schools in the UK do receive significant funding from the state; however, their curriculum has to be mapped against the relevant statutory framework (EYFS or National Curriculum) which gives rise to potentially difficult and sometimes uneasy compromise (see Chapter 6). The same is also the case for Montessori nursery schools in England, although they have had fewer problems in demonstrating compatibility with the EYFS (see Chapter 8). It would be impossible to run a state-funded nursery class/school or EYFS unit (which includes reception) along the lines of a Reggio Emilia school at present in England due to the disparity between the documentation inherent to each framework. The same is true for the Early Years Foundation Phase in Wales, and although the developers of the Curriculum for Excellence in Scotland were showing interest in the Reggio Emilia framework a decade ago, the current indications are that recommended practice in Scotland will become more similar to that of England and Wales rather than that of Reggio Emilia. For more information on this unfolding situation, see the Upstart website: http://www.upstart.scot.

In the 1990s when the standards-based curriculum mandates began in the US, one public school in Salem, Massachusetts built their curriculum around Howard Gardner's multiple intelligence theory. The curriculum for the school has been developed by Gardner himself and his staff of Project Zero at the Harvard Graduate School of Education; see http://www.pz.harvard.edu. This public school is one of the Family Choice Schools in its community. While the school is subjected to all of the education mandates for public education, its mode of instruction is structured on the basis of Gardner's research on intelligence.

> *Howard Gardner's ground-breaking work deepened learning style theory by explor-*
> *ing the meanings and nature of intelligence. Gardner dismissed the traditional*
> *notion that intelligence was a single trait that individuals possessed from birth to a*
> *greater or lesser degree than others. Intelligence was not a characteristic that could*
> *be measured on a single intelligence test, but there were in fact multiple intelligences*
> *or many ways to be 'smart'.*
>
> (Breitborde and Swiniarski 2006, p. 1

The role of teacher training also needs to be considered with regard to how teachers develop their pedagogy within the classroom. If they are trained to construct their role as that of a 'fact and skill transmission engineer', they will find it difficult to fully conceive pedagogies such as those of Pestalozzi, Steiner or Malaguzzi. Wholly school-based training, which both the UK and US are currently trialling, can in particular result in a trainee who is too busy and driven by day-to-day pressures to do anything else other than ensure the relevant material has been 'delivered' in a timely fashion – which of course takes us back to the lack of time to pay attention to what actually matters to children, such as illustrated above: a new shiny pair of shoes or a beloved pet rabbit. Pestalozzi would indeed be disappointed to arrive in the twenty-first century and find his comment that 'We can do very little with people unless the next generation is to have a very different training from that our schools furnish' (Pestalozzi 1801) as true today as it was in his own time, due to the contemporary neo-liberal imperative to immerse very young children in a harsh adult world of performativity at a stage of development where they find this both baffling and morale-sapping. A teacher in England wrote last year in *The Guardian* column, 'Secret Teacher':

> *The last few years have seen creeping demoralisation and the undermining of what essentially a school is – a community. Children (and staff) are measured and assessed at the expense of being valued as people. The children know this too – you can't fool them, they know the score. They can read people. My great-nephew came home for Christmas from his first year in primary school upset that he had not achieved as highly as his best friend. The evidence for this was in his target-setting book. Ben had failed to learn as many key words as expected. It's outrageous that at aged four . . . you need the reassurance of your mum and dad because you feel that you have not performed well enough.*

(The Guardian 2015)

Parents and teachers are key stakeholders in their children's education, hence they currently need to have their voices more clearly heard by policy makers in the UK and US, alongside experts in children's psycho-social development. All of the pioneers in this book would strongly endorse attempts to progress such an initiative.

Conclusion: what now for early years education and care?

There has been a prevailing concern about the nature of Western childhood since the 1980s, articulated in Neil Postman's book, *The Disappearance of Childhood*, and David Elkind's *The Hurried Child*. A professor of Media Ecology at New York University, Postman was primarily concerned with the negative impact media had upon children (Postman 1982). Elkind's research centred on the pressure of children wearing adult modes of dress and expected to exhibit adult-like behaviours. Both authors set out to inform and support efforts to stem the influences that push children beyond their stages of development. 'It is not conceivable that our culture will forget that it needs children. But it is halfway toward forgetting that children need childhood' (Postman 1982, p. 53).

There is a movement to have young children master academic skills and concepts in child care centres, preschools and kindergarten that were once taught in elementary/primary schools. Academic achievements that once were expected in mainstream elementary/primary school are now asked of younger children. Peabody, Blow, McMillan and Isaacs cautioned against kindergartens becoming a mere preparation for elementary education. Froebel's idea of unfolding in childhood was akin to the notion of development. He had a view of the child's cognitive development not impeding on social and emotional development in his aims of the education of the whole young child. Montessori proposed:

> *The ancient and superficial idea of the uniform . . . growth of the personality has remained unaltered and the erroneous belief has persisted that it is the duty of the adult to fashion the child according to the pattern defined by society. . . . When the independent life of the child is not recognised with its own characteristics and its own ends, when the adult man interprets these characteristics and ends, which are different from his, there arises between the strong and the weak a struggle which is fatal to mankind . . . if, during the delicate and precious period of childhood, a sacrilegious form of servitude has been inflicted upon the children, it will no longer be possible for men to accomplish great deeds . . . but when the intrinsic value of the child's personality has been recognised and he has been given room to expand . . . we have had the revelation of an entirely new child [with] astonishing characteristics.*
>
> *(Montessori 1943, pp. 18–20)*

In the UK, the Too Much, Too Soon campaign and the Save Childhood Movement (on which David Elkind is an advisor, see http://www.savechildhood.net/advisors-and-champions.html) have taken up the challenge to persuade policy makers to honour the wisdom of the pioneers, through the voices of their contemporary heirs. In 2007, American Lilian Katz, also an advisor to Save Childhood, expressed her surprise at the move towards earlier and earlier literacy instruction emergent at that time from the British New Labour Government early years strategy, commenting in *The Guardian* that 'teaching younger children [formal literacy] can look OK in the short term but in the long term children who are taught early are not better off. For a lot of children five will be too early' (*The Guardian* 2007). In 2015, Pam Jarvis made the following response to the prospect raised by the Ofsted Chief Inspector of educating two-year-olds in English schools:

> *Schooling infants is . . . commensurate with placing a young animal in a cage. Human beings evolved in a niche in which the requirement to learn how to engage in complex spontaneous interaction is paramount. Taking short cuts in early childhood in pursuit of processing human beings into units of human capital as quickly as possible risks the production of 'damaged goods'.*
>
> *(Jarvis 2015)*

Seventy-four years earlier, fellow Briton Susan Isaacs had similarly advocated 'humanising our town schools . . . [in] the full knowledge and understanding of human nature as a whole' (Giardiello 2012, p. 120). She would have been extremely disappointed to think that the same battle was being fought nearly three quarters of a century later, and with respect to the prospect of the 'schoolification' of much younger children.

Perhaps, however, the most evocative illustration of the toxic impact of neo-liberal culture upon young children was constructed by American researchers Henley, McBride, Milligan and Nichols from Arkansas State University, who wrote:

> *The playground at Maple Street Elementary School is quiet these days. The only movements on the swing sets are a result of a strong west wind edging the swings back and forth. The long lines that once formed for trips down the sliding boards are empty. There are no softball or kickball games nor are there any games of tag or duck-duck-goose being played. . . . No, Maple Street Elementary School is not closing. It is squeezing every minute of the school day to meet the mandates.*
>
> *(Henley et al. 2007, pp. 56–7)*

In conclusion, all of the pioneers in this book would have been horrified at the current state of affairs in which the education and care of young children in the two most prominent Anglophone nations in the world is immersed. They have, however, left us clear blueprints from which to forge more effective liberatory pedagogies for early years and for primary/elementary education; pedagogies that create the foundations within each and every child from which to cognisantly embrace the democratic ideals that both nations hold so dear. It is time for teachers across the world to forge collaborations that effectively 'stand on the shoulders' of these 'giant' early years pioneers; to develop excellent, internationally and culturally flexible liberatory pedagogies worthy of the pioneers' combined legacy. Malaguzzi's concept of democracy was centred on 'mak[ing] space for commitment to a personal knowledge of each being, and to the possibility of being the protagonist of one's own destiny' (Cagliari et al. 2016, p. 12). We propose that this is a very good place to make a start.

References

Bradbury, A. and Roberts-Holmes, G. (2016) *They are Children, not Robots, not Machines: The Introduction of Reception Baseline Testing.* London: National Union of Teachers. Available at: http://www.betterwithoutbaseline.org.uk/uploads/2/0/3/8/20381265/baseline_assessment_2.2.16-_10404.pdf. Accessed 7 March 2016.

Breitborde, M. and Swiniarski, L. (2006) *Teaching on Principle and Promise: The Foundations of Education.* Boston: Houghton Mifflin Company.

Cagliari, P., Castagnetti, M., Giudici, C., Rinaldi, C., Vecchi, V. and Moss, P. (2016) *Loris Malaguzzi and the Schools of Reggio Emilia: A Selection of His Writings and Speeches, 1945–1993.* Abingdon: Routledge.

Elkind, D. (2007). *The Hurried Child*. Cambridge, MA: DaCapo Press.

Giardiello, P. (2013) *Pioneers in Early Childhood Education: The Roots and Legacies of Rachel and Margaret McMillan, Maria Montessori and Susan Isaacs*. Abingdon: Routledge.

Henley, J., McBride, J., Milligan, J. and Nichols, J. (2007) Robbing Elementary Students of Their Childhood: The Perils of No Child Left Behind. *Education*, 128(1), 56–63. Available at: http://kellywilliams.wiki.westga.edu/file/view/perils+of+NCLB.pdf. Accessed 8 March 2016.

Isaacs, S. (1933) *Social Development in Young Children*. London: Routledge and Kegan Paul.

Jarvis, P. and Liebovich, B. (2015) British Nurseries, Head and Heart: McMillan, Owen and the Genesis of the Education/Care Dichotomy. *Women's History Review*, 24(6), 917–937, DOI: 10.1080/09612025.2015.1025662. Available at: http://www.tandfonline.com/doi/pdf/10.1080/09612025.2015.1025662. Accessed 30 May 2016.

Jarvis, P. (2015) It's Against Human Nature to Send Two Year Olds to School. *The Conversation*. Available at: https://theconversation.com/its-against-human-nature-to-send-two-year-olds-to-school-37180. Accessed 30 May 2016.

Montessori, M. (1943) *Peace and Education*. Adyar: The Theosophical Publishing House. Available at: https://ia700409.us.archive.org/5/items/Peace_And_Education_/peace_and_education_.pdf. Accessed 8 March 2016.

Pestalozzi, J. (1801) *Leonard and Gertrude*. Available at: https://archive.org/stream/pestalozzisleona00pestuoft/pestalozzisleona00pestuoft_djvu.txt. Accessed 3 February 2016.

Postman, N. (1982) *The Disappearance of Childhood*. New York: Delacorte Press.

Steedman, C. (1990) *Childhood, Culture and Class in Britain: Margaret McMillan 1860–1931*. New Brunswick: Rutgers University Press.

Swiniarski, L. (ed.) (2014) *The Evolution of Universal Preschool in a Global Age: World Class Initiatives and Practices in Early Education*. Dordrecht, The Netherlands: Springer.

The Guardian (2007) Under-Sevens 'Too Young to Learn to Read'. Available at: http://www.theguardian.com/uk/2007/nov/22/earlyyearseducation.schools. Accessed 7 March 2016.

The Guardian (2015) Secret Teacher: It's Time to Go Old School on Targets. Available at: http://www.theguardian.com/teacher-network/2015/jan/17/secret-teacher-school-targets. Accessed 7 March 2016.

Index

Note: Page references in **bold** refer to glossaries; *f* refers to figures.

academies (UK) **13**, 77, 173
Achtner, W. 156, 158
Addams, Jane 75, 77
Alcott, Amos Bronson 50
Alcott, Louisa May 50, 55
Alexander I 22
Alfred the Great 18
American Froebel Union 55, 56
anthropology 124, 142, 151
anthroposophical education 88–90, 91
Anthroposophical Society 86
anthroposophy 4, 80, 83, 85, 86–7, 88, 91
assessment: Issacs 151; Reggio Emilia 163;
    Steiner 92; United Kingdom 2, 13, 79,
    151–2, 165, 171; United States 62, 172
Association for Childhood Education
    International 54
Association of the Montessori Internationale
    (AMI) 129
Astor, Nancy, Lady 104
attachment theory 150–1

Baker, Charlie 62
Bambini (journal) 158
Barnard, Dr. Henry 52
Baylor, R. 71
BCE (befoe Christian Era) **3**
Bennett, Tess 163–4
Besant, Annie 80, 85, 86
Birch, D. 140, 153
Birth to Three Matters 108
Blatchford, Robert 103–4
Blow, Susan 11, 36, 56, 65, 168, 169
Blow: critical perspectives: philosophical
    discourse 71–2; physical factors 70–1;

religious assumptions and conflicts
    4, 71
Blow's kindergarten movement 38, 65–7: 1873
    public kindergartens 67–8, 67*f*; community
    outreach 69–70; curriculum development
    and teacher training 67, 68–9
Blow's legacy 72, 76–7: antecedent of
    Full Service Schools 75–6; influences
    on Settlement House 75; recognition
    for achievements 73–4; relevance to
    contemporary practice 74
Booth, Charles 98
Bowlby, John 150–1
Bradbury, A. 171
Bradford 100, 101, 103, 140, 141
Bradley, Milton 43, 62
Breitborde, M. 34, 35, 75, 173
Brierley, Susan *see* Isaacs, Susan
Brierley, William 142
British Psychoanalytical Society 143, 144, 146,
    147
Bronfenbrenner, Urie 159
Bruhlmeier, A. 21
Bruner, Jerome 7, 89, 131, 159
Brunson Day, C. 156

Cagliari, P. *et al.* 176
Campill 93
Carter, Paul 98
Catholic Italian Women's Centre 157
CE (Christian Era) **3**
Channing, Rev. William Ellery 50
Charter Schools (US) 76
Child Care Centers (US) **13**
child development 6–7

child minders (UK) **14**
childhood 16–18, 174–5
Children's Centres (UK) 9–10, **14**, 108
Christian Socialism 4–5, 99, 102, 103–4, 108–9, 142
Christianity 3–5, 18
classroom environment 43, 132, 159–60, 165, 170
Cleveland, Grover 57
Cochran, M. 141
Columbia University Teachers College 36, 40, 70, 71, 72, 74
Comenius, John Amos 18, 20, 33, 53
Common School 56, 56*f*, 60, 66
Community Schools *see* Full Service Schools
Concord School of Philosophy 50, 58, 73
constructivism 6–7
cooperative movement 27
Covert, B. 59
Cullough, Mary C. 74
Cunningham, H. 17, 18, 19
Curtis Committee (1945) 151

Dahlberg, G. *et al.* 165
Dale, Caroline 24
Davis, R. 23, 24, 25, 26, 27
daycare provision (UK) 9–10, **14**, 108
democracy 52, 66, 123, 126, 156, 170, 176
Deptford 100, 105–8
developmental stages: Freud's psychosexual theory 143–4; Montessori's planes of development 125, 130; Piaget's stage theory 6–7, 89, 125, 130, 134, 149; Steiner's cycles 89–90, 125
Dewey, John 6, 40, 71–2, 77, 127, 159
Donaldson, Margaret 149
Dozier, Cynthia 74
Dryfoos, Joy 75
D'Souza, D. 5

early childhood education (US) **13**
early years foundation stage (EYFS) 9, 13, 14, 79, 91, 136, 151–2, 155, 165
early years pioneers 1, 2–3, 4–5, 10–12
educare 11, 101–3, 139, 176; *see also* liberatory pedagogy
education in the past: in the family 17–18; mass formal education 19–20
elementary schools (US) **12**
Eliot, Abigail 72
Elizabeth I 18

Elkind, David 174, 175
Emerson, Ralph Waldo 49–50, 59
England *see* United Kingdom
Enlightenment 19
Episcopalianism 4, 71
Erikson, Erik 159
ethology 151
Eunike, Anna 85
eurhythmy 85, 86, 89, 91
Every Child Matters 97
evolutionary psychology 145
EYFS *see* early years foundation stage

Fairhurst, Alice 141
Fairhurst, Bessie 141
Fairhurst, Susan *see* Isaacs, Susan
Fairhurst, William 140–1, 146
feminism 60, 121–2, 129, 131, 142, 145, 146
Fichte, Johann 84
Findlay, John Joseph 141
Finland 42–3, 44, 54
Fisher, K. *et al.* 135
Fisher, Laura 70, 71, 74
France 66, 126, 129; *see also* Rousseau
Frank, Anne 130
free universal preschools (US) **12**
Freire, Paulo 106
Freud, Anna 146, 147, 151
Freud, Sigmund 120, 123, 129, 139, 146; id, ego, superego 143, 144, 145; Oedipus Complex 143–4; psychoanalysis 142–4, 145, 146, 151; psychosexual stages 143–4
Froebel, Frederick 11, 31–2: ancient forebears 32–3; Gliedganzes 4, 34; Idealism 31, 33, 34, 35, 51, 54; importance of nature 31, 35, 43; influence of Pantheism 4, 34; kindergarten 35–6, 127; memorials 44; the romantic age 33–4
Froebel: critical perspectives 37–41: Great Britain 38, 39, 44, 103, 141; Italy 38, 40–1; kindergarten: international model 38; United States 39–40, 71–2
Froebel's kindergarten 35, 52, 66: environment 43; gifts and occupations 34, 35, 36–7, 44; *Mother Play* 52, 69; play 35–6, 42–3; songs 68
Froebel's legacy 42, 72: gifts and occupations 44, 45, 68; practices for today's child 42–3; teacher education for early years 43–4
Froebel Society 38
Full Service Schools 59, 70, 75–6
Fuller, Margaret 51, 60

Gandini, L. 157
Gardner, Howard 173
Gardner, R. 124, 130
Garland, Mary 55
gender differences: child development 146; in education 17, 18, 20, 26, 140; in play 145
gender discrimination 69, 122, 129, 168, 169
The Genographic Project 16
Germany 38, 53, 55; see also Froebe; Steiner
Giardiello, P. 151, 176
Gill, Stephen 50
Gilligan, C. 145
Glass, G. 140
glossary of terms **12–14**
Glover, James 147
grades (US) **12**
Graham, Philip 103, 140, 141, 142, 143, 146, 147, 148, 149, 151
grammar schools (US) **12**
Graves, Robert James 70
Great Britain see United Kingdom
The Guardian 174, 175
Gutek, G. and Gutek, P. 127, 133

Hall, K. et al. 163
Harris, William T. 56, 66, 71, 72, 73
Hawthorne, Nathaniel 49, 51, 59
Head, Caroline Hart 74
Head, Harriet 74
'head, heart and hand' 21, 22
Hegel, G. W. F. 34
Henley, J. et al. 176
Henry VIII 18
high schools (US) **12**
Hill, Patty Smith 40, 72
historical notes 3–5
holistic education 2, 8, 12, 24, 27, 52, 79, 152; see also McMillan, Margaret; Montessori, Maria; Steiner schools
Holland, W. 28
Horney, Karen 144
Hubbard, Clara Benson 69
humours 90

Idealism 31, 33, 34, 35, 51, 54, 71, 170
independent schools (UK) **13**, **14**
independent schools (US) **12**
industrialization 5, 19–20, 23, 24–5, 27, 28, 39, 98, 146
Institute for Deaf Mutes, Paris 123
Institute of Education (OIE), London 150, 151

International Kindergarten Union (IKU) 55, 71, 72
Isaacs, Susan 11–12, 139–40: early life and education 103, 121, 140–2, 168; educare 139, 176; feminism 142, 146; and Klein 148, 169; Malting House School 146–9, 150, 169; and Piaget 148–9; play 145, 146, 150, 152; psychoanalysis 139, 142–6, 147, 149, 150; religion 4, 140, 146
Isaacs' legacy 149–52, 170–1: Cambridge Evacuation Study 150–1; naturalistic observation 12, 134, 139, 146, 147, 148–9, 150, 151–2; writings 143, 146, 148, 149–50, 151, 152
Isaacs, Nathan 146, 147, 149, 169
Italy 38, 40, 53; see also Malaguzzi, Loris; Montessori, Maria
Itard, Jean Marc 120, 123, 131

Jarvis, Josephine 69
Jarvis, P. 8, 28, 145, 152, 175

Kant, Immanuel 80, 83, 88
Katz, Lilian 158–9, 165, 175
Keilhau Froebel School 44
Kilpatrick, William Heard 127
kindergartens: United States 8, **12**, 38, 56, 61–2; see also Froebel's kindergarten; Peabody's kindergarten movement
Klein, Melanie 139, 144–5, 146, 147, 148, 151, 169
Kornig, Karl 93
Kramer, R. 121, 123, 126, 127
Kraus-Boelte, Maria 66
Kriege, Matilde and Alma 55
Kurschner, Joseph 85

language teaching 54
Lawrence, Evelyn 149
learning style theory 173
LeBlanc, M. 157
liberatory pedagogy 97, 106–8, 139, 170
Lillard, A. 40, 133
Lilley, I. 34
Lincoln, Abraham 57, 66
Lindenberg, C. 85, 87
literacy: Comenius 33; in England 2, 13, 93, 165, 175; Montessori 129, 132, 136; Owen 24, 25–6; in the past 17, 19; Peabody 54; Pestalozzi 22; Reggio Emilia 93; Steiner 82, 89, 92, 93; in USA 62

Livesey, Ruth 99, 106
Locke, John 6, 19–20, 21, 24, 25, 28, 168

McClure, Samuel 127
McLuhan, Marshall 171
McMillan, Margaret 28, 40, 97: Christian
    Socialism 4–5, 99, 142; genesis of educare
    and outdoor play 11, 98–105, 131; Night
    Camp and Camp School 101; nurseries 11,
    39, 101–5, 106–9
McMillan's legacy 105–6: liberatory pedagogy
    97, 106–8, 139; relevance to contemporary
    practice 108–9, 172
McMillan, Rachel 39, 40, 99, 100–2, 107, 168–9
Malaguzzi, Loris 12, 155–6, 169, 170: classroom
    environment 159–60, 165; life and work
    156–8; Reggio Emilia 12, 93, 155, 156–8;
    social constructivism 155, 159; theory and
    philosophy 157, 158–60, 176
Malaguzzi's legacy 158–61: documentation
    162–3; Reggio Emilia in the 21st century
    163–5; teaching and curriculum 160, 161–3
Malting House School 146–9, 150, 169
Manchester Guardian 104
Mann, Horace 50–1, 52, 53, 56, 60, 66
Mann, Mary (*née* Peabody) 49, 50, 51, 52, 53,
    55, 168
Mansbridge, Alan 100
Marder, N. 145
Marenholtz-Buelow, Baroness von 38
Martin, J. 40
Marwedel, Emma 39
Mary, Queen 102, 105
Massachusetts Department of Early Education
    and Care 62
maternity leave (UK) **14**
Methodism 4, 140
middle schools (UK) **13**
middle schools (US) **12**
Miner, Myrtilla 57
Molt, Emil 87
Montesano, Giuseppe 124
Montessori, Alessandro 121–2, 124, 127
Montessori, Maria 11, 40, 120, 170: Catholicism
    124, 127, 129; clinical paediatrician 122;
    criticisms of 127; early life and education
    120–2, 168; feminism 121–2, 129, 131; Nobel
    Peace Prize 131
Montessori's legacy: capabilities of the
    individual child 159, 175; Casa dei
    Bambini 40, 125, 135–6, 159; classroom

environment 132, 159–60; democratic
    practice 123, 170; directresses 40–1, 125,
    132–3, 134, 136; nature and nurture 123, 134;
    pedagogic anthropology 123–31; planes of
    development 125, 130; practical skills 35,
    121, 132, 133; relevance to contemporary
    practice 135–6, 172–3; resources 40, 41*f*,
    123, 128, 129–30, 132, 133–4, 136; 'scientific
    pedagogy' 124, 125–6; secondary age
    children 128; teacher training 40, 126, 127,
    128, 129, 130; teaching and curriculum 131–4
Montessori, Mario Montesano 124, 127, 128,
    129–30, 131, 169
Montessori method 40, 125–7, 128, 129, 131–4
Montessori schools 125, 126, 127, 128–30, 132,
    135, 172–3
More, Sir Thomas 18
Moretti, E. 129
Moss, Peter 108
motherhood education 31, 33, 60, 69–70
multiple intelligence theory 173
Mussolini, Benito 129, 156
Myers, Charles 142

National Association for the Education of
    Young Children (NAEYC) 42, 173
National Governors Association Center for
    Best Practices 62
National Society for the Prevention of Cruelty
    to Children (NSPCC) 98
nature 31, 35, 43
nature and nurture 123, 134
neuroscience 93, 135
New, R. 141
Nidi Infanzia 158
Nietzsche, Friedrich 80
numeracy 4: Blow 68; in England 2, 13, 93, 165;
    Froebel 36, 43; Montessori 132–4; Owen 24;
    Piaget 6; Steiner 82, 83, 91, 92; in USA 62
nurseries (UK) **13**, **14**, 102–8; *see also* McMillan,
    Margaret
Nursery School Association (NSA) 39, 102–3,
    105, 141
nursery schools (US) **12**
The Nursery World (magazine) 150
Nutbrown, Cathy 135

observation of children: Isaacs 12, 134, 139,
    146, 147, 148–9, 150, 151–2; Montessori 40,
    122, 123, 125, 130, 132–3, 134; Peabody 63
O'Donnell, M. 122, 127, 134, 135

O'Hagan, F. 23, 24, 25, 26, 27
Organisation for Economic Co-operation and Development (OECD) 43, 76
original sin 18, 19
Orme, N. 17, 18
Orthophrenic School, Rome 124, 131
Owen, David Dale 27
Owen, Grace 141, 142
Owen, Richard Dale 27
Owen, Robert 11, 22–7, 23*f*, 28, 172: New Lanark School 11, 11*f*, 24, 25, 26*f*, 27, 169*f*
Owen, Robert Dale 27

Palmer, Joseph 49
Pantheism 4, 34
parent education 33, 69, 70, 75, 149–50
parents as educators: early pioneers 59, 73, 75, 91–2, 155, 160–2, 170; in the past 17, 32, 33
Parents' Magazine (US) 150
payment by results 140
Peabody, Elizabeth 11, 48: ancestry and influences 48–51; feminism 60; memorial 60; social justice 56–8; Transcendentalism 4, 50, 51, 52, 58, 60, 73
Peabody: critical perspectives 56, 57–8
Peabody's kindergarten movement 38, 51–5, 66–7: curriculum 52–3; gifts and occupations 37, 44, 52; *kindergartner* alumni 55; outreach for professional status 55–6; play 52, 54, 59, 63; prototypes 51–2; reading and language 54; symbolic teaching and learning 54; teacher training reforms 53–4
Peabody's legacy: kindergarten legacy 59–60; kindergarten *vs.* US today 60–2; leadership model 60; personal legacy 58–9
Peabody, Elizabeth Palmer 49
Peabody, Mary *see* Mann, Mary
Peabody, Nathaniel 49
Peabody, Sophia 49, 51
pedagogic anthropology 123–31
Penn, H. 156
Pestalozzi-Froebel Haus, Berlin 38
Pestalozzi, Johann Heinrich 10–11, 21–2, 27–8, 168, 170, 174: influences of 24, 25, 31, 38, 53, 123, 124, 132
Piaget, Jean 6, 129, 148–9, 159: psychological theory 132; schema theory 25, 133, 135; stage theory 6–7, 89, 125, 130, 134, 149
Plato 32, 43, 53
play 153: Froebel 35–6, 42–3; gendered play 145; Isaacs 145, 146, 150, 152; Montessori 41,

134, 135; Peabody 52, 54, 59, 63; Steiner 85, 89; symbolic play 36
playschool (UK) **14**
Postman, Neil 174–5
poverty 5, 98–9
Power, E. 33, 38, 39
preparatory schools (US) **12**
preparatory ("prep") schools (UK) **13**
Presbyterianism 4, 71
preschools (US) 8, **12**
primary schools (UK) **13**
private schools (UK) **13**
private schools (US) **12**
problem solving 43, 135–6
psychoanalysis: Freud 142–4, 145, 146, 151; Isaacs 139, 142–6, 147, 149, 150; Klein 139, 144–5, 146
psychosexual stages 143–4
public schools (UK) **13**
public schools (US) **12**
punishment 22, 123–4, 133, 147, 151
Pyke, Geoffrey 147, 149, 169

Quintilian 32, 43, 53

Rachel McMillan Open Air Nursery School 102, 104, 106, 108
Rachel McMillan Teacher Training College 105, 106
Rambush, Nancy McCormick 127
Rank, Otto 142
reception classes (UK) **13**
Reggio Children 158
Reggio Emilia schools 12, 93, 157–8, 163–5, 173; *see also* Malaguzzi, Loris
Rickman, John 146
Rinaldi, C. 160, 163
Robbins, Lionel 146
Roberts-Holmes, G. 171
Romanticism 33–4
Ronda, B. 50, 57, 60
Ross, Ellen 99, 105
Rousseau, Jean-Jacques 6, 19, 21, 25, 27–8, 80, 155, 168
Runyard, Mary 74
Russell, James Earl 72
Russia 22, 38, 126; *see also* Vygotsky

scaffolding 7
Schelling, F. W. J. 34
schema theory 25, 133, 135

School Boards 99, 100
'schoolification' 79, 93, 103, 172, 176
Schrader-Breymann, Henriette 38
Schroer, Karl 83–4, 85
Schurz, Margarethe and Agatha 38, 52
Scott, Dred 65
secondary schools (UK) **13**
secondary schools (US) **12**
Seguin, Edouard 120, 123, 131
self-discipline 18, 133, 134, 135
Sergi, Giuseppe 124–5
Settlement House movement 58, 59, 70, 75, 77,
    99
Sheldon, Edward A. 52
slavery 5, 51, 57, 65
slum children 102, 103, 105, 125, 130, 135–6
Smith College 40, 72
Smith, Henrietta Brown 104–5(n50)
Smith, Nora Archibald 37
Snider, Denton Jacques 73
Snyder, Agnes 39, 74
social constructivism 89, 125, 155, 159
social justice 56–8
Socialism 99–100
Spain: Montessori 128
'special schools' 92–3
The Spectator 148
Spiral Curriculum 7
Staley, Betty 90
Standing, E. M. 121, 127, 128
Starr, Elizabeth Gates 75
state schools (UK) **13**
Staudenmaier, P. 91
Steedman, Carolyn 99–100, 102, 168–9
Steiner, Rudolf 11, 79, 102, 169, 170:
    anthroposophy 4, 80, 83, 85, 86–7;
    eurhythmy 85, 86, 89, 91; Goetheanum 86,
    88; lectures 84, 87; life and work 79–88; play
    85, 89; as pupil teacher 83; Social Three
    Folding 87–8; spiritualism 80, 83, 84, 87, 89;
    temperaments 90; theosophy 4, 80, 85–6;
    tutoring 84–5
Steiner schools 79, 173: criticisms of 84, 85,
    87–8, 92–4; cycles of child development
    89–90, 125; popularity of 80, 91–2, 93–4;
    reading and writing 82, 89, 92, 93; teaching
    and curriculum 81, 82–3, 90–1
Steiner's legacy: anthroposophical education
    88–90, 91; relevance to contemporary
    practice 91–4; teaching and curriculum 90–1
Sterns, P. 16, 17, 20, 25, 28

Stoppani, Renilde 121, 122
Sweden 77, 164
Swiniarski, L. 34, 35, 42, 43, 53, 55, 57, 58, 59,
    69, 70, 71, 75, 173
Switzerland 21–2, 126; *see also* Piaget
symbolism 36, 69

teacher education for early years 174: Froebel's
    legacy 43–4; Montessori 40, 126, 127, 128,
    129, 130; Peabody 53–4, 55–6, 57
Temple, Alice 40
Temple School 50
Theosophical Society 80, 85, 130
theosophy 4, 80, 85–6
Thompson, Katie 98
Thoreau, Henry David 51
Tolstoy, Countess Tatiana 126
Transcendentalism 4, 50, 51, 52, 58, 60, 71

Ullrich, H. 85, 86, 89
UN Declaration of the Rights of the Child 151
UNESCO 27, 123, 130–1
Union of Italian Women (UDI) 157
Unitarianism 4
United Kingdom: academies **13**, 77, 173;
    assessment 2, 13, 79, 151–2, 165, 171;
    Children's Centres 9–10, **14**, 108; current
    concerns 1–2; daycare 9–10, **14**, 108; early
    years education and care 1, 8–10, 171;
    Education Acts 100, 102; England 1, 2, 9, 10,
    13–14, 27, 88, 92, 103; EYFS 9, 13, 14, 79, 91,
    136, 151–2, 155, 165; Froebel 38, 39, 44, 103,
    141; glossary of terms **13–14**; historical notes
    3–5; inspections 2; literacy 2, 13, 93, 165, 175;
    Montessori 125, 135, 136, 172–3; National
    Children's Day 42; Northern Ireland 2, 9,
    10; NSA 39, 102–3, 105, 141; numeracy 2,
    13, 93, 165; Ofsted 9, 14; Peabody 53; Save
    Childhood Movement 42, 93; Scotland 2,
    4, 9, 10, 27, 93, 164, 173; Steiner schools 88,
    92–3, 173; Sure Start 9–10, 108; Too Much,
    Too Soon 1, 93, 175; Wales 2, 9, 10, 22, 173;
    see also industrialization; Isaacs, Susan;
    Locke, John; McMillan, Margaret; Owen,
    Robert
United States: assessment 62, 172; Charter
    Schools 76; childcare 8; Common Core 62,
    74, 172; current concerns 1–2; Department
    of Education 8; early years education and
    care 1, 7–8, 171, 172; federal funding 61,
    61*f*; Federal Government 8; Full Service

Schools 59, 70, 75–6; glossary of terms **12–13**; Head Start 8, 10, 42; historical notes 3–5; influence of Froebel 39–40, 71–2; kindergartens 8, **12**, 38, 56, 61–2; literacy and numeracy 62; Montessori schools 125, 127, 135, 172–3; NAEYC 42, 173; No Child Left Behind 165; PARCC 62, 172; preschools 8; Race to the Top 165; Reggio Emilia schools 164, 173; teacher education 44; Waldorf/ Steiner schools 79, 173; *see also* Blow, Susan; Peabody, Elizabeth
universal preschools (US) **12**
University of Greenwich Archive 107

values 62, 66–7, 72, 144, 152
Von Laue, Max 80
Von Moltke, Helmuth and Elizabeth 87
Von Sivers, Marie 80, 86
Vygotsky, Lev 7, 89, 131, 132, 159

Waldorf/Waldorf Steiner schools *see* Steiner schools
Weber, Evelyn 36, 71
Wellesley College 40, 72
Wheaton College 40, 72
Wheelock, Lucy 55
Whitbread, N. 139, 151
Wiggin, Kate Douglas 34, 37, 39–40, 45
Winnemucca, Piute Princess 57
Wordsworth, William 50, 58, 60
workhouses 99
Wright, Frank Lloyd 43

year groups (UK) **13**
Yorkshire Daily Observer 100

Zaretsky, E. 144, 145
Zimmerman, Robert 84
Zone of Proximal Development 7, 25, 132